I0089229

Breaking Open the Word

AN OCIA GUIDE TO SUNDAY SCRIPTURE

MARY KATHARINE DEELEY

Liguori
PUBLICATIONS
A Redemptorist Ministry

Imprimi Potest: Stephen T. Rehrauer, CSsR, Provincial, Denver Province, the Redemptorists

Imprimatur: "In accordance with CIC 827, permission to publish has been granted on August 4, 2020, by the Most Reverend Mark S. Rivituso, Auxiliary Bishop, Archdiocese of St. Louis. Permission to publish is an indication that nothing contrary to Church teaching is contained in this work. It does not imply any endorsement of the opinions expressed in the publication; nor is any liability assumed by this permission."

Library of Congress Cataloging-in-Publication Data

Names: Liguori Publications. Title: Breaking Open the Word : An OCIA Guide to Sunday Scripture. Description: First edition. | Liguori : Liguori Publications, 2020 | Includes index. | Contents: Year B | Identifiers: LCCN 2020018311 | ISBN 9780764827662 (paperback) | Subjects: LCSH: Church year meditations. | Catholic Church—Prayers and devotions. | Catholic Church. *Ordo lectionum Missae* (2nd ed., 1998). English. Classification: LCC BX2170.C55 B735 2020 | DDC 242/.3—dc23 | LC record available at lccn.loc.gov/2020018311

Compliant with *The Roman Missal,* Third Edition

To order this book, visit Liguori.org or call 800-325-9521.

The process by which adults are initiated into the Catholic faith throughout the United States is now called the OCIA—the Order of Christian Initiation of Adults. "Order" is a clearer translation of the Latin term for the process formerly known as the RCIA—the Rite of Christian Initiation of Adults. People preparing for baptism and reception into the Church celebrate several rites as part of the order to which those rites belong—an order whose mission is to journey in the faith. The US Conference of Catholic Bishops adopted the name change in 2021, with American dioceses introducing the name thereafter. For more information, please contact your local diocese.

Contents

Overview

What *is* Breaking Open the Word?

The *Lectionary for Sunday Mass* forms the basis for the OCIA process. This is appropriate because the Scriptures tell the story of the faith experienced by the people of God: the relationship between the Chosen People and Yahweh, and the relationship between the early Christian community and Jesus of Nazareth, the Son of God. As we reflect upon these faith stories, our own stories of how God has impacted our lives become more clearly perceived and articulated. The Scriptures convey the stories of a community. So it is fitting that the catechumens and candidates gather in community to break open God's word and apply it to their own lives in the here and now.

In their reflection and linking of the Scriptures to their own lives, the early Christians began to develop official summaries and teachings about the meaning of their communal religious experiences. Since these doctrines and dogmas were born of theological reflection grounded in Scripture, the Church now links these teachings to Scripture in the OCIA process. Therefore, the sessions begin with Scripture reflection and move toward an encounter with Catholic belief. Since it is primarily through the Sunday liturgy that the community hands on its traditions and beliefs, this is also the most opportune time for the catechumens and candidates to be formed by the community. Beginning with the period of the catechumenate, it is urged that they be dismissed from the liturgy following the Prayers of the Faithful to reflect together upon the word of God and the teachings of the Church.

Breaking Open the Word—available for each of the three liturgical years (A, B, and C)—contains all the readings for every Sunday of each year. The readings are arranged so there are twenty-eight weeks between the first Sunday of Advent and Pentecost and twenty-eight weeks between Trinity Sunday and Christ the King. Commentaries for each Sunday, written by Scripture scholar Mary Katharine Deeley, follow the readings and are introduced with titles.

How *to use* Breaking Open the Word

Breaking Open the Word is designed to be useful for all team leaders of Christian initiation groups—adults and adolescents—and it serves as an excellent resource for participants in adult initiation classes. Additionally, it holds value for individual use, separate from Christian initiation: Whether you are planning homilies, involved in small-group faith-sharing, or simply searching for further enrichment and knowledge through the Sunday readings.

Relevant *Journey of Faith* lessons are listed at the end of each reflection. These include lessons related to the theme, as well as at least one lesson that ties most closely to the Scripture readings. Incorporating these lessons ensures that you cover all the lessons in *Journey of Faith* during the liturgical year. Sundays between the first Sunday of Advent and the eighth Sunday in Ordinary Time refer you to lessons from the *Journey of Faith* Catechumenate packet; Sundays between the first Sunday of Lent and Easter refer you to lessons from the Enlightenment packet; Sundays between the second Sunday of Easter and Pentecost refer you to lessons from the Mystagogy packet. Because the twenty-eight weeks between Trinity and Christ the King may be used either for continuing Mystagogy or for beginning a new group of inquirers (or both), all the Sundays between Trinity and Christ the King refer you to both the Mystagogy and the Inquiry packets.

The commentaries, themes, and prayers contained in this book are aids for preparing you to lead inquirers, catechumens, candidates, and neophytes. You are invited and encouraged to familiarize yourself with these resources to better anticipate and stimulate questions and discussions. Leading others to Christ is the most important work you will do in your life; your personal preparation for such significant and rewarding work can never be adequately emphasized. *Breaking Open the Word* is a valuable resource for this type of work.

Included in Breaking Open the Word

- ➤ Readings for all Sundays of liturgical years A, B, and C, Advent through Christ the King

- ➤ Readings for the Easter Triduum

- ➤ Year A readings for the third, fourth, and fifth Sundays of Lent

- ➤ Readings for those occasional Sundays that supersede Ordinary Time Sunday readings

- ➤ Scripture commentary for every set of readings

- ➤ Discussion and/or reflection questions for every set of readings

- ➤ Readings are cross-referenced to the catechetical lessons

- ➤ A brief collection of short gathering prayers and dismissal prayers for each phase of the initiation process

- ➤ A thematic index

All readings are taken directly from the Lectionary for Mass *for use in the dioceses of the United States of America, second typical edition © 2001 Confraternity of Christian Doctrine, Inc., Washington, DC.*

Suggested Agenda for a Sunday Session

30 minutes	Liturgy—all gather in church. Dismissal after the Prayer of the Faithful.
10 minutes	Refreshments and settling in.
15 minutes	Prayer and reflection—Where are we at this moment?
45 minutes	Reread, reflect upon, and share the readings of the day—either all or one chosen for this session. Spouses and sponsors can join this session after Mass.
10 minutes	Evaluation and prayer—How are we going to live the Scriptures this week?

Note: During Precatechumenate (Inquiry) or Mystagogy, this format may be adapted for either a Sunday morning after Mass or for a weekday evening session.

I thank my God every time I remember you, constantly praying with joy in every one of my prayers for all of you, because of your sharing in the gospel from the first day until now. And this is my prayer, that your love may overflow more and more with knowledge and full insight, having produced the harvest of righteousness that comes through Jesus Christ for the glory and praise of God.

Philippians 1:3, 4, 5, 9, 11

First Sunday of Advent, Year B

READING 1, ISAIAH 63:16B–17, 19B; 64:2–7

You, LORD, are our father, our redeemer you are named forever. Why do you let us wander, O LORD, from your ways, and harden our hearts so that we fear you not? Return for the sake of your servants, the tribes of your heritage. Oh, that you would rend the heavens and come down, with the mountains quaking before you, while you wrought awesome deeds we could not hope for, such as they had not heard of from of old. No ear has ever heard, no eye ever seen, any God but you doing such deeds for those who wait for him. Would that you might meet us doing right, that we were mindful of you in our ways! Behold, you are angry, and we are sinful; all of us have become like unclean people, all our good deeds are like polluted rags; we have all withered like leaves, and our guilt carries us away like the wind. There is none who calls upon your name, who rouses himself to cling to you; for you have hidden your face from us and have delivered us up to our guilt. Yet, O LORD, you are our father; we are the clay and you the potter: we are all the work of your hands.

PSALM 80:2–3, 15–16, 18–19

READING 2, 1 CORINTHIANS 1:3–9

Grace to you and peace from God our Father and the Lord Jesus Christ. I give thanks to my God always on your account for the grace of God bestowed on you in Christ Jesus, that in him you were enriched in every way, with all discourse and all knowledge, as the testimony to Christ was confirmed among you, so that you are not lacking in any spiritual gift as you wait for the revelation of our Lord Jesus Christ. He will keep you firm to the end, irreproachable on the day of our Lord Jesus Christ. God is faithful, and by him you were called to fellowship with his Son, Jesus Christ our Lord.

GOSPEL, MARK 13:33–37

Jesus said to his disciples: "Be watchful! Be alert! You do not know when the time will come. It is like a man traveling abroad. He leaves home and places his servants in charge, each with his own work, and orders the gatekeeper to be on the watch. Watch, therefore; you do not know when the Lord of the house is coming, whether in the evening, or at midnight, or at cockcrow, or in the morning. May he not come suddenly and find you sleeping. What I say to you, I say to all: 'Watch!'"

Remembering God

When he gave his first interview to the press as the 266th pontiff, Pope Francis was asked, "Who is Jorge Mario Bergoglio?" His notable first response was: "I am a sinner." He said it with a candor and humility that awed the world. How many of us are so willing to admit our faults? Even more to the point, how many of us truly kneel before God in prayer and confess that we are sinners? We might wonder what God's reaction would be and whether such an admission could truly set us free.

At the beginning of the Advent season as we prepare for Christmas and the coming of Jesus Christ, Isaiah the prophet describes the terrible situation in which the Israelites found themselves. They were in exile, their temple destroyed. They felt abandoned by God. Perhaps they were even angry with God because of what had happened. If we were to read all of Isaiah we would learn that many of the Israelites had failed to follow God's law. Now in a foreign country, the people realized that without the familiar prayers, ritual, and community to guide and support them, they were falling further away from God. Isaiah acknowledges that God was justified in his anger, but he doesn't turn his back. Instead, Isaiah calls out to God in an act of absolute trust. Isaiah helps us remember that God is our Father who works awesome feats for his people. When we remember God, even in the midst of sorrow and hurt, we open ourselves to him. But it's important to note that Isaiah is a model servant of humility before the Lord. God is the potter, we are the clay, and allowing God to work on us throughout this season prepares us for his coming.

Spiritual Strength

Throughout Scripture, we see that God continually reached out to his people even when they failed to be steadfast in their faith and were lured away by temptations of the world or their own desires. This *falling away* often happens during periods of prosperity. When things are going well, we forget about God. It isn't until bad things happen that we remember him. We usually ask, "Where is God?" and cry out to him during times of suffering and distress. In his First Letter to the Corinthians, Paul tries to encourage the early Christians to stay strong when life gets tough. He doesn't want them to fall into sin when confronted with persecution; he wants them to know in their hearts that God has given them the spiritual strength to withstand any difficulty. Through the grace of Jesus Christ, they are able to withstand the temptation of sin or of despair when sorrow comes.

The word for the season is "watch." Jesus compares God to the master who leaves his servants to do the household work while he is away. His implicit warning that they keep alert for the Master's return is an admonition that serves us well. This season isn't about getting Christmas presents. It's about preparing our hearts and minds for the coming of the Lord. May we also find ourselves awake and waiting.

Good News for All of Us

Advent is often hijacked by our focus on family gatherings, decorating, giving gifts, and end-of-school terms. But these four weeks before Christmas mark the beginning of a new liturgical year and a renewed dedication to the Lord's place in our lives. As the people of God, we juxtapose comfort and challenge. Though God gives us everything we need for our journey, we aren't promised it will always be easy. When difficulty comes, we may be tempted to turn away from God or begin to believe that he has abandoned us. Let us not forget we have turned away from him many times and he has always welcomed us back. We must stay awake to guard against those temptations, and remember that God will always return. Both Isaiah and Paul use the image of a pregnant woman to describe us as a people who wait for the Lord. And we wait now, in this season, for God who has already come and who will come again.

Questions for Reflection and Discussion

➤ *Describe a time when you felt like you had been abandoned by family or friends. Who did you turn to? What got you through that period in your life?*

➤ *Advent is the premier time of expectation and waiting. Was there ever a time you expected something and had a hard time waiting for it? How did you get through that waiting period?*

Related Journey of Faith Lessons

C10, "The People of God"

Themes

Conversion
    C3, "The Sacrament of Baptism"
    C4, "The Sacrament of Confirmation"
Covenant
    C10, "The People of God"
    C12, "Church History"
Remembrance
    C2, "The Sacraments: An Introduction"
    C11, "The Early Church"

Second Sunday of Advent, Year B

READING 1, ISAIAH 40:1–5, 9–11

Comfort, give comfort to my people, says your God. Speak tenderly to Jerusalem, and proclaim to her that her service is at an end, her guilt is expiated; indeed, she has received from the hand of the LORD double for all her sins. A voice cries out: In the desert prepare the way of the LORD! Make straight in the wasteland a highway for our God! Every valley shall be filled in, every mountain and hill shall be made low; the rugged land shall be made a plain, the rough country, a broad valley. Then the glory of the LORD shall be revealed, and all people shall see it together; for the mouth of the LORD has spoken. Go up on to a high mountain, Zion, herald of glad tidings; cry out at the top of your voice, Jerusalem, herald of good news! Fear not to cry out and say to the cities of Judah: Here is your God! Here comes with power the Lord GOD, who rules by his strong arm; here is his reward with him, his recompense before him. Like a shepherd he feeds his flock; in his arms he gathers the lambs, carrying them in his bosom, and leading the ewes with care.

PSALM 85:9–10–11–12, 13–14

READING 2, 2 PETER 3:8–14

Do not ignore this one fact, beloved, that with the Lord one day is like a thousand years and a thousand years like one day. The Lord does not delay his promise, as some regard "delay," but he is patient with you, not wishing that any should perish but that all should come to repentance. But the day of the Lord will come like a thief, and then the heavens will pass away with a mighty roar and fire, and the earth will dissolve the elements and everything done on it will be found out. Since everything is to be dissolved in this way, what sort of persons ought you to be, conducting yourselves in holiness and devotion, waiting for and hastening the coming of the day of God, because of which the heavens will be dissolved in flames and the elements melted by fire. But according to his promise we await new heavens and a new earth in which righteousness dwells. Therefore, beloved, since you await these things, be eager to be found without spot or blemish before him, at peace.

GOSPEL, MARK 1:1–8

The beginning of the good news of Jesus Christ, the Son of God. As it is written in Isaiah the prophet: Behold, I am sending my messenger ahead of you; he will prepare your way. A voice of one crying out in the desert: "Prepare the way of the Lord, make straight his paths." John the Baptist appeared in the desert proclaiming a baptism of repentance for the forgiveness of sins. People of the whole Judean countryside and all the inhabitants of Jerusalem were going out to him and were being baptized by him in the Jordan River as they acknowledged their sins. John was clothed in camel's hair, with a leather belt around his waist. He fed on locusts and wild honey. And this is what he proclaimed: "One mightier than I is coming after me. I am not worthy to stoop and loosen the thongs of his sandals. I have baptized you with water; he will baptize you with the Holy Spirit."

Comfort My People

The coming of the Messiah meant good news for the Israelites. Isaiah spoke to them at the end of their long exile in Babylon—the result of their disobedience to God's law. The prophets and others who were faithful to that law warned them to change their ways, but old habits are hard to break, and sin continued to fill the land.

About forty years passed until, as Scripture says, God raised up Cyrus the Persian to free the Israelites from captivity (Isaiah 45:13). Isaiah's joyful shout of comfort tells them what has happened and relates that they have served their time. In Isaiah's vision, God's coming will turn things upside down. Inherent in that message is the encouragement to renew their zeal to hear and obey the word of God. The rest of the prophecy includes commands to love and serve the Lord alone, to care for the widow, the orphan, and the sojourner, and to promote the justice of the Lord in the land. A new start in their homeland meant a new start in their faith.

New Heaven and New Earth

Peter's letter speaks about the coming of the Lord with somewhat more challenging images. He reminds us that the Lord is patient because he wants us to repent, but Peter also presents us with an image of judgment that is less than comforting. "The elements will be dissolved by fire...the earth and everything done on it will be found out." The early Christians were viewed with suspicion and persecuted. When Peter speaks to them, his exhortation is to be patient and renew their commitment to the Lord, even in persecution. He reminds them that God will bring a new heaven and earth when God wills it, not when we do. Could it be that God is waiting for the whole world to come to repentance before he comes again? This is something only God knows. We should heed Peter's encouragement to reform our lives and not worry about God's plan.

Prepare the Way of the Lord

John the Baptist shared a message with the people: "Something is coming." It was the prophet Malachi who said that Elijah would appear before the coming of the Lord. In Mark's Gospel, John shows up looking like Elijah the Prophet coming out of the desert dressed in a hairy coat with a leather belt around his waist. John's message echoes the first reading: "Prepare the way of the Lord." Mark sees his entrance as the only appropriate beginning to the Good News of Christ, and John plays his part as he baptizes all who come to him as they confess their sins. Mark knows we can't reform our lives or be transformed by God's grace unless we first acknowledge that we are sinners. John's baptism was itself a preparation for Jesus' coming. Repentance helps us turn our lives around and become more open to grace. But John knows that the one who is to come will baptize with the Holy Spirit—a hint that this person is more powerful than anyone could ever imagine. All of us can benefit from more preparation.

Good News for All of Us

Every year, we prepare for the coming of Christ in a world plagued by war, discrimination, economic and social injustice, and polarization that threatens to split families and societies. I suspect both the Israelites and early Christians experienced similar circumstances. But baptism tells us that the coming of Christ into the world and into our souls has given us a choice. Through grace, we can change old habits, turn away from sin, and turn toward God. We can embrace God's justice and mercy and bring it into the world by allowing God to work through us. Advent is the time to renew our commitment to fulfill God's work.

Questions for Reflection and Discussion

➤ *Are there behaviors or thoughts in your life that you would like to call on the grace of God to help you change?*

➤ *Think about injustices or discrimination occurring in your school, neighborhood, or the country at large. How could you help initiate change, even in a small way?*

Related Journey of Faith Lesson

C2, "The Sacraments: An Introduction"

Themes

Justice
    C13, "Christian Moral Living"
    C16, "Social Justice"
New Creation
    Q4, "Who Is Jesus Christ?"
Reconciliation
    C6, "The Sacrament of Penance and Reconciliation"
    C7, "The Sacrament of the Anointing of the Sick"

Third Sunday of Advent, Year B

READING 1, ISAIAH 61:1–2A, 10–11

The spirit of the Lord God is upon me, because the Lord has anointed me; he has sent me to bring glad tidings to the poor, to heal the brokenhearted, to proclaim liberty to the captives and release to the prisoners, to announce a year of favor from the Lord and a day of vindication by our God. I rejoice heartily in the Lord, in my God is the joy of my soul; for he has clothed me with a robe of salvation and wrapped me in a mantle of justice, like a bridegroom adorned with a diadem, like a bride bedecked with her jewels. As the earth brings forth its plants, and a garden makes its growth spring up, so will the Lord God make justice and praise spring up before all the nations.

LUKE 1:46–48, 49–50, 53–54

READING 2, 1 THESSALONIANS 5:16–24

Brothers and sisters: Rejoice always. Pray without ceasing. In all circumstances give thanks, for this is the will of God for you in Christ Jesus. Do not quench the Spirit. Do not despise prophetic utterances. Test everything; retain what is good. Refrain from every kind of evil. May the God of peace make you perfectly holy and may you entirely, spirit, soul, and body, be preserved blameless for the coming of our Lord Jesus Christ. The one who calls you is faithful, and he will also accomplish it.

GOSPEL, JOHN 1:6–8, 19–28

A man named John was sent from God. He came for testimony, to testify to the light, so that all might believe through him. He was not the light, but came to testify to the light. And this is the testimony of John. When the Jews from Jerusalem sent priests and Levites to him to ask him, "Who are you?" He admitted and did not deny it, but admitted, "I am not the Christ." So they asked him, "What are you then? Are you Elijah?" And he said, "I am not." "Are you the Prophet?" He answered, "No." So they said to him, "Who are you, so we can give an answer to those who sent us? What do you have to say for yourself?" He said: "I am *the voice of one crying out in the desert, 'make straight the way of the Lord,'* as Isaiah the prophet said." Some Pharisees were also sent. They asked him, "Why then do you baptize if you are not the Christ or Elijah or the Prophet?" John answered them, "I baptize with water; but there is one among you whom you do not recognize, the one who is coming after me, whose sandal strap I am not worthy to untie." This happened in Bethany across the Jordan, where John was baptizing.

Rejoice Always

The First Letter to the Thessalonians tells us to rejoice always (*semper gaudete*), pray constantly, and give thanks in all circumstances because "this is the will of God for you in Christ Jesus." We might be tempted to think, *of course I can't do it constantly; I'm really busy.* But if God has done what we believe he's done, praying, giving thanks, and rejoicing are the least we can do. Advent is a good time to reassess how we live our lives. Paul's letter touches on that. Though it may be difficult, at times, the recipe to prepare for the Lord is not complicated. Turn away from evil and do that which is good. If we strive to always choose what's good, we will be well on our way.

Testifying to the Light

The Gospel of John seemingly repeats the story of John the Baptist found in Mark's Gospel, but John provides crucial details about the Baptist and the Messiah. John the Baptist comes as a witness to the light. Much like today, witnesses were very important in the ancient Near East. The testimony of two witnesses was needed to prove a case in court. John the Baptist is the first witness named in this story of Jesus. As the priests and the Levites question him, he continually reports that he is not the Messiah or Elijah or the prophet (the prophet like Moses whom God promised to raise up in Deuteronomy 18:15). He identifies himself with the "voice of one crying in the wilderness" (see Isaiah 40). When they question his baptism, he implies that his baptism is nothing compared to the one who is to come. Then he drops the bombshell. "Among you is one whom you do not know...." Jesus is among them even now. Before him, even John the Baptist bows and considers himself unworthy. The rest of John's Gospel unfolds John the Baptist's early witness.

Good News for All of Us

Both Advent and Lent set aside one Sunday in the midst of preparation or repentance to reflect on the absolute joy of Christ in the world. In Advent, it's the third Sunday and is known by the Latin word in the entrance antiphon: *Gaudete* (rejoice). The word is a summons to all people to praise and thank God for the gift of the Incarnation. The readings today recall God's blessing and mercy and encourage us to live in faithfulness to him and in anticipation of his return.

We return to Isaiah for the prophetic words of God's servant. Isaiah was prophesying to a people that had returned from exile, and who faced many challenges in their return, including the question of who had the authentic word of God and how they could remain faithful in their new circumstances. The one who spoke in Isaiah's prophecy proclaimed Good News for not just the rich and powerful, but for everyone. Though we don't know the identity of the one speaking, we do know that Jesus used this passage as the Scripture for his first public proclamation (Luke 4:18–20). Upon finishing the reading, Jesus said: "Today this Scripture has been fulfilled in your hearing." The effect must have been electrifying. It was what people longed for—a return to fullness and a renewed relationship with God.

Questions for Reflection and Discussion

➤ *What are you most grateful for in your life? How do you show your appreciation?*

➤ *If you were to be a witness to what brought you to Catholicism or what keeps you in the Church, what would you say?*

Related Journey of Faith Lesson

C4, "The Sacrament of Confirmation"

Themes

Change of Heart
    C3, "The Sacrament of Baptism"
Holiness
    C13, "Christian Moral Living"
    C15, "A Consistent Ethic of Life"
Ministry
    C9, "The Sacrament of Holy Orders"
    C10, "The People of God"

Fourth Sunday of Advent, Year B

READING 1, 2 SAMUEL 7:1–5, 8B–12, 14A, 16

When King David was settled in his palace, and the LORD had given him rest from his enemies on every side, he said to Nathan the prophet, "Here I am living in a house of cedar, while the ark of God dwells in a tent!" Nathan answered the king, "Go, do whatever you have in mind, for the LORD is with you." But that night the LORD spoke to Nathan and said: "Go, tell my servant David, 'Thus says the LORD: Should you build me a house to dwell in?' "It was I who took you from the pasture and from the care of the flock to be commander of my people Israel. I have been with you wherever you went, and I have destroyed all your enemies before you. And I will make you famous like the great ones of the earth. I will fix a place for my people Israel; I will plant them so that they may dwell in their place without further disturbance. Neither shall the wicked continue to afflict them as they did of old, since the time I first appointed judges over my people Israel. I will give you rest from all your enemies. The LORD also reveals to you that he will establish a house for you. And when your time comes and you rest with your ancestors, I will raise up your heir after you, sprung from your loins, and I will make his kingdom firm. I will be a father to him, and he shall be a son to me. Your house and your kingdom shall endure forever before me; your throne shall stand firm forever."

PSALM 89:2–3, 4–5, 27, 29

READING 2, ROMANS 16:25–27

Brothers and sisters: To him who can strengthen you, according to my gospel and the proclamation of Jesus Christ, according to the revelation of the mystery kept secret for long ages but now manifested through the prophetic writings and, according to the command of the eternal God, made known to all nations to bring about the obedience of faith, to the only wise God, through Jesus Christ be glory forever and ever. Amen.

GOSPEL, LUKE 1:26–38

The angel Gabriel was sent from God to a town of Galilee called Nazareth, to a virgin betrothed to a man named Joseph, of the house of David, and the virgin's name was Mary. And coming to her, he said, "Hail, full of grace! The Lord is with you." But she was greatly troubled at what was said and pondered what sort of greeting this might be. Then the angel said to her, "Do not be afraid, Mary, for you have found favor with God. Behold, you will conceive in your womb and bear a son, and you shall name him Jesus. He will be great and will be called Son of the Most High, and the Lord God will give him the throne of David his father, and he will rule over the house of Jacob forever, and of his kingdom there will be no end." But Mary said to the angel, "How can this be, since I have no relations with a man?" And the angel said to her in reply, "The Holy Spirit will come upon you, and the power of the Most High will overshadow you. Therefore the child to be born will be called holy, the Son of God. And behold, Elizabeth, your relative, has also conceived a son in her old age, and this is the sixth month for her who was called barren; for nothing will be impossible for God." Mary said, "Behold, I am the handmaid of the Lord. May it be done to me according to your word." Then the angel departed from her.

The House of God

Christmas is almost here. The anticipation of the holidays causes joyous expectation in some and a little panic in others. Many are overcome by the thought: *How will I get everything done?* Today's readings turn to the home that the Lord will find when he comes. David worries about a suitable place for the Ark of the Covenant, and Luke narrates the miraculous story of the annunciation when Mary learns that she will become the first *home* to the Lord on earth where he will dwell among us.

When Moses received the Ten Commandments, the tablets were placed in the Ark of the Covenant, which traveled with the Israelites as they journeyed through the desert in its own "tent of meeting." The tent was a visible sign of God's presence to Israel. The Book of Exodus records that when the cloud settled on the tent, the Lord's glory filled it (Exodus 40:34–38). The reading from 2 Samuel opens shortly after David ascends to the throne of Israel. When David was anointed king, he was installed in a great palace and remembered the relatively poor dwelling of the Ark of the Covenant. He announces his plan to build a more permanent house as a sign of God's presence with the people.

God had other plans. The House of David (that is, his descendants) would be built up. They would prosper and God would remain with them forever. David's son, Solomon, would go on to build the temple, which would be destroyed, by the Babylonians. But despite this, God's promise to be with the house of David remained. That promise reaches its ultimate fulfillment in the birth of Jesus, who is of the House of David.

Open to God's Work

In Luke's Gospel, Mary had no designs to build anything. She knew the stories of David and grew up going to the great temple, which had been rebuilt. In her story, the annunciation captures our imaginations. When Gabriel appears to Mary, she is little more than a girl and her confusion is to be expected. Why should she be favored above anyone else? The words, "The Lord is with you," were usually reserved for prophets,

kings, or warriors and were a predictor of their success. Now an angel was telling Mary that God had found favor with her and she would give birth to a Son who would be named Jesus, which means "God saves."

Mary was a model of humility; she wondered how this could happen. The angel tells her that the Most High would overshadow her. The Greek word has the sense of a shadow cast by a cloud, similar in idea to the cloud that covered the tent of meeting. The implication is that God is filling Mary. Mary's response is simply to open herself to God's will. We are not in control of what God decides to do. God simply waits for us to say yes.

God Is with Us Still

As if in response to Mary's yes, the Apostle Paul tells us that God is with us still and is able to strengthen us for anything that happens. This last part of the Epistle to the Romans is a celebration of the Lord Jesus who is the revelation of God himself to us. Paul also notes that the revelation of God is not just for the Jews but for the entire world so that all might be obedient, just as Mary was.

Good News for All of Us

Even now, God continues to seek a home in our broken world and in our hearts. Though we aren't always as open as we would like to be and can easily be distracted from the will of God, what God seeks is an open and willing heart. Let us follow the example of Mary, who listens and humbly places herself in God's service. Mary showed us that the only proper response to the Incarnation is to make a home for Christ in ourselves and in our world.

Questions for Reflection and Discussion

➤ If you had a beloved guest coming to your house for a long visit, how would you prepare? Relate this to preparing yourself as a vessel for Christ.

➤ God chose to come to earth as a baby rather than a king or warrior. What does that choice tell us about God?

Related Journey of Faith Lesson

Q11, "Places in the Church"

Themes

Ark of the Covenant
    C12, "Church History"
Mother of God
    Q4, "Who Is Jesus Christ?"
Temple
    C10, "The People of God"

Feast of the Holy Family, Year B

READING 1, SIRACH 3:2–6, 12–14

God sets a father in honor over his children; a mother's authority he confirms over her sons. Whoever honors his father atones for sins, and preserves himself from them. When he prays, he is heard; he stores up riches who reveres his mother. Whoever honors his father is gladdened by children, and, when he prays, is heard. Whoever reveres his father will live a long life; he who obeys his father brings comfort to his mother. My son, take care of your father when he is old; grieve him not as long as he lives. Even if his mind fail, be considerate of him; revile him not all the days of his life; kindness to a father will not be forgotten, firmly planted against the debt of your sins—a house raised in justice to you.

PSALM 128:1–2, 3, 4–5

READING 2, COLOSSIANS 3:12–21

Brothers and sisters: Put on, as God's chosen ones, holy and beloved, heartfelt compassion, kindness, humility, gentleness, and patience, bearing with one another and forgiving one another, if one has a grievance against another; as the Lord has forgiven you, so must you also do. And over all these put on love, that is, the bond of perfection. And let the peace of Christ control your hearts, the peace into which you were also called in one body. And be thankful. Let the word of Christ dwell in you richly, as in all wisdom you teach and admonish one another, singing psalms, hymns, and spiritual songs with gratitude in your hearts to God. And whatever you do, in word or in deed, do everything in the name of the Lord Jesus, giving thanks to God the Father through him. Wives, be subordinate to your husbands, as is proper in the Lord. Husbands, love your wives, and avoid any bitterness toward them. Children, obey your parents in everything, for this is pleasing to the Lord. Fathers, do not provoke your children, so they may not become discouraged.

GOSPEL, MATTHEW 2:13–15, 19–23

When the magi had departed, behold, the angel of the Lord appeared to Joseph in a dream and said, "Rise, take the child and his mother, flee to Egypt, and stay there until I tell you. Herod is going to search for the child to destroy him." Joseph rose and took the child and his mother by night and departed for Egypt. He stayed there until the death of Herod, that what the Lord had said through the prophet might be fulfilled, *Out of Egypt I called my son.* When Herod had died, behold, the angel of the Lord appeared in a dream to Joseph in Egypt and said, "Rise, take the child and his mother and go to the land of Israel, for those who sought the child's life are dead." He rose, took the child and his mother, and went to the land of Israel. But when he heard that Archelaus was ruling over Judea in place of his father Herod, he was afraid to go back there.

And because he had been warned in a dream, he departed for the region of Galilee. He went and dwelt in a town called Nazareth, so that what had been spoken through the prophets might be fulfilled, *He shall be called a Nazorean.*

A Family Full of Grace

The feast of the Holy Family isn't just the celebration of the ideal family; it is also the time we remember that God chose to be born into a family with all its joys and challenges. Like us, Jesus learned from parents and obeyed them. As he grew, his parents loved him and worried about him. The family of the Messiah didn't always find life easy. Imagine how difficult it was for Mary to keep vigil at the foot of the cross while he died.

Our readings begin with the description of ideal families. The Book of Sirach is a part of the Wisdom literature, which provides proverbial advice for how to live our lives. Here the author says that children are to honor and respect their parents, both father and mother. The rewards are great for the children who do so, even in the father's old age.

Our families extend beyond blood relatives. The Church is our family, too. We are to treat one another with the same love and respect our own families deserve. Paul instructs us on the characteristics we should have as disciples and as brothers and sisters in Christ: compassion, kindness, and humility. In addition, he places special emphasis on love, which is above all. As a final admonition, Paul also asks that we be grateful and give thanks for what God has given us.

The last part of Paul's letter frequently causes consternation among both women and men. Paul was the first theologian of the Church, but he was also a man of his time. Paul speaks of wives being subject to their husbands and husbands loving their wives. He also says that slaves must obey their masters and masters should treat slaves fairly. Paul's mission was not to upset the status quo but to make sure that husbands and masters do not abuse their power. Today we acknowledge that slavery is immoral and marriage is seen more as a partnership. But all of us are to treat each other as brothers and sisters in faith, as God intended.

A Light for the World

Luke's Gospel shows us the real joy and challenge of family. The purification was for Mary, who was rendered unclean by childbirth (Leviticus 12). The law dictated that the woman present herself with an offering to be made clean again. Another law said that the firstborn male of every human or animal family should be dedicated to the Lord (Exodus 13). In response, Mary, Joseph, and Jesus made their way to the Temple at the designated time. They were met by Simeon who, when he saw Jesus, praised God for allowing him to see the salvation of Israel before his death. Simeon's words echoed those of Isaiah who calls God's servant the light of the nations (Isaiah 42:6 and 49:6). On a darker note, Simeon also explains to Mary the opposition Jesus will face from many people and the suffering she will endure as she watches this happen.

Simeon wasn't the only one to see Jesus. The prophet, Anna, who never left the Temple, proclaimed the redemption of Jerusalem to all who would listen to her. In the Old Testament, it was a prophet's job to point out where God was present and working his will in the world. Anna did exactly that when she saw Jesus. When Luke tells us that God's favor was upon Jesus, we remember that it was also on his Mother at the annunciation.

Good News for the Rest of Us

Being family isn't always easy. We are called to love and forgive even when we don't feel like it. We experience joy when someone accepts us as we are and perhaps we get irritated or even angry when someone challenges us to be better. The wonder of Christmas is that Christ entered our weakness and made it holy simply by doing so. Through him we learn how to become family. Mary and Joseph, the many disciples that followed Jesus, and the millions who have joined Christianity since have given witness to the possibility that we can be one family in God and brothers and sisters to all.

Questions for Reflection and Discussion

➤ *Name one joy and one challenge of being part of your family today.*

➤ *What does the ideal family look like to you? What influences that ideal?*

Related Journey of Faith Lessons

M7, "Family Life"
C8, "The Sacrament of Matrimony"

Themes

Catholic
    C2, "The Sacraments: An Introduction"
    C12, "Church History"
Family Life
    C8, "The Sacrament of Matrimony"
Messiah
    Q4, "Who Is Jesus Christ?"

Epiphany of the Lord, Year B

READING 1, ISAIAH 60:1–6

Rise up in splendor, Jerusalem! Your light has come, the glory of the Lord shines upon you. See, darkness covers the earth, and thick clouds cover the peoples; but upon you the LORD shines, and over you appears his glory. Nations shall walk by your light, and kings by your shining radiance. Raise your eyes and look about; they all gather and come to you: your sons come from afar, and your daughters in the arms of their nurses. Then you shall be radiant at what you see, your heart shall throb and overflow, for the riches of the sea shall be emptied out before you, the wealth of nations shall be brought to you. Caravans of camels shall fill you, dromedaries from Midian and Ephah; all from Sheba shall come bearing gold and frankincense, and proclaiming the praises of the LORD.

PSALM 72:1–2, 7–8, 10–11, 12–13

READING 2, EPHESIANS 3:2–3A, 5–6

Brothers and sisters: You have heard of the stewardship of God's grace that was given to me for your benefit, namely, that the mystery was made known to me by revelation. It was not made known to people in other generations as it has now been revealed to his holy apostles and prophets by the Spirit: that the Gentiles are coheirs, members of the same body, and copartners in the promise in Christ Jesus through the gospel.

GOSPEL, MATTHEW 2:1–12

When Jesus was born in Bethlehem of Judea, in the days of King Herod, behold, magi from the east arrived in Jerusalem, saying, "Where is the newborn king of the Jews? We saw his star at its rising and have come to do him homage." When King Herod heard this, he was greatly troubled, and all Jerusalem with him. Assembling all the chief priests and the scribes of the people, He inquired of them where the Christ was to be born. They said to him, "In Bethlehem of Judea, for thus it has been written through the prophet: *And you, Bethlehem, land of Judah, are by no means least among the rulers of Judah; since from you shall come a ruler, who is to shepherd my people Israel.*" Then Herod called the magi secretly and ascertained from them the time of the star's appearance. He sent them to Bethlehem and said, "Go and search diligently for the child. When you have found him, bring me word, that I too may go and do him homage." After their audience with the king they set out. And behold, the star that they had seen at its rising preceded them, until it came and stopped over the place where the Child was.

They were overjoyed at seeing the star, and on entering the house they saw the child with Mary his mother. They prostrated themselves and paid him homage. Then they opened their treasures and offered him gifts of gold, frankincense, and myrrh. And having been warned in a dream not to return to Herod, they departed for their country by another way.

The Glory of the Lord Is Upon You

When people talk about having an epiphany, it usually means a sudden insight or thought that makes things clearer. The word itself comes from the Greek word meaning "to appear over or upon." In the Bible, the word is used almost exclusively in relation to God appearing to Israel or to the birth, post-resurrection appearances, or Second Coming of Christ. In nearly every instance, the appearance of the Divine was surprising and, for some, a little intimidating. When the Lord comes, the world is turned upside down—mountains are made low; rough places are made smooth; the poor have enough to eat; and the rich are sent away empty. Through it all, the justice and peace of the Lord fills the earth.

Today, Isaiah evokes a vision of the glory of God shining like a great light over a dark world. God's light is so bright that all nations will be drawn to it. Paul picks up that theme as he talks about his "epiphany" that the Gentiles are also heirs to the kingdom of God, sharing in the promise first given to the Jews. Finally, Matthew records the story of a light that appeared suddenly in the sky to three Magi. It isn't clear who these figures were. Many scholars think they were astrologers, but whether they were astrologers, kings, or just wise men, what they saw compelled them to go and find out what it meant.

A Beacon to the World

Isaiah patterns the heavenly city and the holy mountain after Mount Zion and the city of Jerusalem, the place God chose "for my name to be there" (2 Chronicles 6:6). When this passage was written, the Israelites had already been freed from exile. Isaiah's vision is an encouragement in a still turbulent time as Israel determines how to hold fast to its faith and live according to God's law even though its land was under foreign rule. The Jerusalem of Isaiah's vision is more than the city of David; it's the city of God. On the day of the Lord, God's light will draw all nations and kings to it and they will know that God rules the world.

A Clarion Call to Believers and Nonbelievers

When Paul presents the promises of God, he is influenced by the teachings of Jesus. He also draws inspiration from the prophet Isaiah to help people understand the message of Jesus. His Letter to the Ephesians emphasizes a mystery revealed by the Holy Spirit: Gentiles will also be heirs of Abraham—an idea that was controversial to many. The Old Testament cautioned or even prohibited the Israelites from intermingling with Gentiles. To do so meant turning away from the law. In fact, the first council of the Church was convened to deal with this issue (see Acts 15). It was unveiled that "Gentiles would also be heirs of Abraham," Jesus opened the Church to the entire world.

Matthew's Gospel speaks to the fulfillment of Isaiah's prophecy. It tells the story of nations who come to the light of the Lord. Three Wise Men from the East represent great kingdoms—certainly with more power than Herod who was under Rome's rule. When they saw the star, they came to pay homage to a king. What they found was a child with his mother, Mary. The Wise Men "prostrated" in this Child's presence and presented gifts of gold, frankincense and myrrh (Matthew 2:11). Fearful, Herod plotted to use the wise men to find the child and destroy him. Scripture records that the wise men were warned not to return to Herod and that they went home by another road.

Good News for All of Us

Jesus is indeed the light of the world. This tells us three things: We're not the center of the universe—God is. Without the light of Christ, our sight is hindered—it shows us where we are going and how to get there. We are all brothers and sisters trying to make our way back to God, and we must love and serve one another. No one has the exclusive right to the light.

Questions for Reflection and Discussion

> How can we reflect the light of Christ to others in our day-to-day living as well as in times of despair and trouble?

> How can we develop and strengthen our compassion and empathy for others?

Related Journey of Faith Lesson

C5, "The Sacrament of the Eucharist"

Themes

Ecumenism
    C13, "Christian Moral Living"
Epiphany
    C2, "The Sacraments: An Introduction"
Oppression
    C14, "The Dignity of Life"
    C16, "Social Justice"

Baptism of the Lord, Year B

READING 1, ISAIAH 42:1–4, 6–7

Thus says the LORD: Here is my servant whom I uphold, my chosen one with whom I am pleased, upon whom I have put my spirit; he shall bring forth justice to the nations, not crying out, not shouting, not making his voice heard in the street. A bruised reed he shall not break, and a smoldering wick he shall not quench, until he establishes justice on the earth; the coastlands will wait for his teaching. I, the LORD, have called you for the victory of justice, I have grasped you by the hand; I formed you, and set you as a covenant of the people, a light for the nations, to open the eyes of the blind, to bring out prisoners from confinement, and from the dungeon, those who live in darkness.

PSALM 29:1–2, 3–4, 3, 9–10

READING 2, ACTS 10:34–38

Peter proceeded to speak to those gathered in the house of Cornelius, saying: "In truth, I see that God shows no partiality. Rather, in every nation whoever fears him and acts uprightly is acceptable to him. You know the word that he sent to the Israelites as he proclaimed peace through Jesus Christ, who is Lord of all, what has happened all over Judea, beginning in Galilee after the baptism that John preached, how God anointed Jesus of Nazareth with the Holy Spirit and power. He went about doing good and healing all those oppressed by the devil, for God was with him."

GOSPEL, MARK 1:7–11

This is what he proclaimed: "One mightier than I is coming after me. I am not worthy to stoop and loosen the thongs of his sandals. I have baptized you with water; he will baptize you with the Holy Spirit." It happened in those days that Jesus came from Nazareth of Galilee and was baptized in the Jordan by John. On coming up out of the water he saw the heavens being torn open and the Spirit, like a dove, descending upon him. And a voice came from the heavens, "You are my beloved Son; with you I am well pleased."

The Servant of the Lord

The Baptism of the Lord marks the end of the Christmas season and prepares us for Ordinary Time. For the early Christians, Jesus was unlike anything they had encountered, and they searched for the words to describe him. As they looked at their Scriptures, they found passages that reflected what they experienced: Isaiah's prophesies spoke of God's servant who is a light to the nations; Deuteronomy describes a prophet like Moses whom God will raise up; Malachi speaks about the coming day of the Lord for whom the appearance of Elijah will be a sign. When Jesus appears at the Jordan to be baptized, Mark records a voice coming from heaven announcing that Jesus is "my beloved Son; with you I am well pleased." The words seem to echo Isaiah's vision of God's servant whom God has chosen and in whom God delights

Justice in the World

Isaiah's prophecy is the first of four "servant songs" in Isaiah (others appear in chapters 49, 50, and 52). This one contrasts the power of God to bring justice to the world with the apparent quiet manner of the servant who will not cry out or lift up his voice until his mission is accomplished. Jesus fits the description of this "servant". It confirms the belief that he was God's chosen one, come to set his people free. This early belief revealed the truth that Jesus was God. And, much later, it defined the formulation of the Trinitarian doctrine.

God's servant has a mission to bring justice to the world, to be a covenant between the people and God. He will open blind eyes, free prisoners, and release those who sit in darkness. Notice that it is not the mission of the servant to defeat great armies or to make earthly laws. The servant's mission is God's mission. Jesus was sent by God to reconcile the people to him, open their eyes to his presence, and free them from whatever was keeping them from following him.

In the second reading, Peter confirms that mission and its divine origin. He reminds the people that God welcomes all who fear him and do what is right. This idea, first found in Deuteronomy, was lifted up and emphasized by the preaching of Jesus. Peter is clear—God sent a message of peace through Jesus. Just as he was meant to do, Jesus went through Galilee "doing good and healing all who were oppressed" through the power of God and the Holy Spirit.

God's Beloved Son, Our Brother

Mark's version of Jesus' baptism is the shortest. The bare-bones story tells us that many people came to be baptized by John. The ritual cleansing for the forgiveness of sins was potent medicine for spiritual sickness. In Mark's description, the dramatic moment arrives when Jesus submits himself and then rises out of the water to a heavenly voice and something like a dove descends on him. Mark says the heavens were torn apart. This is the answer to the cry in Isaiah 63:17–19.

By contrast, John is humble and meek, and when he contrasts his baptism by water with the baptism of the Holy Spirit that Jesus will bring, we understand how much more powerful it will be. God's appearance is always powerful and awe-inspiring.

Good News for All of Us

At our baptisms, we were anointed into the mission of Jesus as priest, prophet, and king. The priest always and everywhere offered praise and sacrifice to God. The prophet's job was to point to God and call people to faithfulness in line with God's law. The job of the king was not to enact laws or lead armies, but to be an example of obedience to God's law. In our lives we can pray daily, work for justice, give witness to faith, and always encourage others to do the same. Paul tells us that Jesus was obedient even to dying on a cross. We may not be called to go that far, but Jesus is the example of what we can and should be if we live our baptismal promises to the fullest.

Questions for Reflection and Discussion

> *How can you or do you live out your baptismal mission? How do you invite others to do so?*

> *What would it take to bring justice to your little corner of the world? To the world in general?*

Related Journey of Faith Lesson

C3, "The Sacrament of Baptism"

Themes

Baptism
    C3, "The Sacrament of Baptism"
Holy Spirit
    C4, "The Sacrament of Confirmation"
Power
    C15, "The Consistent Ethic of Life"
    C16, "Social Justice"

Second Sunday in Ordinary Time, Year B

READING 1, 1 SAMUEL 3:3B–10, 19

Samuel was sleeping in the temple of the LORD where the ark of God was. The LORD called to Samuel, who answered, "Here I am." Samuel ran to Eli and said, "Here I am. You called me." "I did not call you, "Eli said. "Go back to sleep." So he went back to sleep. Again the LORD called Samuel, who rose and went to Eli. "Here I am, "he said. "You called me." But Eli answered, "I did not call you, my son. Go back to sleep." At that time Samuel was not familiar with the LORD, because the LORD had not revealed anything to him as yet. The LORD called Samuel again, for the third time. Getting up and going to Eli, he said, "Here I am. You called me." Then Eli understood that the LORD was calling the youth. So he said to Samuel, "Go to sleep, and if you are called, reply, Speak, LORD, for your servant is listening." When Samuel went to sleep in his place, the LORD came and revealed his presence, calling out as before, "Samuel, Samuel!" Samuel answered, "Speak, for your servant is listening." Samuel grew up, and the LORD was with him, not permitting any word of his to be without effect.

PSALM 40:2, 4, 7–8, 8–9, 10

READING 2, 1 CORINTHIANS 6:13C–15A, 17–20

Brothers and sisters: The body is not for immorality, but for the Lord, and the Lord is for the body; God raised the Lord and will also raise us by his power. Do you not know that your bodies are members of Christ? But whoever is joined to the Lord becomes one Spirit with him. Avoid immorality. Every other sin a person commits is outside the body, but the immoral person sins against his own body. Do you not know that your body is a temple of the Holy Spirit within you, whom you have from God, and that you are not your own? For you have been purchased at a price. Therefore glorify God in your body.

GOSPEL, JOHN 1:35–42

John was standing with two of his disciples, and as he watched Jesus walk by, he said, "Behold, the Lamb of God." The two disciples heard what he said and followed Jesus. Jesus turned and saw them following him and said to them, "What are you looking for?" They said to him, "Rabbi"—which translated means Teacher—,"where are you staying?" He said to them, "Come, and you will see." So they went and saw where Jesus was staying, and they stayed with him that day. It was about four in the afternoon. Andrew, the brother of Simon Peter, was one of the two who heard John and followed Jesus. He first found his own brother Simon and told him, "We have found the Messiah"—which is translated Christ—. Then he brought him to Jesus. Jesus looked at him and said, "You are Simon the son of John; you will be called Cephas"—which is translated Peter.

The Beginning of Discipleship—Listening

We don't always know the voice of God when he calls us. In the first reading, the young Samuel isn't sure who he heard in the middle of the night, but he goes to Eli and responds, "Here I am." Eli assumes Samuel has been dreaming until he comes in the third time saying that someone called him. Eli, who spent a lifetime listening for the Lord, suggests it is God himself who is calling the young prophet. When he sends Samuel back to listen again, he tells him to simply lie quietly. The first step of discipleship is listening to what the master says.

The Second Step of Discipleship—Come and See

The call of the disciples in John's Gospel doesn't take place on the seashore as in the other Gospels. The day after testifying that Jesus is the Son of God, John the Baptist sees Jesus walk by. He announces to the two disciples in his presence: "Behold the Lamb of God," and the disciples proceed to follow Jesus (John 1:34–35). John gave no thought to keeping his disciples with him. He didn't cling to his power but freely pointed to one who was greater than he.

Like the young Samuel, John's disciples aren't sure who they're following. When Jesus asks what they're looking for, their response seems absurd. "Where are you staying?" Jesus issues the perfect invitation: "Come and see." In John's Gospel, seeing is interpreted as understanding and accepting the significance of what's happening; by contrast, blindness is the refusal to understand or accept. If the first step of discipleship is listening, the second is seeing all we can.

After their encounter, Andrew, the only one of the two whose name we know, tells his brother Simon about the man he met. Andrew refers to Jesus as "the Messiah." Amazed, Simon also goes to see. When he arrives, Jesus looks at him and changes his name to Cephas (the Latin word is *Petros,* meaning "rock.") In the Old Testament, when God changed a person's name, it was a sign that God had a mission for that person. We don't hear about Peter's mission in John's Gospel, but it's recorded in Matthew 16:18: "You are Peter, and upon this rock I will build my church."

The Third Step of Discipleship—Live the Life

Disciple means "student" or "scholar." The disciples of Jesus, particularly the Twelve, spent their time with Jesus trying to learn everything they could and obey what he said. After the resurrection, they shared their good news with others and taught them. In today's epistle, Paul is concerned with giving in to the desires of the body. Paul expected Jesus to come soon, so he warned against getting entangled with earthly pleasure. Paul also plays on the understanding that the relationship between God and Israel is analogous to a marriage. To worship other gods was to be a prostitute or a fornicator. Both our physical bodies and the body of the Church are temples where God dwells. We are cautioned to keep them pure and free from sin.

Good News for All of Us

As we reflect on Jesus and what he taught, we may wonder: *How do we best hear and obey him? How do we become the disciples we are meant to be?* Samuel relied on Eli to tell him what to do. John's disciples would not have followed Jesus if John had not pointed him out. Even Paul needed help to see the Lord clearly. We also have guides. Think about the holy men and women who quietly do things in such a way that we want to know them and be more like them. We also have the saints who have heard the voice of God and listened. Additionally, there are likely teachers, friends, priests, and family members with whom we share spiritual moments experienced in the sacraments and in prayer. In these conversations, we learn the practice of faith. Together we move closer to God and invite others to do the same. Listen, see, follow, and invite. It is important to remember these steps always. Ultimately, they will lead us home to God.

Questions for Reflection and Discussion

➤ *Where do you think you are now in your journey to follow Jesus?*

➤ *Have you talked to anyone about becoming (or being) Catholic? How did they respond? If you haven't talked to anyone about it, consider why?*

Related Journey of Faith Lesson

C11, "The Early Church"

Themes

Call
    C2, "The Sacraments: An Introduction"
Confirmation
    C4, "The Sacrament of Confirmation"
Discipleship
    C10, "The People of God"
    C13, "Christian Moral Living"

Third Sunday in Ordinary Time, Year B

READING 1, JONAH 3:1–5, 10

The word of the LORD came to Jonah, saying: "Set out for the great city of Nineveh, and announce to it the message that I will tell you." So Jonah made ready and went to Nineveh, according to the LORD's bidding. Now Nineveh was an enormously large city; it took three days to go through it. Jonah began his journey through the city, and had gone but a single day's walk announcing, "Forty days more and Nineveh shall be destroyed," when the people of Nineveh believed God; they proclaimed a fast and all of them, great and small, put on sackcloth. When God saw by their actions how they turned from their evil way, he repented of the evil that he had threatened to do to them; he did not carry it out.

PSALM 25:4–5, 6–7, 8–9

READING 2, 1 CORINTHIANS 7:29–31

I tell you, brothers and sisters, the time is running out. From now on, let those having wives act as not having them, those weeping as not weeping, those rejoicing as not rejoicing, those buying as not owning, those using the world as not using it fully. For the world in its present form is passing away.

GOSPEL, MARK 1:14–20

After John had been arrested, Jesus came to Galilee proclaiming the gospel of God: "This is the time of fulfillment. The kingdom of God is at hand. Repent, and believe in the gospel." As he passed by the Sea of Galilee, he saw Simon and his brother Andrew casting their nets into the sea; they were fishermen. Jesus said to them, "Come after me, and I will make you fishers of men." Then they abandoned their nets and followed him. He walked along a little farther and saw James, the son of Zebedee, and his brother John. They too were in a boat mending their nets. Then he called them. So they left their father Zebedee in the boat along with the hired men and followed him.

The Time Is Now

This week, our emphasis is on responding to God's call as soon as possible, even if that response comes at a cost. We join Jonah in the middle of his story. When God told him to go to Nineveh, he tried to run away. We know how the story goes. When a storm arises, Jonah knows it is God's work and tells the frightened sailors to throw him overboard. A great fish swallows him. Jonah prays to God and promises to obey. After the fish vomits him onto the shore, Jonah goes to Nineveh where the power of his preaching is so great that the people believe his message and immediately turn away from sin. God "changes his mind" about the destruction he intended. A little further in the book, we learn Jonah is unhappy about that.

How could the Ninevites be so sure they did the right thing? We rarely feel that clear. When we read the epistle and Gospel, we are struck again by the immediacy of Paul's warning that the present age is passing away and the way the first disciples left everything to follow Jesus. Can we do the same?

Waiting for the End

Paul's belief that Jesus would return soon shaped his message. It was also part of the reason he didn't advocate a change in the social constructs of the time. Rather, he urged the Christian community to live very differently than their pagan counterparts and remember that all the baptized were welcome to the eucharistic table regardless of who they were. The Corinthians disagreed about who was most important. Paul reminds them that the Lord is coming soon, and the world's values and cares aren't nearly as important.

Similarly, we get mixed messages today about what's important. Paul urges a detachment from the world's values saying: "Keep your mind on God, not on what the world tells you is important." It seems to echo the commands to watch for the Master we heard about in Advent. That message is good whether Christ is coming tomorrow or a millennium from now.

Leaving Our Old Selves Behind

In Mark's characteristically terse writing, Jesus simply calls to Simon, Andrew, James, and John and says, "Follow me." Amazingly, they immediately leave everything to follow this itinerant preacher whom they did not know. A closer look reveals the enormity of their action. They left their nets, a primary component of their livelihood as fishermen. When Simon and Andrew drop them, they imply complete trust that God will provide for them. James and John hear the call and leave not only their nets but their boat. Only wealthy fishermen had boats; James and John turn their back on this wealth. They also leave their families, which was very important in Hebrew life.

Jesus was compelling. Jesus called fishermen to be more authentically and deeply who they were and gave them a mission: to be fishers of all people. He called fishermen to fulfill their trade, calling in a way they had not imagined. I think they had to follow and did so with a glad heart, even when the going got rough.

Good News for All of Us

Following Jesus takes more than a willing heart. We must have the courage to leave our old selves behind and become someone who sees the world differently and acts accordingly. Like the Ninevites, we must repent of our sins and turn away from the things that keep us from God. Like the Corinthians, we must detach ourselves from our need to control our lives and become more aware of God's presence in the world. Finally, we must trust completely in the Lord in order to respond as quickly as possible to Jesus' call to follow him. The grace is there for us to do it if we open ourselves to listen.

Questions for Reflection and Discussion

➤ *How would you know that God was calling you? What are some of the signs you would look for?*

➤ *What do you think are some of the obstacles in your life that may keep you from following Jesus or the call he has for you?*

Related Journey of Faith Lesson

C12, "Church History"

Themes

Prophet
     C10, "The People of God"
Rebirth
     C4, "The Sacrament of Confirmation"
Repentance
     C6, "The Sacrament of Penance and
     Reconciliation"

READING 1, DEUTERONOMY 18:15–20

Moses spoke to all the people, saying: "A prophet like me will the LORD, your God, raise up for you from among your own kin; to him you shall listen. This is exactly what you requested of the LORD, your God, at Horeb on the day of the assembly, when you said, 'Let us not again hear the voice of the LORD, our God, nor see this great fire any more, lest we die.' And the LORD said to me, 'This was well said. I will raise up for them a prophet like you from among their kin, and will put my words into his mouth; he shall tell them all that I command him. Whoever will not listen to my words which he speaks in my name, I myself will make him answer for it. But if a prophet presumes to speak in my name an oracle that I have not commanded him to speak, or speaks in the name of other gods, he shall die.'"

PSALM 95:1–2, 6–7, 7–9

READING 2, 1 CORINTHIANS 7:32–35

Brothers and sisters: I should like you to be free of anxieties. An unmarried man is anxious about the things of the Lord, how he may please the Lord. But a married man is anxious about the things of the world, how he may please his wife, and he is divided. An unmarried woman or a virgin is anxious about the things of the Lord, so that she may be holy in both body and spirit. A married woman, on the other hand, is anxious about the things of the world, how she may please her husband. I am telling you this for your own benefit, not to impose a restraint upon you, but for the sake of propriety and adherence to the Lord without distraction.

GOSPEL, MARK 1:21–28

Then they came to Capernaum, and on the sabbath Jesus entered the synagogue and taught. The people were astonished at his teaching, for he taught them as one having authority and not as the scribes. In their synagogue was a man with an unclean spirit; he cried out, "What have you to do with us, Jesus of Nazareth? Have you come to destroy us? I know who you are—the Holy One of God!" Jesus rebuked him and said, "Quiet! Come out of him!" The unclean spirit convulsed him and with a loud cry came out of him. All were amazed and asked one another, "What is this? A new teaching with authority. He commands even the unclean spirits and they obey him." His fame spread everywhere throughout the whole region of Galilee.

The One with Authority

In our daily lives, most of us can do what needs to be done. We do our jobs, we cook, and we clean and care for our families and friends. When we get stuck on something, we ask for advice or we look on the internet, all of which gives us a feeling of competence. But when things get difficult in our lives, we turn to those who have real expertise to help us out of the rough spot. Today's readings encourage us to look in the direction of God's help.

The Prophet Like Moses

Deuteronomy records the last address Moses gave to the people before they entered the Promised Land. He reminds them of their time in Egypt and the giving of the Ten Commandments. He speaks in the name of God and with such authority that it is sometimes difficult to tell whether Moses or God is speaking. Moses delineates the laws that will govern the people in the Promised Land, beginning with the great "Shema" in Deuteronomy 6:4–5: "Hear, O Israel, the Lord is our God, the Lord alone. You shall love the Lord your God with all your heart and all your soul and all your might." Moses also talked about the characteristics of priests, prophets, and kings in the new land. We hear God's promise to raise up a prophet like Moses when it's needed (Deuteronomy 18:15–19). At the very end of the book, we are told there has not arisen a prophet like Moses since Moses died. The Israelites were waiting for that person to appear.

The Appearance of the Holy One of God

In the first five chapters of Mark's Gospel, Jesus gradually but inexorably establishes his authority over the whole of human life. His first public appearance is in the synagogue, the center of Jewish life. There, Jesus taught in a compelling and completely natural manner; his teaching astounds his listeners. When a possessed man enters, the unclean spirit identifies Jesus as the "Holy One of God." Unclean spirits recognized Jesus often when others did not. Jesus rebukes the spirit, silences him, and commands him to come out. Jesus' authority over unclean spirits makes him the talk of the town. Over time, and under the guidance of the Holy Spirit, the Church was able to recognize and define connections between prophets like Moses and Jesus with greater clarity.

How Are We to Live Our Lives?

At first glance, Paul clearly thinks that marriage is a distraction to serving the Lord, and he wants people to serve the Lord wholeheartedly. Remember, Paul believed that the Lord was coming soon and he wanted people to be ready. We have come to a different appreciation for the vocation of marriage. Each of us is called to make the world holy in whatever vocation we find ourselves, including marriage, the priesthood, and consecrated life, and to do the same within the various careers or ministries we work. To grow in love is to grow in God and help build our Christian community for God's glory.

Good News for All of Us

Regardless of the responsibilities or worries we carry, we are all asked to follow God's call in our lives and to become disciples of Jesus wherever we are. While this is a tall order, we can look to Jesus to reinforce God's love for us and his everlasting mercy. This does not give us permission to do whatever we want without consequences.

Remember what Deuteronomy says: "Whoever will not listen to my words which he speaks in my name, I myself will make him answer for it." Our duty is to listen to what Jesus says and obey it in whatever state of life we find ourselves. It is hard to balance the cares of this world with the command to obey and serve the Lord. But grace abounds, as St. Paul says, and Jesus will not abandon us in our efforts to follow God and his commands.

Questions for Reflection and Discussion

➤ How do you find quiet time to pray to God and reflect on the way God has been active in your life?

➤ Saint Ignatius says we should do everything for the greater glory of God. Consider how you can more fully heed this admonition.

Related Journey of Faith Lesson

C13, "Christian Moral Living"

Themes

Authority
    C12, "Church History"
Holy Orders
    C9, "The Sacrament of Holy Orders"
Marriage
    C8, "The Sacrament of Matrimony"

Fifth Sunday in Ordinary Time, Year B

READING 1, JOB 7:1–4, 6–7

Job spoke, saying: Is not man's life on earth a drudgery? Are not his days those of hirelings? He is a slave who longs for the shade, a hireling who waits for his wages. So I have been assigned months of misery, and troubled nights have been allotted to me. If in bed I say, "When shall I arise?" then the night drags on; I am filled with restlessness until the dawn. My days are swifter than a weaver's shuttle; they come to an end without hope. Remember that my life is like the wind; I shall not see happiness again.

PSALM 147:1–2, 3–4, 5–6

READING 2, 1 CORINTHIANS 9:16–19, 22–23

Brothers and sisters: If I preach the gospel, this is no reason for me to boast, for an obligation has been imposed on me, and woe to me if I do not preach it! If I do so willingly, I have a recompense, but if unwillingly, then I have been entrusted with a stewardship. What then is my recompense? That, when I preach, I offer the gospel free of charge so as not to make full use of my right in the gospel. Although I am free in regard to all, I have made myself a slave to all so as to win over as many as possible. To the weak I became weak, to win over the weak. I have become all things to all, to save at least some. All this I do for the sake of the gospel, so that I too may have a share in it.

GOSPEL, MARK 1:29–39

On leaving the synagogue Jesus entered the house of Simon and Andrew with James and John. Simon's mother-in-law lay sick with a fever. They immediately told him about her. He approached, grasped her hand, and helped her up. Then the fever left her and she waited on them. When it was evening, after sunset, they brought to him all who were ill or possessed by demons. The whole town was gathered at the door. He cured many who were sick with various diseases, and he drove out many demons, not permitting them to speak because they knew him. Rising very early before dawn, he left and went off to a deserted place, where he prayed. Simon and those who were with him pursued him and on finding him said, "Everyone is looking for you." He told them, "Let us go on to the nearby villages that I may preach there also. For this purpose have I come." So he went into their synagogues, preaching and driving out demons throughout the whole of Galilee.

God and the Human Condition

As we move deeper into Ordinary Time, Jesus moves closer to the human condition. In today's readings, we hear Job's cry of anguish as he reflects on the turn his life has taken. His success, wealth, and family have been taken from him. Job becomes destitute, a condition brought about by a wager between Satan and God. Job might be forgiven for his wailing and his feelings of emptiness. Here he reflects on the mortal nature of human beings and their swift passing in this world.

By contrast, Jesus enters into the human condition. He takes on mortality and walks with people in their illness and suffering. For good measure he invites the disciples to share in the mission for which he was sent. Paul, who met Jesus only in a vision, takes up his mission to proclaim the Good News to all who would listen. He talks about his obligation to preach even if he doesn't want to for the sake of sharing in the blessings of the gospel.

Jesus Enters Our Lives

Here we meet Jesus in the center of social life, in Simon Peter's house in the middle of town. The miraculous healing of Simon's mother-in-law tells us that not only can Jesus cast out demons, but he also has power over physical ailments. By the end of the day, the townspeople bring all who are sick or possessed to Jesus for his healing touch. Mark records that the whole city came to the door.

When the marathon healing session is finished, Jesus withdraws to pray. In his human nature, Jesus must take time alone with his Father, knowing that all power comes from God. When his disciples find him, they tell him, "Everyone is looking for you." Jesus includes them in his work knowing that proclaiming God's kingdom will become their mission soon enough: "Let us go on to the nearby villages...." Jesus moves through each town, preaching in the synagogues and casting out demons. More and more people begin to follow him.

Good News for All of Us

Job felt alone and hurt. He was suffering and miserable. He wondered where God was. His visiting friends were no help. They insisted he or his children must have done something wrong. They thought he might have disrespected God. This ideology supported the prevailing theology of the time—misfortune was the result of sin. The story of Job is meant to dispel that myth, but old thinking doesn't die quickly, and many continue to think a sudden tragedy is the result of sin.

The people who encountered Jesus were suffering as well. Roman rule oppressed them. Many were very poor; some were very sick; and more than a few seemed to be possessed by demons. The Romans didn't help them, and the promise of a Messiah seemed very far away. Jesus entered their midst. He spoke with great authority and displayed power that could have only come from God.

Mark tells us God walks with us in our suffering. Faith in God doesn't guarantee that no pain or sorrow will ever befall us. Natural disasters happen, human bodies and minds are frail, human hearts and souls sometimes give in to evil. Despite this, we have hope. God promises he will be with us always. He offers healing when that is called for, brings peace in troubled times, and stands with us even to the end of our lives. When Jesus suffered on the cross, he not only freed us from sin, but he entered into the deep mystery of life—the mystery of suffering and evil. In his resurrection, Jesus proves that suffering and death is not the end. We will live in Christ and he will be Lord of all.

Questions for Reflection and Discussion

> *Have you ever felt like you were alone or abandoned by God when something bad happened? How did you get over that feeling? What would you recommend to someone who is feeling similarly?*

> *Who would you give almost anything to see in person? What draws you to that individual?*

Related Journey of Faith Lesson

C7, "The Sacrament of the Anointing of the Sick"

Themes

Healing
    C7, "The Sacrament of the Anointing of the Sick"
Persecution
    C14, "The Dignity of Life"
Solidarity
    C16, "Social Justice"

Sixth Sunday in Ordinary Time, Year B

READING 1, LEVITICUS 13:1–2, 44–46

The LORD said to Moses and Aaron, "If someone has on his skin a scab or pustule or blotch which appears to be the sore of leprosy, he shall be brought to Aaron, the priest, or to one of the priests among his descendants. If the man is leprous and unclean, the priest shall declare him unclean by reason of the sore on his head. "The one who bears the sore of leprosy shall keep his garments rent and his head bare, and shall muffle his beard; he shall cry out, 'Unclean, unclean!' As long as the sore is on him he shall declare himself unclean, since he is in fact unclean. He shall dwell apart, making his abode outside the camp."

PSALM 32:1–2, 5, 11

READING 2, 1 CORINTHIANS 10:31—11:1

Brothers and sisters, whether you eat or drink, or whatever you do, do everything for the glory of God. Avoid giving offense, whether to the Jews or Greeks or the church of God, just as I try to please everyone in every way, not seeking my own benefit but that of the many, that they may be saved. Be imitators of me, as I am of Christ.

GOSPEL, MARK 1:40–45

A leper came to Jesus and kneeling down begged him and said, "If you wish, you can make me clean." Moved with pity, he stretched out his hand, touched him, and said to him, "I do will it. Be made clean." The leprosy left him immediately, and he was made clean. Then, warning him sternly, he dismissed him at once. He said to him, "See that you tell no one anything, but go, show yourself to the priest and offer for your cleansing what Moses prescribed; that will be proof for them." The man went away and began to publicize the whole matter. He spread the report abroad so that it was impossible for Jesus to enter a town openly. He remained outside in deserted places, and people kept coming to him from everywhere.

Sin and Sickness

In biblical times, diseases like chicken pox would have rendered a person unclean. Part of that is because of the contagious nature of the disease and part is because of the chance the person would begin to bleed from his or her sores. Blood was synonymous with life. If someone was bleeding, life was spilling out of him and he was thought to be unclean. The priests knew the difference between transitory rashes or burns and diseases like leprosy. The critical element was the presence of raw flesh.

The method of dealing with such diseases might strike us as extreme, but the reading from Leviticus represents both the medical and spiritual reaction to such things. Medically, those with open sores and lesions were quarantined so others wouldn't get sick. Spiritually, the concern was that the disease might be the result of sin, and so the verdict of unclean or clean was left to the priest who examined the sores for signs of more serious conditions. If the person recovered, he was examined by the priest to see if he had been cured physically, and he offered sacrifice for sin and in praise of God for ritual purity.

A Radical Cure

As Jesus continues healing and teaching in Mark's Gospel, he encounters a leper and does something unthinkable for his time. Jesus touches the leper as he cures him. In a simple but radical way, Jesus demonstrates that the power of God is greater than this disease. He also shows his compassion in reaching out to those who are ostracized. He commands the leper to show himself to the priest and offer sacrifice as was written in the law. Oddly, he tells the man to say nothing about this. Jesus does not want people coming to him simply because he can heal. The man, of course, spreads the news of his cure, and Mark tells us people came to him from every quarter.

Many of us don't like asking for help when we're suffering or ill, particularly if the illness is psychological or emotional. The Gospel has two pieces of good news for us. The first is that Jesus wants to make us whole. This does not always mean cured, but God can work through friends, doctors, counselors, and family to bring peace to our minds and hearts. Jesus doesn't shun us; he walks with us in our isolation. The second is this: we hear again that everyone was coming to Jesus—everyone. Whatever might be wrong with us, we are not alone. We join many who are already coming to Jesus and asking for what they need. The answer may not come in the way we expect or be the answer we thought we wanted, but it will come. And we will find ourselves face to face with Jesus just as we are.

Good News for All of Us

People who are sick for a long time begin to feel isolated and alone. Others go on with their lives and forget that the sick can use some compassion and cheering up. The lepers in the Bible were ordered to be apart from the community. No one came to visit them because they were unclean. Jesus defies convention with a kind word, a soothing touch, and the healing the leper most wanted to have.

Questions for Reflection and Discussion

> *Has there been a time when it was difficult to ask friends or family for help? What made you able to do so?*

> *Is there anyone you know who is isolated from the community because of physical or psychological illness? How can you reach out to that person?*

Related Journey of Faith Lesson

C7, "The Sacrament of the Anointing of the Sick"

Themes

Renewal
    C7, "The Sacrament of the Anointing the Sick"
Sin
    C6, "The Sacrament of Penance and Reconciliation"
Suffering
    C14, "The Dignity of Life"

Seventh Sunday in Ordinary Time, Year B

READING 1, ISAIAH 43:18–19, 21–22, 24B–25

Thus says the LORD: Remember not the events of the past, the things of long ago consider not; see, I am doing something new! Now it springs forth, do you not perceive it? In the desert I make a way, in the wasteland, rivers. The people I formed for myself, that they might announce my praise. Yet you did not call upon me, O Jacob, for you grew weary of me, O Israel. You burdened me with your sins, and wearied me with your crimes. It is I, I, who wipe out, for my own sake, your offenses; your sins I remember no more.

PSALM 41:2–3, 4–5, 13–14

READING 2, 2 CORINTHIANS 1:18–22

Brothers and sisters: As God is faithful, our word to you is not "yes" and "no." For the Son of God, Jesus Christ, who was proclaimed to you by us, Silvanus and Timothy and me, was not "yes" and "no," but "yes" has been in him. For however many are the promises of God, their Yes is in him; therefore, the Amen from us also goes through him to God for glory. But the one who gives us security with you in Christ and who anointed us is God; he has also put his seal upon us and given the Spirit in our hearts as a first installment.

GOSPEL, MARK 2:1–12

When Jesus returned to Capernaum after some days, it became known that he was at home. Many gathered together so that there was no longer room for them, not even around the door, and he preached the word to them. They came bringing to him a paralytic carried by four men. Unable to get near Jesus because of the crowd, they opened up the roof above him. After they had broken through, they let down the mat on which the paralytic was lying. When Jesus saw their faith, he said to the paralytic, "Child, your sins are forgiven." Now some of the scribes were sitting there asking themselves, "Why does this man speak that way? He is blaspheming. Who but God alone can forgive sins?" Jesus immediately knew in his mind what they were thinking to themselves, so he said, "Why are you thinking such things in your hearts? Which is easier, to say to the paralytic, 'Your sins are forgiven,' or to say, 'Rise, pick up your mat and walk?' But that you may know that the Son of Man has authority to forgive sins on earth"—he said to the paralytic, "I say to you, rise, pick up your mat, and go home." He rose, picked up his mat at once, and went away in the sight of everyone. They were all astounded and glorified God, saying, "We have never seen anything like this."

Something New

In the Church year, we are fast approaching Lent. From healing illness to casting out demons in synagogues, homes, and towns, Jesus has walked into our lives without hesitancy. In today's reading, Jesus touches someone's soul with forgiveness. No one ever saw anything like it. Only God forgave sins.

To help us understand, the Church chose the reading from Isaiah, which tells the people to forget the past and look at what is new. Remembering and forgetting are important themes in both Old Testament and the New Testament. If God remembered someone, God acted toward that person, usually in some good way. If God forgot someone, that person would cease to exist. When God doesn't remember sin, it isn't swept under the rug; it's gone. The sinner gets to start anew and transform his or her life.

God's Promise Is Always Yes

Paul's brief passage from 2 Corinthians is an encouragement to the people of Corinth. God's promise through his Son, Jesus, is that God himself will bring justice to the world. It is understandable that people who have been waiting a long time for justice and freedom might be discouraged as the Roman Empire continues to hold sway. Also in that time, many people were claiming to be the Messiah or to have a new teaching. Paul reminds the Corinthians that Jesus was God's faithful yes. Paul also points out that the God they heard in Isaiah's passage was the same God who sent Jesus and now sends Paul and his companions to them. The Spirit the people sense in Paul is the first fruit of Paul's faith in Jesus.

Faith, Forgiveness, and Healing

Mark's Gospel is the only one where we hear about Jesus being at home. In our imaginations, we might see Jesus sitting down relaxing, but as has been the case, people crowd around the house hoping to get in. The paralyzed man would never have made it before Jesus except that the man's four friends remove part of the roof from Jesus' home and lower the man inside.

In this story, Jesus does something new. When he sees the faith of the man's friends, he turns to the paralytic and forgives his sin. The words caused consternation among the scribes who dared not say anything. Rather, they questioned in their hearts how Jesus could do this. Jesus does another new thing. He calls them out, showing that he knows what they are thinking and feeling. They do not think he has the authority to forgive sin. Jesus proves his authority by curing the paralytic. In Mark's Gospel, Jesus is the embodiment of God's new thing.

Good News for All of Us

The New Testament emphasizes how forgiveness plays an important role in allowing an individual to feel they renewed their relationship with God. In the Lord's Prayer, one of the hardest parts is praying, "Forgive us our trespasses as we forgive those who trespass against us." The connection between God's mercy and ours is profound. Before Jesus ascended into heaven, he gave the gift of forgiveness to the Church by giving the power to forgive to the apostles. Over the years, the Church developed the ritual that is the sacrament of penance and reconciliation, in which we confess our sins to a priest and receive the assurance of God's pardon and the absolution of sins by the Church.

Every time we enter into the sacrament with a willing and contrite heart, we affirm God's promise to forget our sins and allow us to begin anew and turn our lives to Christ. We model the sacramental forgiveness of the Church by forgiving one another when our relationships become broken. We can also ask God's help in forgiving ourselves for not being perfect or living up to the standards we set for ourselves. Knowing that God can forgive us makes our own ability to forgive a little easier.

Questions for Reflection and Discussion

➤ Which do you think is easier to say: "Your sins are forgiven" or "Take up your mat and walk"?

➤ Why can't we simply pray directly to God for forgiveness? Why do we need to go to a priest?

Related Journey of Faith Lesson

C6, "The Sacrament of Penance and Reconciliation"

Themes

Anointing
    C7, "The Sacrament of the Anointing of the Sick"
Christology
    Q4, "Who Is Jesus Christ?"
Forgiveness
    C6, "The Sacrament of Penance and Reconciliation"

Eighth Sunday in Ordinary Time, Year B

READING 1, HOSEA 2:16B, 17B, 21–22

Thus says the LORD: I will lead her into the desert and speak to her heart. She shall respond there as in the days of her youth, when she came up from the land of Egypt. I will espouse you to me forever: I will espouse you in right and in justice, in love and in mercy; I will espouse you in fidelity, and you shall know the LORD.

PSALM 103:1–2, 3–4, 8, 10, 12–13

READING 2, 2 CORINTHIANS 3:1B–6

Brothers and sisters: Do we need, as some do, letters of recommendation to you or from you? You are our letter, written on our hearts, known and read by all, shown to be a letter of Christ ministered by us, written not in ink but by the Spirit of the living God, not on tablets of stone but on tablets that are hearts of flesh. Such confidence we have through Christ toward God. Not that of ourselves we are qualified to take credit for anything as coming from us; rather, our qualification comes from God, who has indeed qualified us as ministers of a new covenant, not of letter but of spirit; for the letter brings death, but the Spirit gives life.

GOSPEL, MARK 2:18–22

The disciples of John and of the Pharisees were accustomed to fast. People came to him and objected, "Why do the disciples of John and the disciples of the Pharisees fast, but your disciples do not fast?" Jesus answered them, "Can the wedding guests fast while the bridegroom is with them? As long as they have the bridegroom with them they cannot fast. But the days will come when the bridegroom is taken away from them, and then they will fast on that day. No one sews a piece of unshrunken cloth on an old cloak. If he does, its fullness pulls away, the new from the old, and the tear gets worse. Likewise, no one pours new wine into old wineskins. Otherwise, the wine will burst the skins, and both the wine and the skins are ruined. Rather, new wine is poured into fresh wineskins."

Remembering Who We Are

In the days of the prophet Hosea, the Israelites became intrigued with the gods of the foreign nations. They saw nothing wrong with combining the worship of the Lord with the worship of these others. *Wasn't one god as good as another?* Hosea uses an example from his own life to talk about God's relationship with Israel as a marriage. He likened the worship of other gods to adultery. In a beautiful image, Hosea relays that God himself will lure Israel back to the wilderness—the place where God first made a covenant with the people. He wants to remind the people who they are and to whom they belong so that God can renew his covenant with them. The fact that God continuously renews his covenant with his people is a miracle of love and mercy. When we read Hosea, we gain some insight into just how much God loves us.

You Are Our Letter

When people know they are loved, it shows in their facial expressions and mannerisms. They are confident, happy, and at peace. When people know God loves them, they exude joy and act with compassion and serve others. Paul's Second Letter to the Corinthians tells them they don't need to write a letter of recommendation for Paul to the next town—their actions are proof of their belief. Paul gives all credit to God whose grace moves him to preach the gospel. Jeremiah once prophesied that the new covenant will not be carved in stone but carved directly in the heart (Jeremiah 31:31–34). For Paul, the Corinthian people serve as proof that the Holy Spirit is present among them.

A New Covenant Requires a New People

At first glance, the Gospel seems to have little to do with the other two readings, but a closer look yields some parallels. Jesus draws on the reality of marriage when the question of fasting comes up. He rightfully proclaims that the guests will not fast when the bridegroom is present. The Pharisees were probably puzzled by his words because they would not have assumed that he was talking about the relationship between God and Israel. They could not dispute the truth of his words, however. Jesus goes on to talk about what happens when something new is put together with something old. Anyone who has ever mended a sweater or a pair of pants knows that the ends of a hole are often frayed and weak. The mender must be careful to reinforce the patch so it will hold.

Mark's Gospel relates the notion of new wine in a new wineskin, but the message remains the same. Israel had to go back to the wilderness to accept God's loving covenant and live as the children of God. The new teaching that Jesus gives required all who heard it to become new so that the teaching could take root in their hearts and grow. We also must allow the Good News to infiltrate our whole beings before we can be the "letter" that shares the gospel with others.

Good News for All of Us

God remains ever faithful and loving in our relationship with him. In our theology of marriage, we say that the relationship of each partner to the other should be such that the presence of God is evident in his or her love. Such marriages are fruitful. Unfortunately, due to human frailty and weakness, some marriages also end in divorce. Here is where the relationship experienced in marriage differs from our relationship with God. We may leave God, but God will never leave us. Instead, he waits patiently for our return. In response to God's never-ending mercy, we humbly ask to begin anew as we try to become a person that can hold all that God has to offer and share it with others.

Questions for Reflection and Discussion

> *Where are you in your relationship with God? Is this the honeymoon phase? Or is this a renewal of a past relationship?*

> *If you were the letter sent by Paul or Jesus, what would people read in you?*

Related Journey of Faith Lesson

C6, "The Sacrament of Penance and Reconciliation"

Themes

Eucharist
    C5, "The Eucharist"
    C11, "The Early Church Liturgy"
Liturgy
    C10, "The People of God"
    C12, "Church History"
Love
    C8, "The Sacrament of Matrimony"

READING 1, GENESIS 9:8–15

God said to Noah and to his sons with him: "See, I am now establishing my covenant with you and your descendants after you and with every living creature that was with you: all the birds, and the various tame and wild animals that were with you and came out of the ark. I will establish my covenant with you, that never again shall all bodily creatures be destroyed by the waters of a flood; there shall not be another flood to devastate the earth." God added: "This is the sign that I am giving for all ages to come, of the covenant between me and you and every living creature with you: I set my bow in the clouds to serve as a sign of the covenant between me and the earth. When I bring clouds over the earth, and the bow appears in the clouds, I will recall the covenant I have made between me and you and all living beings, so that the waters shall never again become a flood to destroy all mortal beings."

PSALM 25:4–5, 6–7, 8–9

READING 2, 1 PETER 3:18–22

Beloved: Christ suffered for sins once, the righteous for the sake of the unrighteous, that he might lead you to God. Put to death in the flesh, he was brought to life in the Spirit. In it he also went to preach to the spirits in prison, who had once been disobedient while God patiently waited in the days of Noah during the building of the ark, in which a few persons, eight in all, were saved through water. This prefigured baptism, which saves you now. It is not a removal of dirt from the body but an appeal to God for a clear conscience, through the resurrection of Jesus Christ, who has gone into heaven and is at the right hand of God, with angels, authorities, and powers subject to him.

GOSPEL, MARK 1:12–15

The Spirit drove Jesus out into the desert, and he remained in the desert for forty days, tempted by Satan. He was among wild beasts, and the angels ministered to him. After John had been arrested, Jesus came to Galilee proclaiming the gospel of God: "This is the time of fulfillment. The kingdom of God is at hand. Repent, and believe in the gospel."

A Time for Change

In an effort to change for the better and become the people Jesus wants us to be, we do three things during Lent:

- Pray more fervently and frequently than before.
- Fast from little pleasures with the understanding that our fasting is more than an endurance test until Easter but a real effort to share in Christ's suffering.
- Give alms, to place ourselves in solidarity with those who have less.

The lure to renew our lives is so great that Ash Wednesday often brings great crowds to church.

Today's readings mark the beginning of our Lenten journey. Genesis tells the story of God's first covenant with Noah, a promise never again to destroy the earth with a flood. The epistle emphasizes God's new covenant in the blood of Christ. Finally, Jesus goes into the wilderness to be tempted and overcomes Satan. Renewed in spirit, Jesus comes preaching about the kingdom of God and inviting people to repent and believe. All three readings are a clarion call to transform our hearts.

The Flood as New Creation

The first chapters of Genesis tell the story of the world from creation to the Fall of Adam and Eve to the spread of humanity on the earth. Though there were some good people, the earth and its inhabitants were corrupted by sin and seemed destined for ruin. God's plan to send a great flood echoes the original creation when the Spirit of God moved across the waters. Warned by God to build an ark, Noah obeys, and God delivers his family and the animals through the Flood.

Water has always been a symbol of chaos. The story of Noah and the Flood, passed down from generation to generation, seems to have taken its final written form when the Israelites had just suffered the chaos of exile. These first stories of Genesis reflect an emphasis on themes of God's plan and God's control over the world. It was a way of helping people cope with what had happened. In chaotic times we want to know that someone is in charge. The Flood was God's way of giving a new start to those who needed it.

Baptism as New Creation

Peter was clear. Christ died for us in order to bring us to God. After his resurrection, Christ also went to preach the Good News to the souls who were imprisoned. Just as the Flood renewed the world, baptism makes us a new creation through Jesus. The promise of salvation is fulfilled in Christ. Peter points out that only eight people were saved by the ark in the great Flood. He reveals a fuller understanding of baptism: "...It is not a removal of dirt from the body by an appeal to a God for a clear conscience, through the resurrection of Jesus Christ..." (1 Peter 3:21).

Repentance—a Change of Mind and Heart

After the baptism of Jesus, Mark says that the Spirit immediately drove Jesus into the wilderness. In Jesus' story, the connection between his baptism and temptation shows us that baptismal grace does not eliminate our encounter with temptations. But we can take solace in the fact that the power of the Holy Spirit and the love of God, can help overcome these temptations. The mention of angels and wild beasts suggest Jesus' power over both heavenly and earthly beings. After his wilderness battle, Jesus began his own preaching. His call to repent is a plea to change one's life. Jesus' message is clear: the kingdom of God is very near. To prepare, we open ourselves to God's invitation to a change of mind and heart.

Good News for All of Us

We might think we're too set in our ways or question how God could possibly want us in our broken state. But nothing is impossible for God. Jesus visits the spirits in prison after his crucifixion to proclaim the Good News. Similarly, we should consider the possibility that Jesus is speaking to us now through our own prison walls to proclaim our freedom to follow him in obedience to God. Whether it's our mind, heart, or an impossible situation that impedes our progress, the Lord invites our conversion. We can always begin anew—it is never too late to work toward change and become who God wants us to be.

Questions for Reflection and Discussion

➤ What will you do to make your Lenten disciplines last beyond six weeks?

➤ What tempts you away from living your best life? How do you defeat temptation?

Related Journey of Faith Lessons

E1, "Election: Saying Yes to Jesus"; and E2, "Living Lent"

Themes

Lent
    E2, "Living Lent"
Temptation
    E3, "Scrutinies: Looking Within"

Second Sunday of Lent, Year B

READING 1, GENESIS 22:1–2, 9A, 10–13, 15–18

God put Abraham to the test. He called to him, "Abraham!" "Here I am!" he replied. Then God said: "Take your son Isaac, your only one, whom you love, and go to the land of Moriah. There you shall offer him up as a holocaust on a height that I will point out to you." When they came to the place of which God had told him, Abraham built an altar there and arranged the wood on it. Then he reached out and took the knife to slaughter his son. But the Lord's messenger called to him from heaven, "Abraham, Abraham!" "Here I am!" he answered. "Do not lay your hand on the boy," said the messenger. "Do not do the least thing to him. I know now how devoted you are to God, since you did not withhold from me your own beloved son." As Abraham looked about, he spied a ram caught by its horns in the thicket. So he went and took the ram and offered it up as a holocaust in place of his son. Again the Lord's messenger called to Abraham from heaven and said: "I swear by myself, declares the Lord, that because you acted as you did in not withholding from me your beloved son, I will bless you abundantly and make your descendants as countless as the stars of the sky and the sands of the seashore; your descendants shall take possession of the gates of their enemies, and in your descendants all the nations of the earth shall find blessing—all this because you obeyed my command."

PSALM 116:10, 15, 16–17, 18–19

READING 2, ROMANS 8:31B–34

Brothers and sisters: If God is for us, who can be against us? He who did not spare his own Son but handed him over for us all, how will he not also give us everything else along with him? Who will bring a charge against God's chosen ones? It is God who acquits us, who will condemn? Christ Jesus it is who died—or, rather, was raised—who also is at the right hand of God, who indeed intercedes for us.

GOSPEL, MARK 9:2–10

Jesus took Peter, James, and John and led them up a high mountain apart by themselves. And he was transfigured before them, and his clothes became dazzling white, such as no fuller on earth could bleach them. Then Elijah appeared to them along with Moses, and they were conversing with Jesus. Then Peter said to Jesus in reply, "Rabbi, it is good that we are here! Let us make three tents: one for you, one for Moses, and one for Elijah." He hardly knew what to say, they were so terrified. Then a cloud came, casting a shadow over them; from the cloud came a voice, "This is my beloved Son. Listen to him." Suddenly, looking around, they no longer saw anyone but Jesus alone with them. As they were coming down from the mountain, he charged them not to relate what they had seen to anyone, except when the Son of Man had risen from the dead. So they kept the matter to themselves, questioning what rising from the dead meant.

Hidden Glory

The readings of Lent follow a pattern each year. The first Sunday, which relates Jesus' temptation in the desert, relates Jesus' humanity. The second Sunday gives a glimpse of Jesus' divinity in the transfiguration. Many scholars believe this story took place after the resurrection, but the synoptic Gospels (Matthew, Mark, and Luke) place it just before Jesus enters Jerusalem in the last chapter of his life. Peter, James, and John—who accompany Jesus in important stories in Mark's Gospel—go up the mountain with Jesus and are astounded by what they see and hear.

Accompanying the Gospel is the story of the sacrifice of Isaac from Genesis, which is described as a test from God. There is more than one test here, as we see. Paul expresses a confidence we also should adopt: If God was willing to sacrifice his own Son, how can we doubt that God will provide everything we need?

I Give Everything to You

Isaac is the long-awaited child promised by God to Abraham and Sarah. In the ancient Near East, many cultures worshiped gods who required human sacrifice. When the command comes to sacrifice his beloved son, Abraham has a choice to make. Even though God had promised Abraham his descendants would be through Isaac, Abraham is willing to offer his son as a sacrifice. "He reasoned that God was able to raise even from the dead, and he received Isaac back as a symbol" (Hebrews 11:19). After going to the designated place, Abraham gathers the wood and puts it on Isaac's shoulder. Isaac carries the wood for his own sacrifice! Just as Abraham is about to slay Isaac, an angel calls from a bush and tells him not to sacrifice Isaac. Abraham and Isaac's faith was being tested. They chose to obey God's command. God was pleased with Abraham's obedience. God blesses him, promises numerous descendants, and foretells that the nations will gain blessings because of his reverence.

Listen to Him

Mark underscores God's command to listen and, by inference, to obey Jesus. On the mountain, the disciples are speechless at the sight of Moses, who represents the law; Elijah, who represents the prophets; and the glorified Jesus, who is the fulfillment of both. Peter can't think of anything else to do but build three tents (reminiscent of the tent of meeting in the desert). When a cloud descends, we are reminded of the cloud on Mount Sinai. God's voice echoes the words spoken at Jesus' baptism. "This is my beloved Son."

In our lives, we relate mountaintop experiences as life-changing events. But we always have to come down. When Jesus and the others descend, he commands them not to tell anyone until "the Son of Man has risen from the dead." This foreshadows the crucifixion and resurrection, trials that are not quite understood at this point.

Good News for All of Us

When we make a change in our lives, it often means letting go of our old self and becoming someone new. When we get married, we let go of single life and its joys and challenges to embrace the new reality of a being part of a couple. We are willing to make that change because we believe we have found something better. When we become Christian, we let go of habits that keep us from obeying the commandments or the call to become more like Christ. As we embrace our new self who by grace is able to choose to follow Jesus, it is important to pray every day for the will of God to make itself known. Along with Abraham, we also lift our head to God and say, "Here I am."

Questions for Reflection and Discussion

➤ What was the last thing you did—small or great—that changed your life? How did your life change and why did you make the decision to go through with it?

➤ Have you ever given up something for someone else? Why? What could you sacrifice now for God?

Related Journey of Faith Lesson

E3, "Scrutinies: Looking Within"

Themes

Change
   E1, "Election: Saying Yes to Jesus"
Life-giving
   E3, "Scrutinies: Looking Within"
Love
   E5, "The Way of the Cross"

Third Sunday of Lent, Year B

READING 1, EXODUS 20:1–17

In those days, God delivered all these commandments: "I, the LORD, am your God, who brought you out of the land of Egypt, that place of slavery. You shall not have other gods besides me. You shall not carve idols for yourselves in the shape of anything in the sky above or on the earth below or in the waters beneath the earth; you shall not bow down before them or worship them. For I, the LORD, your God, am a jealous God, inflicting punishment for their fathers' wickedness on the children of those who hate me, down to the third and fourth generation; but bestowing mercy down to the thousandth generation on the children of those who love me and keep my commandments. You shall not take the name of the LORD, your God, in vain. For the LORD will not leave unpunished the one who takes his name in vain. Remember to keep holy the sabbath day. Six days you may labor and do all your work, but the seventh day is the sabbath of the LORD, your God. No work may be done then either by you, or your son or daughter, or your male or female slave, or your beast, or by the alien who lives with you. In six days the Lord made the heavens and the earth, the sea and all that is in them; but on the seventh day he rested. That is why the LORD has blessed the sabbath day and made it holy. Honor your father and your mother, that you may have a long life in the land which the LORD, your God, is giving you. You shall not kill. You shall not commit adultery. You shall not steal. You shall not bear false witness against your neighbor. You shall not covet your neighbor's house. You shall not covet your neighbor's wife, nor his male or female slave, nor his ox or ass, nor anything else that belongs to him."

PSALM 19:8, 9, 10, 11

READING 2, 1 CORINTHIANS 1:22–25

Brothers and sisters: Jews demand signs and Greeks look for wisdom, but we proclaim Christ crucified, a stumbling block to Jews and foolishness to Gentiles, but to those who are called, Jews and Greeks alike, Christ the power of God and the wisdom of God. For the foolishness of God is wiser than human wisdom, and the weakness of God is stronger than human strength.

GOSPEL, JOHN 2:13–25

Since the Passover of the Jews was near, Jesus went up to Jerusalem. He found in the temple area those who sold oxen, sheep, and doves, as well as the money changers seated there. He made a whip out of cords and drove them all out of the temple area, with the sheep and oxen, and spilled the coins of the money changers and overturned their tables, and to those who sold doves he said, "Take these out of here, and stop making my Father's house a marketplace." His disciples recalled the words of Scripture, *Zeal for your house will consume me.* At this the Jews answered and said to him, "What sign can you show us for doing this?" Jesus answered and said to them, "Destroy this temple and in three days I will raise it up." The Jews said, "This temple has been under construction for forty-six years, and you will raise it up in three days?" But he was speaking about the temple of his body. Therefore, when he was raised from the dead, his disciples remembered that he had said this, and they came to believe the Scripture and the word Jesus had spoken. While he was in Jerusalem for the feast of Passover, many began to believe in his name when they saw the signs he was doing. But Jesus would not trust himself to them because he knew them all, and did not need anyone to testify about human nature. He himself understood it well.

The Power and Wisdom of God

We forget that sometimes God's love challenges us to do right and use the guidelines we receive to determine what that looks like. Today's readings focus on the first set of laws the Israelites (and we likely) received. The Ten Commandments lay out rules for God's relationship with his people and the people with each other. The commandments were meant to put people in right relationships with God and community.

In the Gospel, Jesus drives out the moneychangers partly because he sees what they are doing as a violation of the sanctity of the Temple and thus a violation against God. In between the two readings, Paul points to Christ crucified as the power and wisdom of God, a stumbling block to the Jews who sought a Messiah to overturn Rome and foolishness to the Gentiles who thought their philosophers were the sources of wisdom.

I Am the Lord Your God

The Ten Commandments begin with God's self-identification as the Lord who "brought you out of the land of Egypt." For Jews, that alone is the first commandment or "word" (Hebrew translation). Once we know who is speaking, the message is met with deep gratitude. Of course, we want to follow his teaching—we owe him our very lives. We see that God demands faithfulness, a refusal to take his name in vain, and regular observance of the Lord's day. The laws also demand respect for parents and reverence for the dignity of every human being. The commandments are designed to allow each person to live in peace. With these laws, God makes a covenant with Israel. Every law that follows is derived in some way from the Ten Commandments.

Cleansing and Rebuilding the Temple

It was the custom for moneychangers and animal sellers to occupy the outer court of the Temple. The moneychangers exchanged the various coins people brought in for the common coin that paid the Temple tax. Those with animals often sold them to those who had no animals of their own to sacrifice in the Temple. It would seem that both activities were necessary to carry on Temple business. But Jesus drives them out for two reasons. First, he takes seriously the injunction from Isaiah that God's house be a house of prayer and not a marketplace. But even more, Jesus feels an urgency to stop the Temple sacrifices, not because he disagreed with the animal sacrifices *per se*, but because he knew he was the fulfillment of their symbolism. He was the true Lamb of God who would sacrifice himself and then reign in glory at the right hand of God. We see the hint of this in his exchange with the Jewish authorities. They thought he meant he would raise the Temple of stone in three days. Jesus meant the temple of his own body. Not surprisingly, those gathered didn't understand. Only after the resurrection did the disciples even remember it.

Good News For All of Us

The Ten Commandments remain our guide in our relationships with God and others. In the Old Testament, lawbreakers had to atone. A sacrifice in the Temple was required for serious offenses. Yearly, the nation paid for the sins of all. Jesus is the Lamb who was sacrificed for our sake once and for all. We can atone for our sins by turning to God and being disciples of Christ. At every Mass the sacrifice of the once-for-all true Lamb of God is re-presented for the forgiveness of our sins and the nourishment of our being as we partake of the Body and Blood of Christ in the Holy Eucharist. We have no greater example of self-giving love than Jesus Christ, who followed the Ten Commandments and was obedient to his Father.

Questions for Reflection and Discussion

➤ Are the Ten Commandments still valid for us today? What other guidelines from the New Testament do we follow?

➤ Paul talks about Christ crucified as a stumbling block to those who do not believe. What challenges do you think Catholics face today because of what they believe?

Related Journey of Faith Lesson

E4, "The Creed"

Themes

Cross
    E5, "The Way of the Cross"
Law
    E4, "The Creed"
Trust
    E1, "Election: Saying Yes to Jesus"

READING 1, 2 CHRONICLES 36:14–16, 19–23

In those days, all the princes of Judah, the priests, and the people added infidelity to infidelity, practicing all the abominations of the nations and polluting the LORD's temple, which he had consecrated in Jerusalem. Early and often did the LORD, the God of their fathers, send his messengers to them, for he had compassion on his people and his dwelling place. But they mocked the messengers of God, despised his warnings, and scoffed at his prophets, until the anger of the LORD against his people was so inflamed that there was no remedy. Their enemies burnt the house of God, tore down the walls of Jerusalem, set all its palaces afire, and destroyed all its precious objects. Those who escaped the sword were carried captive to Babylon, where they became servants of the king of the Chaldeans and his sons until the kingdom of the Persians came to power. All this was to fulfill the word of the LORD spoken by Jeremiah: "Until the land has retrieved its lost Sabbaths, during all the time it lies waste it shall have rest while seventy years are fulfilled." In the first year of Cyrus, king of Persia, in order to fulfill the word of the LORD spoken by Jeremiah, the LORD inspired King Cyrus of Persia to issue this proclamation throughout his kingdom, both by word of mouth and in writing: "Thus says Cyrus, king of Persia: All the kingdoms of the earth the LORD, the God of heaven, has given to me, and he has also charged me to build him a house in Jerusalem, which is in Judah. Whoever, therefore, among you belongs to any part of his people, let him go up, and may his God be with him!"

PSALM 137:1–2, 3, 4–5, 6

READING 2, EPHESIANS 2:4–10

Brothers and sisters: God, who is rich in mercy, because of the great love he had for us, even when we were dead in our transgressions, brought us to life with Christ— by grace you have been saved—, raised us up with him, and seated us with him in the heavens in Christ Jesus, that in the ages to come He might show the immeasurable riches of his grace in his kindness to us in Christ Jesus. For by grace you have been saved through faith, and this is not from you; it is the gift of God; it is not from works, so no one may boast. For we are his handiwork, created in Christ Jesus for the good works that God has prepared in advance, that we should live in them.

GOSPEL, JOHN 3:14–21

Jesus said to Nicodemus: "Just as Moses lifted up the serpent in the desert, so must the Son of Man be lifted up, so that everyone who believes in him may have eternal life." For God so loved the world that he gave his only Son, so that everyone who believes in him might not perish but might have eternal life. For God did not send his Son into the world to condemn the world, but that the world might be saved through him. Whoever believes in him will not be condemned, but whoever does not believe has already been condemned, because he has not believed in the name of the only Son of God. And this is the verdict, that the light came into the world, but people preferred darkness to light, because their works were evil. For everyone who does wicked things hates the light and does not come toward the light, so that his works might not be exposed. But whoever lives the truth comes to the light, so that his works may be clearly seen as done in God.

Rejoice All You Who Mourn

The entrance antiphon for this Sunday begins, "Rejoice, Jerusalem…Be joyful all who were in mourning." This is *Laetare* (Latin for "rejoice") Sunday. Long ago, it signaled a brief respite from the heavy Lenten fast of the time. But what is there to rejoice in? Our first reading from 2 Chronicles details the terrible punishment of exile, the last resort of God, who had sent many messengers to tell the people to repent of their sins. When they did not, the Babylonian victory was the result so that the people might learn to "keep Sabbath" and reverence the Lord. But God's mercy reasserts itself and he raises up Cyrus the Persian to free the people from exile and build a Temple in Jerusalem.

Paul's Letter to the Ephesians lightens the load a bit more when he tells us that God loved us even when we were dead in our sins. It was God's merciful love that raises us up with Christ. Finally, Christ tells Nicodemus that God sent him out of love, not to condemn the world, but to save it. From beginning to end, our readings celebrate the mercy of God, which is so much greater than his judgment.

Destruction Gives Way to Salvation

Stories like this one from 2 Chronicles are the reason people think the Old Testament God is angry and mean. Though God's anger is evident here, his mercy abounds even more. We're told that God's wrath lasts until the third or fourth generation, but his loving mercy lasts until the thousandth generation. In his compassion, God sent the prophets to steer people in the right direction. After the exile and again in compassion, the Lord uses Cyrus the Persian as his instrument. Cyrus wasn't an Israelite so it's amazing that he heard and obeyed God's voice when it came to him. The Psalms tell us the people went back to Israel rejoicing.

The mercy of God is what the Letter to the Ephesians highlights as well. We were sinners; of that Paul has no doubt. But God gave us a free gift of grace through Jesus. Similar to the Israelites who did nothing to earn their freedom by Cyrus, we did nothing to deserve such a gift. We were dead in sin. God made us alive in Christ.

God So Loved the World

In a passage in the Book of Numbers, the people grumble against the Lord and are bitten by poisonous snakes. When they complain, God tells Moses to lift up an image of the serpent that anyone who looks at it might live. John uses that analogy to talk about Christ being lifted up on the cross. We know, of course, that the people in Moses' time would die again. John says those who believe will have eternal life. For John, eternal life began with belief right now, not just when we died. This is the enormity of God's love for us. Our faith in the Son of God allows us to triumph over death.

Good News for All of Us

It's sometimes hard to be merciful, especially to someone who has messed things up for the umpteenth time. We find it hard to love others when we're tired or stressed. We don't know how to act when yet another beggar in the street seeks a donation. Celtic Christian spirituality often talks about the well at the bottom of the soul. That well is filled with God's love and mercy so that when we find ourselves running dry, we can come and drink deeply of what God has so freely given to us. It's an image we might find helpful as we make our way. And it's good to remember that love and compassion don't always come easy. Jesus gave his life for it and for us. Responding to others with love is an act of gratitude.

Questions for Reflection and Discussion

➤ *In what ways do you see the image of God in the Old and New Testaments alike and different?*

➤ *God is both a merciful and a just judge. How do we think God's justice and mercy are manifested today?*

Related Journey of Faith Lesson

E5, "The Way of the Cross"

Themes

Compassion
    E5, "The Way of the Cross"
Family
    E1, "Election: Saying Yes to Jesus"

Fifth Sunday of Lent, Year B

READING 1, JEREMIAH 31:31–34

The days are coming, says the LORD, when I will make a new covenant with the house of Israel and the house of Judah. It will not be like the covenant I made with their fathers the day I took them by the hand to lead them forth from the land of Egypt; for they broke my covenant, and I had to show myself their master, says the LORD. But this is the covenant that I will make with the house of Israel after those days, says the LORD. I will place my law within them and write it upon their hearts; I will be their God, and they shall be my people. No longer will they have need to teach their friends and relatives how to know the LORD. All, from least to greatest, shall know me, says the LORD, for I will forgive their evildoing and remember their sin no more.

PSALM 51:3–4, 12–13, 14–15

READING 2, HEBREWS 5:7–9

In the days when Christ Jesus was in the flesh, he offered prayers and supplications with loud cries and tears to the one who was able to save him from death, and he was heard because of his reverence. Son though he was, he learned obedience from what he suffered; and when he was made perfect, he became the source of eternal salvation for all who obey him.

GOSPEL, JOHN 12:20–33

Some Greeks who had come to worship at the Passover Feast came to Philip, who was from Bethsaida in Galilee, and asked him, "Sir, we would like to see Jesus." Philip went and told Andrew; then Andrew and Philip went and told Jesus. Jesus answered them, "The hour has come for the Son of Man to be glorified. Amen, amen, I say to you, unless a grain of wheat falls to the ground and dies, it remains just a grain of wheat; but if it dies, it produces much fruit. Whoever loves his life loses it, and whoever hates his life in this world will preserve it for eternal life. Whoever serves me must follow me, and where I am, there also will my servant be. The Father will honor whoever serves me. "I am troubled now. Yet what should I say? 'Father, save me from this hour'? But it was for this purpose that I came to this hour. Father, glorify your name." Then a voice came from heaven, "I have glorified it and will glorify it again." The crowd there heard it and said it was thunder; but others said, "An angel has spoken to him." Jesus answered and said, "This voice did not come for my sake but for yours. Now is the time of judgment on this world; now the ruler of this world will be driven out. And when I am lifted up from the earth, I will draw everyone to myself." He said this indicating the kind of death he would die.

We Have Come to See Jesus

As we move closer to Holy Week, our desire to come even closer to Jesus grows. Where does that desire come from? The reading from Jeremiah talks about the new covenant that God will write on the hearts of his people. God says, "Then they shall know me...." On the feast of the Baptism of the Lord, Isaiah spoke of the servant who is given as a covenant to the people and a light to the nations. At the Last Supper, Jesus talks about the "new covenant in my blood." The desire to seek God comes from God himself who longs for his people. The covenant written on the heart begins to take shape when Jesus comes. And just as Isaiah predicted, even the nations will come to the light that Jesus brings into the world.

A New Covenant

Like sections of Isaiah's prophecy, Jeremiah addresses the Israelite exiles in Babylon. Having recognized their sinfulness, they now hear a word of comfort from God who now promises something new. In drawing a contrast with Mosaic law, God does not imply that the law was bad; rather the people broke that covenant, perhaps because they did not know God for themselves.

The word Jeremiah uses for "write" actually means "carve." Just as the old law was carved on tablets of stone, this new one will be carved on the hearts of the people so they will know God from the inside out—his steadfast love and mercy. He will forgive their sins and allow them to start over.

The extent of God's steadfast love is depicted in the Letter to the Hebrews. This recalls Jesus' own agony as he realized the time for his crucifixion was at hand.

Jesus prays and cries to the father who can save him. The letter notes that God heard his prayer and that Jesus learned obedience through his suffering. What we realize, of course, is that he suffered and died for our sake so that we might have salvation. No greater love can be found.

The Hour has Come

The Greeks have asked to see Jesus. Greeks are pagans, according to the Jews. At first, Jesus' response to the disciples when they tell him seems odd. Jesus starts talking about grain and wheat and a troubled soul. A couple of things have happened. Remember, as stated in John's Gospel, to see is to understand. They want to know Jesus. Jesus wants all of them, including the disciples, to know who he is. And so he begins to tell them about the coming events. The hour Jesus refers to isn't a chronological time but the right time for something to happen. He makes an analogy—though admittedly one that's difficult to understand—between a grain of wheat that dies and the need for those who serve him to also follow him. The message asks for faithfulness and the courage to stay until the end.

Jesus does not even think about asking his Father to save him. He sees in the coming events that the Father's name will be glorified. In the Old Testament, this would have been followed by the phrase: "And all will know the Lord." The voice that comes confirms the divine presence, and Jesus speaks more plainly about his coming death.

Good News for All of Us

Recent scientific research has suggested the presence of a "God gene" that predisposes people to seek spiritual comfort. We can't prove that's true, but we can say this. Our faith tells us that God breathed his spirit into us when we were formed and that God knows us before we are born. From faith, we know that the world became broken through sin and we were alienated from God. And we believe that Jesus restored that relationship with God. Whatever draws us closer to him might be the Holy Spirit whispering, "Go and see Jesus." We see him in prayer, the sacraments, and in other people, so that we might come to know him.

Questions for Reflection and Discussion

> *If you were told you could come and see Jesus, what would you talk about or ask him?*

> *Consider a broken relationship in your life that later was renewed. Why did it break? What brought it back to life?*

Related Journey of Faith Lesson

E6, "The Lord's Prayer"

Theme

Forgiveness
    E3, "Scrutinies: Looking Within"
Suffering
    E5, "The Way of the Cross"

Passion (Palm) Sunday, Year B

PROCESSION WITH PALMS, MARK 11:1–10

When Jesus and his disciples drew near to Jerusalem, to Bethphage and Bethany at the Mount of Olives, he sent two of his disciples and said to them, "Go into the village opposite you, and immediately on entering it, you will find a colt tethered on which no one has ever sat. Untie it and bring it here. If anyone should say to you, 'Why are you doing this?' reply, 'The Master has need of it and will send it back here at once.'" So they went off and found a colt tethered at a gate outside on the street, and they untied it. Some of the bystanders said to them, "What are you doing, untying the colt?" They answered them just as Jesus had told them to, and they permitted them to do it. So they brought the colt to Jesus and put their cloaks over it. And he sat on it. Many people spread their cloaks on the road, and others spread leafy branches that they had cut from the fields. Those preceding him as well as those following kept crying out: "Hosanna! Blessed is he who comes in the name of the Lord! Blessed is the kingdom of our father David that is to come! Hosanna in the highest!"

READING 1, ISAIAH 50:4–7

The Lord GOD has given me a well-trained tongue, that I might know how to speak to the weary a word that will rouse them. Morning after morning he opens my ear that I may hear; and I have not rebelled, have not turned back. I gave my back to those who beat me, my cheeks to those who plucked my beard; my face I did not shield from buffets and spitting. The Lord GOD is my help, therefore I am not disgraced; I have set my face like flint, knowing that I shall not be put to shame.

PSALM 22:8–9, 17–18, 19–20, 23–24

READING 2, PHILIPPIANS 2:6–11

Christ Jesus, though he was in the form of God, did not regard equality with God something to be grasped. Rather, he emptied himself, taking the form of a slave, coming in human likeness; and found human in appearance, he humbled himself, becoming obedient to the point of death, even death on a cross. Because of this, God greatly exalted him and bestowed on him the name which is above every name, that at the name of Jesus every knee should bend, of those in heaven and on earth and under the earth, and every tongue confess that Jesus Christ is Lord, to the glory of God the Father.

GOSPEL, MARK 14:1—15:47

The Passover and the Feast of Unleavened Bread were to take place in two days' time. So the chief priests and the scribes were seeking a way to arrest him by treachery and put him to death. They said, "Not during the festival, for fear that there may be a riot among the people."

When he was in Bethany reclining at table in the house of Simon the leper, a woman came with an alabaster jar of perfumed oil, costly genuine spikenard. She broke the alabaster jar and poured it on his head. There were some who were indignant. "Why has there been this waste of perfumed oil? It could have been sold for more than three hundred days' wages and the money given to the poor." They were infuriated with her. Jesus said, "Let her alone. Why do you make trouble for her? She has done a good thing for me. The poor you will always have with you, and whenever you wish you can do good to them, but you will not always have me. She has done what she could. She has anticipated anointing my body for burial. Amen, I say to you, wherever the gospel is proclaimed to the whole world, what she has done will be told in memory of her."

Then Judas Iscariot, one of the Twelve, went off to the chief priests to hand him over to them. When they heard him they were pleased and promised to pay him money. Then he looked for an opportunity to hand him over.

On the first day of the feast of Unleavened Bread, when they sacrificed the Passover lamb, his disciples said to him, "Where do you want us to go and prepare for you to eat the Passover?" He sent two of his disciples and said to them, "Go into the city and a man will meet you, carrying a jar of water. Follow him. Wherever he enters, say to the master of the house, 'The Teacher says, Where is my guest room where I may eat the Passover with my disciples?' Then he will show you a large upper room furnished and ready. Make the preparations for us there." The disciples then went off, entered the city, and found it just as he had told them; and they prepared the Passover.

When it was evening, he came with the Twelve. And as they reclined at table and were eating, Jesus said, "Amen, I say to you, one of you will betray me, one who is eating with me." They began to be distressed and to say to him, one by one, "Surely it is not I?" He said to them, "One of the Twelve, the one who dips with me into the dish. For the Son of Man indeed goes, as it is written of him, but woe to that man by whom the Son of Man is betrayed. It would be better for that man if he had never been born."

While they were eating, he took bread, said the blessing, broke it, and gave it to them, and said, "Take it; this is my body." Then he took a cup, gave thanks, and gave it to them, and they all drank from it. He said to them, "This is my blood of the covenant, which will be shed for many. Amen, I say to you, I shall not drink again the fruit of the vine until the day when I drink it new in the kingdom of God." Then, after singing a hymn, they went out to the Mount of Olives.

Then Jesus said to them, "All of you will have your faith shaken, for it is written: *I will strike the shepherd, and the sheep will be dispersed.* But after I have been raised up, I shall go before you to Galilee." Peter said to him, "Even though all should have their faith shaken, mine will not be." Then Jesus said to him, "Amen, I say to you, this very night before the cock crows twice you will deny me three times." But he vehemently replied, "Even though I should have to die with you, I will not deny you." And they all spoke similarly.

Then they came to a place named Gethsemane, and he said to his disciples, "Sit here while I pray." He took with him Peter, James, and John, and began to be troubled and distressed. Then he said to them, "My soul is sorrowful even to death. Remain here and keep watch." He advanced a little and fell to the ground and prayed that if it were possible the hour might pass by him; he said, "Abba, Father, all things are possible to you. Take this cup away from me, but not what I will but what you will." When he returned he found them asleep. He said to Peter, "Simon, are you asleep? Could you not keep watch for one hour? Watch and pray that you may not undergo the test. The spirit is willing but the flesh is weak." Withdrawing again, he prayed, saying the same thing. Then he returned once more and found them asleep, for they could not keep their eyes open and did not know what to answer him. He returned a third time and said to them, "Are you still sleeping and taking your rest? It is enough. The hour has come. Behold, the Son of Man is to be handed over to sinners. Get up, let us go. See, my betrayer is at hand."

Then, while he was still speaking, Judas, one of the Twelve, arrived, accompanied by a crowd with swords and clubs who had come from the chief priests, the scribes, and the elders. His betrayer had arranged a signal with them, saying, "The man I shall kiss is the one; arrest him and lead him away securely." He came and immediately went over to him and said, "Rabbi." And he kissed him. At this they laid hands on him and arrested him. One of the bystanders drew his sword, struck the high priest's servant, and cut off his ear. Jesus said to them in reply, "Have you come out as against a robber, with swords and clubs, to seize me? Day after day I was with you teaching in the temple area, yet you did not arrest me; but that the Scriptures may be fulfilled." And they all left him and fled. Now a young man followed him wearing nothing but a linen cloth about his body. They seized him, but he left the cloth behind and ran off naked.

They led Jesus away to the high priest, and all the chief priests and the elders and the scribes came together. Peter followed him at a distance into the high priest's courtyard and was seated with the guards, warming himself at the fire. The chief priests and the entire Sanhedrin kept trying to obtain testimony against Jesus in order to put him to death, but they found none. Many gave false witness against him, but their testimony did not agree. Some took the stand and testified falsely against him, alleging, "We heard him say, 'I will destroy this temple made with hands and within three days I will build another not made with hands.'" Even so their testimony did not agree. The high priest rose before the assembly and questioned Jesus, saying, "Have you no answer? What are these men testifying against you?" But he was silent and answered nothing. Again the high priest asked him and said to him, "Are you the Christ, the son of the Blessed One?" Then Jesus answered, "I am; and 'you will see the Son of Man seated at the right hand of the Power and coming with the clouds of heaven.'" At that the high priest tore his garments and said, "What further need have we of witnesses? You have heard the blasphemy. What do you think?" They all condemned him as deserving to die. Some began to spit on him. They blindfolded him and struck him and said to him, "Prophesy!" And the guards greeted him with blows.

While Peter was below in the courtyard, one of the high priest's maids came along. Seeing Peter warming himself, she looked intently at him and said, "You too were with the Nazarene, Jesus." But he denied it saying, "I neither know nor understand what you are talking about." So he went out into the outer court. Then the cock crowed. The maid saw him and began again to say to the bystanders, "This man is one of them." Once again he denied it. A little later the bystanders said to Peter once more, "Surely you are one of them; for you too are a Galilean." He began to curse and to swear, "I do not know this man about whom you are talking." And immediately a cock crowed a second time. Then Peter remembered the word that Jesus had said to him, "Before the cock crows twice you will deny me three times." He broke down and wept.

As soon as morning came, the chief priests with the elders and the scribes, that is, the whole Sanhedrin held a council. They bound Jesus, led him away, and handed him over to Pilate. Pilate questioned him, "Are you the king of the Jews?" He said to him in reply, "You say so." The chief priests accused him of many things. Again Pilate questioned him, "Have you no answer? See how many things they accuse you of." Jesus gave him no further answer, so that Pilate was amazed.

Now on the occasion of the feast he used to release to them one prisoner whom they requested. A man called Barabbas was then in prison along with the rebels who had committed murder in a rebellion. The crowd came forward and began to ask him to do for them as he was accustomed. Pilate answered, "Do you want me to release to you the king of the Jews?" For he knew that it was out of envy that the chief priests had handed him over. But the chief priests stirred up the crowd to have him release Barabbas for them instead. Pilate again said to them in reply, "Then what do you want me to do with the man you call the king of the Jews?" They shouted again, "Crucify him." Pilate said to them, "Why? What evil has he done?" They only shouted the louder, "Crucify him."

So Pilate, wishing to satisfy the crowd, released Barabbas to them and, after he had Jesus scourged, handed him over to be crucified. The soldiers led him away inside the palace, that is, the praetorium, and assembled the whole cohort. They clothed him in purple and, weaving a crown of thorns, placed it on him. They began to salute him with, "Hail, King of the Jews!" and kept striking his head with a reed and spitting upon him. They knelt before him in homage. And when they had mocked him, they stripped him of the purple cloak, dressed him in his own clothes, and led him out to crucify him.

They pressed into service a passerby, Simon, a Cyrenian, who was coming in from the country, the father of Alexander and Rufus, to carry his cross.

They brought him to the place of Golgotha—which is translated Place of the Skull. They gave him wine drugged with myrrh, but he did not take it. Then they crucified him and divided his garments by casting lots for them to see what each should take. It was nine o'clock in the morning when they crucified him. The inscription of the charge against him read, "The King of the Jews." With him they crucified two revolutionaries, one on his right and one on his left. Those passing by reviled him, shaking their heads and saying, "Aha! You who would destroy the temple and rebuild it in three days, save yourself by coming down from the cross." Likewise the chief priests, with the scribes, mocked him among themselves and said, "He saved others; he cannot save himself. Let the Christ, the King of Israel, come down now from the cross that we may see and believe." Those who were crucified with him also kept abusing him.

At noon darkness came over the whole land until three in the afternoon. And at three o'clock Jesus cried out in a loud voice, "*Eloi, Eloi, lema sabachthani*?" which is translated, "My God, my God, why have you forsaken me?" Some of the bystanders who heard it said, "Look, he is calling Elijah." One of them ran, soaked a sponge with wine, put it on a reed and gave it to him to drink saying, "Wait, let us see if Elijah comes to take him down." Jesus gave a loud cry and breathed his last.

Here all kneel and pause for a short time.

The veil of the sanctuary was torn in two from top to bottom. When the centurion who stood facing him saw how he breathed his last he said, "Truly this man was the Son of God!" There were also women looking on from a distance. Among them were Mary Magdalene, Mary the mother of the younger James and of Joses, and Salome. These women had followed him when he was in Galilee and ministered to him. There were also many other women who had come up with him to Jerusalem. When it was already evening, since it was the day of preparation, the day before the Sabbath, Joseph of Arimathea, a distinguished member of the council, who was himself awaiting the kingdom of God, came and courageously went to Pilate and asked for the body of Jesus.

Pilate was amazed that he was already dead. He summoned the centurion and asked him if Jesus had already died. And when he learned of it from the centurion, he gave the body to Joseph. Having bought a linen cloth, he took him down, wrapped him in the linen cloth, and laid him in a tomb that had been hewn out of the rock. Then he rolled a stone against the entrance to the tomb.

Mary Magdalene and Mary the mother of Joses watched where he was laid.

From Praise to Crucifixion

As we come into Holy Week, we hear two Gospels. The first recounts Jesus' entry into Jerusalem when the crowd shouted "Hosanna!" The word comes from the Hebrew "Hoshea-na" and means, "Save us, Lord, we beseech you." They thought Jesus was the Messiah who would free them from Rome. When he entered Jerusalem, they hailed him. Even the word, Hosanna, implies praise rather than petition. But at the beginning of Holy Week and in recognition of our own weaknesses and sin, the original meaning is appropriate.

How quickly things changed. In the first two readings, we realize that this Messiah is unlike anything or anyone we expected. Isaiah's servant may preach eloquently, but he is despised. Perhaps his message wasn't one people wanted to hear. Regardless, the servant continues in his quest, confident that God is with him. That knowledge gives him courage to continue his work.

Paul reminds us that Jesus didn't deem equality with God as something that could be achieved. Nor did Jesus see humanity as something to be despised. Jesus emptied himself to become like us so that he might show us how to be obedient to God. Mark, in his uncluttered style tells us of a horrific death. The very people who shouted Hosanna at the beginning now shout, "Crucify him." The story begins with a symbolic anointing and the account of the Last Supper. By the end, only a stone marks the entrance to the tomb, and we are left to wonder who was in there.

Passion (Palm) Sunday, Year B

Truly This Was the Son of God

Jesus may not have been the one we expected. He is so much more than we could have ever imagined. Embedded in Isaiah's prophecy is the single sure line, "The Lord GOD is my help." Though despised by others, this servant knows God was with him.

We don't expect servants to be saviors or crucified people to be divine. Yet the Letter to the Philippians tells us Jesus was both and his death was not the end. Because Jesus was obedient, God exalted him. Paul then paraphrases another passage from Isaiah, which reads: "Turn to me and be safe, / all you ends of the earth, / for I am God; there is no other! / By myself I swear, / uttering my just decree, / a word that will not return: / To me every knee shall bend; / by me every tongue shall swear, / Saying, "Only in the LORD / are just deeds and power...." (Isaiah 45:22–24a).

Jesus is the word that God sent, and God has given him the name above all so that we can proclaim that Jesus Christ is Lord. Thus, we glorify God. While it's the shortest of all the Gospels, Mark's depiction of the crucifixion is filled with hints about the identity of Jesus. He is not the Messiah that many people expected. Rather Jesus is called variously, "the Teacher," "the Son of Man," "Rabbi," "Messiah, Son of the Blessed One," "King of the Jews," "Messiah, King of Israel," and "God's Son." The first two are self-identifications by Jesus. Of the remainder, people who expected a great leader say all but the last mockingly. All of them were true, but the people saying them didn't know how they were true. The last statement comes from the Roman centurion who had no reason to believe Jesus at all. But he is awestruck by this man and this death, and so he properly identifies Jesus for all to hear.

Good News for All of Us

Jesus Christ isn't just a great prophet or philosopher. He isn't just a teacher or ruler. Jesus is God. If we say he failed because the kingdom of God didn't come at once or because sin and sadness still exist in the world, then we are making the same mistake the people of Jerusalem did. Jesus didn't come to fix all our problems. He came to bring salvation to the world and show us the way back to God. Whether we follow him or not is entirely up to us. Our success will be measured by the love we show, and we will know how we did on the day we see God face to face.

Questions for Reflection and Discussion

➤ *When you pray, what do you hope to hear in return? Have you ever been surprised by an answer?*

➤ *Jesus laid down his life for us. How can this reality inspire the type of relationships we build with others?*

Related Journey of Faith Lesson

E7, "The Meaning of Holy Week"

Themes

Death
    E2, "Living Lent"
Prophecy
    E7, "The Meaning of Holy Week"

Easter Sunday, Year B

READING 1, ACTS 10:34A, 37–43

Peter proceeded to speak and said: "You know what has happened all over Judea, beginning in Galilee after the baptism that John preached, how God anointed Jesus of Nazareth with the Holy Spirit and power. He went about doing good and healing all those oppressed by the devil, for God was with him. We are witnesses of all that he did both in the country of the Jews and in Jerusalem. They put him to death by hanging him on a tree. This man God raised on the third day and granted that he be visible, not to all the people, but to us, the witnesses chosen by God in advance, who ate and drank with him after he rose from the dead. He commissioned us to preach to the people and testify that he is the one appointed by God as judge of the living and the dead. To him all the prophets bear witness, that everyone who believes in him will receive forgiveness of sins through his name."

PSALM 118:1–2, 16–17, 22–23

READING 2, COLOSSIANS 3:1–4

Brothers and sisters: If then you were raised with Christ, seek what is above, where Christ is seated at the right hand of God. Think of what is above, not of what is on earth. For you have died, and your life is hidden with Christ in God. When Christ your life appears, then you too will appear with him in glory.

GOSPEL, JOHN 20:1–9

On the first day of the week, Mary of Magdala came to the tomb early in the morning, while it was still dark, and saw the stone removed from the tomb. So she ran and went to Simon Peter and to the other disciple whom Jesus loved, and told them, "They have taken the Lord from the tomb, and we don't know where they put him." So Peter and the other disciple went out and came to the tomb. They both ran, but the other disciple ran faster than Peter and arrived at the tomb first; he bent down and saw the burial cloths there, but did not go in. When Simon Peter arrived after him, he went into the tomb and saw the burial cloths there, and the cloth that had covered his head, not with the burial cloths but rolled up in a separate place. Then the other disciple also went in, the one who had arrived at the tomb first, and he saw and believed. For they did not yet understand the Scripture that he had to rise from the dead.

From Death into Life

After six long weeks, we joyfully proclaim "Alleluia" on Easter. But the Gospel tells us that the first thing we see is emptiness. Mary Magdalene didn't know what it meant; she presumed the body had been taken. Peter and the other disciple saw only the linen wrappings. What happened? The other disciple believed something had happened that defied expectation. We saw Jesus hanging from the cross and expected that he was gone. But he is not in the tomb. Along with the disciples, we come to know that he has risen from the dead. Easter is a feast of defied expectations.

In the reading from Acts, Peter preaches the truth that God raised Jesus. Peter was a witness to the empty tomb and a witness to the resurrected Jesus who ate and drank with the disciples afterward. No one could have expected it, but Peter understood that his mission now was to preach the Good News so that everyone could receive the forgiveness of sins.

Such glad tidings demand a change in our lives and a transformation of heart. Paul reminds us that we have been raised with Christ. This is not a reference to physical death, but to the fact that we have died to sin and to our old selves. Our new life is now in Christ. We are still living in the world, but we are also looking forward to that time when Christ will be revealed in full glory, for then we shall be revealed as well.

First Witness

Mary Magdalene was coming to the tomb to care for the body and to mourn for Jesus. When she sees the empty tomb, she is shocked. She runs to Peter and the disciple whom Jesus loved, as mentioned in John's Gospel. They corroborate her story. If we were to continue the passage, we would find that Mary lingered in the garden after Peter and the other disciple left. Jesus appears first to her, though she didn't recognize him until he called her name. When she realizes it is Jesus, he gives her a mission to preach the resurrection to all the disciples. For that reason, she is called the apostle to the apostles in the Orthodox tradition. Giving such an important task to a woman defied the expectations of the time. Jesus continues to do after the resurrection what he did before it.

Good News for All of Us

The first thing we saw was the empty tomb, but emptiness is not always bad. Our faith tells us that God created the entire world out of nothing. We could not have expected such a thing, but everything is possible for God. The blind can see, a virgin can conceive a son, a person can be crucified and raised from the dead, and a disciple can believe without understanding everything that happened. What God touches bursts with life. It is no wonder that we are joyful this season. But we are challenged in that joy to be an Easter people. Raised with Christ, we are compelled to share the Good News as Mary and Peter did; we are bound to help the sick, the imprisoned, the poor, and the marginalized as Jesus did. We are to live our lives in every way as followers of Christ and not of the world. It's good to be reminded of that every year.

Questions for Reflection and Discussion

➤ *Have you ever experienced something good coming from a difficult or bad event?*

➤ *Christ has given us new life. What is one thing you can do to reflect that new life?*

Related Journey of Faith Lesson

E8, "Easter Vigil Retreat"

Themes

Easter
    E7, "The Meaning of Holy Week"
Faith
    E4, "The Creed"
Resurrection
    E8, "Easter Vigil Retreat"

Second Sunday of Easter, Year B

READING 1, ACTS 4:32–35

The community of believers was of one heart and mind, and no one claimed that any of his possessions was his own, but they had everything in common. With great power the apostles bore witness to the resurrection of the Lord Jesus, and great favor was accorded them all. There was no needy person among them, for those who owned property or houses would sell them, bring the proceeds of the sale, and put them at the feet of the apostles, and they were distributed to each according to need.

PSALM 118:2–4, 13–15, 22–24

READING 2, 1 JOHN 5:1–6

Beloved: Everyone who believes that Jesus is the Christ is begotten by God, and everyone who loves the Father loves also the one begotten by him. In this way we know that we love the children of God when we love God and obey his commandments. For the love of God is this, that we keep his commandments. And his commandments are not burdensome, for whoever is begotten by God conquers the world. And the victory that conquers the world is our faith. Who indeed is the victor over the world but the one who believes that Jesus is the Son of God? This is the one who came through water and blood, Jesus Christ, not by water alone, but by water and blood. The Spirit is the one that testifies, and the Spirit is truth.

GOSPEL, JOHN 20:19–31

On the evening of that first day of the week, when the doors were locked, where the disciples were, for fear of the Jews, Jesus came and stood in their midst and said to them, "Peace be with you." When he had said this, he showed them his hands and his side. The disciples rejoiced when they saw the Lord. Jesus said to them again, "Peace be with you. As the Father has sent me, so I send you." And when he had said this, he breathed on them and said to them, "Receive the Holy Spirit. Whose sins you forgive are forgiven them, and whose sins you retain are retained." Thomas, called Didymus, one of the Twelve, was not with them when Jesus came. So the other disciples said to him, "We have seen the Lord." But he said to them, "Unless I see the mark of the nails in his hands and put my finger into the nailmarks and put my hand into his side, I will not believe." Now a week later his disciples were again inside and Thomas was with them. Jesus came, although the doors were locked, and stood in their midst and said, "Peace be with you." Then he said to Thomas, "Put your finger here and see my hands, and bring your hand and put it into my side, and do not be unbelieving, but believe." Thomas answered and said to him, "My Lord and my God!" Jesus said to him, "Have you come to believe because you have seen me? Blessed are those who have not seen and have believed." Now Jesus did many other signs in the presence of his disciples that are not written in this book. But these are written that you may come to believe that Jesus is the Christ, the Son of God, and that through this belief you may have life in his name.

We Are Alive in Christ!

What happened after Jesus rose from the dead? From today's first reading to the last, we are shown evidence that lives were changed. The reading from Acts talks about how believers lived, which was certainly different than the prevailing culture. The epistle from John states very plainly that we are born of God, and those who love God obey his commandments. In his Gospel, John says Jesus gave new authority to the apostles, who can now forgive sins. And for Thomas, the experience resulted in greater faith. It took him a while, but the presence of Jesus in their midst was a powerful and convincing catalyst.

It's a remarkable thing, but the early Christian community believed that Christ was alive among them even after the ascension. They did not have to see him to believe he was there. That knowledge, along with the preaching of the apostles, compelled them to live their lives differently. The description in Acts seems nearly unbelievable or, at the very least, fodder for an interesting political debate when compared with today's society. The apostles must have been doing some powerful preaching!

Encounter with Jesus

Shortly after Mary Magdalene meets Jesus in the garden outside the tomb, John records that the disciples were hiding behind locked doors. The first inkling we have that things are different is the sudden appearance of Jesus, who was simply in their midst. John has talked about the peace that he wishes on them. Earlier in the Gospel, Jesus tells them that the peace he gives is not like the peace the world gives. Rather, his peace is everlasting.

Take note that he shows them his hands and side. This was no imposter. Then he commissions them by breathing the Holy Spirit on them and the power of forgiveness. This is one of the passages the Church uses as a foundation for the sacrament of reconciliation.

Thomas was absent that day. When the others tell him Jesus was with them, he says, "I want to see his wounds too, then I will believe." It always strikes me as odd that Thomas is mocked because he wants what they had—proof that Jesus appeared. Whatever the reason, Jesus comes again, wishes them peace, and invites Thomas to touch the wounds. And it is Thomas who utters a profound statement of faith, "My Lord and my God!" Jesus' remarks following Thomas' statement are for the community to whom John is writing. "Blessed are those who have not seen and have believed."

Good News for All of Us

Jesus is alive in the world and, particularly, in the Church which is his body. No, we are not a perfect society; in fact we are a refuge for sinners. There have been wars and scandals throughout our history and the whole Church has suffered for it. But Christ is alive in every person who reaches out to the poor, every family that passes on the faith to their children, and the named and unnamed saints who labor in every corner of the world to give witness to God who is love.

For more than 2,000 years, through bad times and good, the Church has continued to be a place where people are spiritually fed and then go out to set the world on fire. And so we continue to believe that Christ is here through the Holy Spirit to the glory of God the Father.

Questions for Reflection and Discussion

➤ If someone said to you, "I have seen the Lord," would you believe him or her? What proof would you want?

➤ What can you do now to live the Christian life to its fullest?

Related Journey of Faith Lesson

M1, "Conversion: A Lifelong Process"

Themes

Charity
> M2, "The Role of the Laity"

Faith
> M1, "Conversion: A Lifelong Process"

Third Sunday of Easter, Year B

READING 1, ACTS 3:13–15, 17–19

Peter said to the people: "The God of Abraham, the God of Isaac, and the God of Jacob, the God of our fathers, has glorified his servant Jesus, whom you handed over and denied in Pilate's presence when he had decided to release him. You denied the Holy and Righteous One and asked that a murderer be released to you. The author of life you put to death, but God raised him from the dead; of this we are witnesses. Now I know, brothers, that you acted out of ignorance, just as your leaders did; but God has thus brought to fulfillment what he had announced beforehand through the mouth of all the prophets, that his Christ would suffer. Repent, therefore, and be converted, that your sins may be wiped away."

PSALM 4:2, 4, 7–8, 9

READING 2, 1 JOHN 2:1–5A

My children, I am writing this to you so that you may not commit sin. But if anyone does sin, we have an Advocate with the Father, Jesus Christ the righteous one. He is expiation for our sins, and not for our sins only but for those of the whole world. The way we may be sure that we know him is to keep his commandments. Those who say, "I know him," but do not keep his commandments are liars, and the truth is not in them. But whoever keeps his word, the love of God is truly perfected in him.

GOSPEL, LUKE 24:35–48

The two disciples recounted what had taken place on the way, and how Jesus was made known to them in the breaking of bread. While they were still speaking about this, he stood in their midst and said to them, "Peace be with you." But they were startled and terrified and thought that they were seeing a ghost. Then he said to them, "Why are you troubled? And why do questions arise in your hearts? Look at my hands and my feet, that it is I myself. Touch me and see, because a ghost does not have flesh and bones as you can see I have." And as he said this, he showed them his hands and his feet. While they were still incredulous for joy and were amazed, he asked them, "Have you anything here to eat?" They gave him a piece of baked fish; he took it and ate it in front of them. He said to them, "These are my words that I spoke to you while I was still with you, that everything written about me in the law of Moses and in the prophets and psalms must be fulfilled." Then he opened their minds to understand the Scriptures. And he said to them, "Thus it is written that the Christ would suffer and rise from the dead on the third day and that repentance, for the forgiveness of sins, would be preached in his name to all the nations, beginning from Jerusalem. You are witnesses of these things."

Your Sins Are Forgiven

During the Easter season, we continue to reflect on the purpose of the passion, death, and resurrection of Jesus. In various ways, the epistles and Gospels come back to one thing: Christ died for our sins—a reflection of his love for us so we might be reconciled to God. Each of today's readings pulls out a piece of that message. Peter recalls the story of Jesus and tells his listeners that they acted in ignorance. The good news is that they can repent (or change their hearts) and turn to God and their sins will be wiped out.

John reminds us that Jesus is the sacrifice for the sins of the whole world and encourages his listeners not to sin. But he also reminds them that if they do, Jesus is the Advocate with the Father. Luke's Gospel is similar to last week's Gospel. Here, the disciples are witnesses who will proclaim repentance and forgiveness in his name to all the nations. It's no wonder confession and reconciliation play such an important role in our sacraments!

The Proof That We Know God
Both the First and Second Letters of John address the early Christian community as members in the family of believers, children of God and brothers and sisters to one another. As far as John is concerned, it is their behavior that proves they are children of God. He particularly emphasizes "knowing" God. Like the Old Testament prophets, John uses the word "know," in the sense of an intimate family relationship. In this reading, he says: "By this we may be sure we know him, if we obey his commandments." John has a very high moral standard with simple parameters. For John, knowing God automatically results in proper action. Those who say they know him but disobey the commandments are liars. Those who obey have the love of God in them.

We Are Witnesses
The events of the Gospel take place when two disciples met Jesus on the way to Emmaus. As they recount the story, Jesus comes into the midst of them. It's not strange to think Jesus was a ghost. They saw him die. But he shows them his wounds and then as further proof, he asks them for something to eat. The disciples who went to Emmaus only knew Christ in the breaking of the bread. Now others get to know him as they enjoy a meal together. Jesus sees it as an opportunity to teach what the Scriptures said about him. He opened their minds to understand. It is their great commission as witnesses to the Good News.

Good News for All of Us

The 1960s folk hymn "They'll Know We Are Christians By Our Love" helps us draw the connection between faith and works. If we have faith in Christ who does so much for us, we are compelled to be good to others. We don't always get it right, due to the limitations of our human nature. Sometimes we are deliberate in our sin, but more often we sin out of ignorance or because our feelings overwhelm our sense of reason. The truly Good News is that through Christ we are offered forgiveness and a chance to start over. We can do the same for others. Another Christian hymn, "What Wondrous Love Is This," relates a sentiment that just about sums it up.

Questions for Reflection and Discussion

> *Is there someone in your life you find it hard to forgive? What steps could you take to get a little closer to forgiving that person?*

> *Sometimes the hardest person to forgive is ourselves. Is there anything you have done in your life that you feel is unforgivable? How would you bring that to God in prayer?*

Related Journey of Faith Lesson

M4, "Discernment"

Themes

Conversion
    M1, "Conversion: A Lifelong Process"
Forgiveness
    M2, "The Role of the Laity"
Sin
    M4,"Discernment"

Fourth Sunday of Easter, Year B

READING 1, ACTS 4:8–12

Peter, filled with the Holy Spirit, said: "Leaders of the people and elders: If we are being examined today about a good deed done to a cripple, namely, by what means he was saved, then all of you and all the people of Israel should know that it was in the name of Jesus Christ the Nazorean whom you crucified, whom God raised from the dead; in his name this man stands before you healed. He is *the stone rejected by you, the builders, which has become the cornerstone.* There is no salvation through anyone else, nor is there any other name under heaven given to the human race by which we are to be saved."

PSALM 118:1, 8–9, 21–23, 26, 28, 29

READING 2, 1 JOHN 3:1–2

Beloved: See what love the Father has bestowed on us that we may be called the children of God. Yet so we are. The reason the world does not know us is that it did not know him. Beloved, we are God's children now; what we shall be has not yet been revealed. We do know that when it is revealed we shall be like him, for we shall see him as he is.

GOSPEL, JOHN 10:11–18

Jesus said: "I am the good shepherd. A good shepherd lays down his life for the sheep. A hired man, who is not a shepherd and whose sheep are not his own, sees a wolf coming and leaves the sheep and runs away, and the wolf catches and scatters them. This is because he works for pay and has no concern for the sheep. I am the good shepherd, and I know mine and mine know me, just as the Father knows me and I know the Father; and I will lay down my life for the sheep. I have other sheep that do not belong to this fold. These also I must lead, and they will hear my voice, and there will be one flock, one shepherd. This is why the Father loves me, because I lay down my life in order to take it up again. No one takes it from me, but I lay it down on my own. I have power to lay it down, and power to take it up again. This command I have received from my Father."

The Stone the Builders Rejected

In Advent, we listened to prophecies about God turning things upside down. Mountains would be laid low and rough places made smooth. When God comes, things will not be as they were. We hear that in Peter's preaching when he replies to a crippled man's petition for money. Peter replies, "I have neither silver nor gold, but what I do have I give you: in the name of Jesus Christ the Nazorean, [rise and] walk" (Acts 3:6). The miracle astonished the onlookers and gave Peter a chance to preach to them. The authorities arrested him, which leads to confrontation.

Peter credits only Christ with the healing and reminds them that they crucified Jesus and God raised him up. He then quotes verse 22 of Psalm 118 (part of today's Psalm reading). "The stone the builders rejected / has become the cornerstone." God has turned the tables once again. Jesus, whom they rejected, is the foundation for all Christianity and only in his name will all be saved (Acts 4:12, John 14:6).

See What Love the Father Shows Us

I have a couple of friends who were adopted as children. They especially appreciate the references to Christians as the adopted children of God because they know, better than many, what it is to be chosen by someone and loved as their own. First John reminds us that we are children of God now who at our baptism began a long journey of life with God. "What we shall be has not yet been revealed." John knows that becoming a disciple is not an easy task. Throughout life, we move ahead, we fall, we slip backward, and we start over again. Along the way we catch little glimpses of the person God dreams for us to be and we try to lean into that as best we can—a process that differs for each of us. John promises that one thing is certain. "When it is revealed we shall be like him, for we shall see him as he is." That promise is enough to keep us going.

The Good Shepherd

John's Gospel borrows some imagery from Ezekiel 34, where God identifies himself as the shepherd of his people. John adds the word "good" to the description. Jesus does more than the hired help who run away when the wolf comes. But even more, he gathers the sheep who are lost, but not part of the flock (he is referring here to the Gentiles). He even lays down his life for his sheep, not because he must, but because he has the power to do so. In the Gospel of John, Jesus has control throughout; even his crucifixion happened because he allowed it to happen. Jesus lets go of his power, given to him by the Father, in order to die for his "sheep." This exemplifies the infinite love he has for those in his care.

Good News for All of Us

Most of us don't know much about being sheep. But we know a great deal about being children. We know that care, love, and discipline help us grow. We can look back on our childhood and think about what might have been done differently, but we also can come to realize that our parents or guardians did the best they could. They were limited. So are we.

God adopted us into his family. He has blessed us with unceasing love. He sent his Son to suffer what we suffer and to show us what it is to be a child of God. This doesn't mean that nothing bad will happen to us. But it does mean that God sticks by our side and will show us how new life can rise out of something terrible. God will also be with us at the end of life when we make our transition from this pasture to the heavenly one. We listen for his voice all the way.

Questions for Reflection and Discussion

➤ *Jesus says there are other sheep not of this flock that he will bring in. How do you welcome people who are different than you into your church and community?*

➤ *What does it mean that Catholics believe that the Church has the fullness of the means of salvation through Jesus Christ?*

➤ *Can people of other faiths find God or go to heaven?*

Related Journey of Faith Lesson

M2, "The Role of the Laity"

Themes

Interpretation
    M4, "Discernment"
Reality
    M3, "Your Spiritual Gifts"
Relationships
    M7, "Family Life"

Fifth Sunday of Easter, Year B

READING 1, ACTS 9:26–31

When Saul arrived in Jerusalem he tried to join the disciples, but they were all afraid of him, not believing that he was a disciple. Then Barnabas took charge of him and brought him to the apostles, and he reported to them how he had seen the Lord, and that he had spoken to him, and how in Damascus he had spoken out boldly in the name of Jesus. He moved about freely with them in Jerusalem, and spoke out boldly in the name of the Lord. He also spoke and debated with the Hellenists, but they tried to kill him. And when the brothers learned of this, they took him down to Caesarea and sent him on his way to Tarsus. The church throughout all Judea, Galilee, and Samaria was at peace. It was being built up and walked in the fear of the Lord, and with the consolation of the Holy Spirit it grew in numbers.

PSALM 118:1, 8–9, 21–23, 26, 28, 29

READING 2, 1 JOHN 3:18–24

Children, let us love not in word or speech but in deed and truth. Now this is how we shall know that we belong to the truth and reassure our hearts before him in whatever our hearts condemn, for God is greater than our hearts and knows everything. Beloved, if our hearts do not condemn us, we have confidence in God and receive from him whatever we ask, because we keep his commandments and do what pleases him. And his commandment is this: we should believe in the name of his Son, Jesus Christ, and love one another just as he commanded us. Those who keep his commandments remain in him, and he in them, and the way we know that he remains in us is from the Spirit he gave us.

GOSPEL, JOHN 15:1–8

Jesus said to his disciples: "I am the true vine, and my Father is the vine grower. He takes away every branch in me that does not bear fruit, and every one that does he prunes so that it bears more fruit. You are already pruned because of the word that I spoke to you. Remain in me, as I remain in you. Just as a branch cannot bear fruit on its own unless it remains on the vine, so neither can you unless you remain in me. I am the vine, you are the branches. Whoever remains in me and I in him will bear much fruit, because without me you can do nothing. Anyone who does not remain in me will be thrown out like a branch and wither; people will gather them and throw them into a fire and they will be burned. If you remain in me and my words remain in you, ask for whatever you want and it will be done for you. By this is my Father glorified, that you bear much fruit and become my disciples."

A Fruitful Life

Nearly all the readings during the Easter season encourage us to grow in our faith and act according to that growth. This is the fruit of which Jesus speaks in the Gospels. No one is exempt, and we see that in the first reading. Saul had been imprisoning and murdering Christians. His reputation was well-known. But after an encounter with Christ on the road to Damascus, he was transformed, underwent a miraculous conversion. The Christians might be forgiven for being suspicious. But on the word of Barnabas, who witnessed his transformation and heard him preach about Jesus in Damascus, the believers took him in. The fruit of Paul's conversion was the power of his preaching. The fruit of the believers was their willingness to help him escape from those who wanted to do him harm.

Love in Action

Of all the New Testament writings, John's Gospel and epistles speak the most about love. It is John who first articulates that God is love, the evidence of which we see throughout the Bible. For John, the fruit of being a disciple is borne out in words and deeds. He urges his hearers to make their love visible, because then they will know that they are from the truth. He reminds them that God knows everything.

That is both a comfort and a challenge. We can't hide anything from God. If we do not love or if we love less than wholeheartedly, God will know. The fruit of our life in God is that we obey his commandments. John names two: Believe in the name of Jesus and love one another. By doing these actions, we will abide in God and he in us. And people will know this, John says, because of the Spirit he has given us.

Vine and Branches

There are two great images of the Church. The most well-known is Paul's "Body of Christ." The second is the one in today's Gospel. "The vine and the branches...." Like Paul's image, this one is organic—a living entity whose life is rooted in Christ. Paul talked about the head and members of the body. John acknowledges only one life-giving source—the vine— and all disciples are branches on that living vine.

Hidden in that reality is the work the vine grower must do to have as great a yield. Anyone who has grown vegetables or fruit trees knows that care must be taken to prune away dead leaves, keep the plant fertilized, and occasionally thin out buds so it may flower more abundantly. This is how Jesus talks about the Father. He watches over the branches to see that they are continually drawing nourishment from the vine. When they have gotten too far away from their source of life or have withered away, he prunes them in order that they might bear all the fruit they are able.

How do we become a part of the vine? We do so by believing in Jesus and listening to his words. Jesus says, "Abide in me." The word means "to dwell." If we live in him, the fruit we bear will all be for the greater glory of God.

Good News for All of Us

We know many examples of people who exude goodness. Pope Francis, who may have one of the hardest jobs in the world, nearly always seems to invoke a sense of peace about him. Examples of Good Samaritans and ordinary people doing extraordinary acts of kindness are remembered on the internet and in the stories of local heroes in the news. In our own families and neighborhoods, we have undoubtedly run across a person who is always willing to lend a hand. John would recognize these as children of God—those who allow God's light to shine in them so brightly it spills out for everyone to see. That could be any one of us who draw life from the living vine and bear fruit for the world.

Questions for Reflection and Discussion

➤ *Jesus says we are to love one another. Consider a time in your life when putting that love into action was difficult. What did you do?*

➤ *What are the "fruits" that you are bearing into the world right now?*

Related *Journey of Faith* Lesson

M6, "Living the Virtues"

Themes

Community
    Q7, "Your Prayer Life"
Ministry
    M3, "Your Spiritual Gifts"

Sixth Sunday of Easter, Year B

READING 1, ACTS 10:25–26, 34–35, 44–48

When Peter entered, Cornelius met him and, falling at his feet, paid him homage. Peter, however, raised him up, saying, "Get up. I myself am also a human being." Then Peter proceeded to speak and said, "In truth, I see that God shows no partiality. Rather, in every nation whoever fears him and acts uprightly is acceptable to him." While Peter was still speaking these things, the Holy Spirit fell upon all who were listening to the word. The circumcised believers who had accompanied Peter were astounded that the gift of the Holy Spirit should have been poured out on the Gentiles also, for they could hear them speaking in tongues and glorifying God. Then Peter responded, "Can anyone withhold the water for baptizing these people, who have received the Holy Spirit even as we have?" He ordered them to be baptized in the name of Jesus Christ.

PSALM 98:1, 2–3, 3–4

READING 2, 1 JOHN 4:7–10

Beloved, let us love one another, because love is of God; everyone who loves is begotten by God and knows God. Whoever is without love does not know God, for God is love. In this way the love of God was revealed to us: God sent his only Son into the world so that we might have life through him. In this is love: not that we have loved God, but that he loved us and sent his Son as expiation for our sins.

GOSPEL, JOHN 15:9–17

Jesus said to his disciples: "As the Father loves me, so I also love you. Remain in my love. If you keep my commandments, you will remain in my love, just as I have kept my Father's commandments and remain in his love. I have told you this so that my joy may be in you and your joy might be complete. This is my commandment: love one another as I love you. No one has greater love than this, to lay down one's life for one's friends. You are my friends if you do what I command you. I no longer call you slaves, because a slave does not know what his master is doing. I have called you friends, because I have told you everything I have heard from my Father. It was not you who chose me, but I who chose you and appointed you to go and bear fruit that will remain, so that whatever you ask the Father in my name he may give you. This I command you: love one another."

A Spirit-filled Church

Could Gentiles become Christian without first submitting to Mosaic law? This was the first controversial question that the new community of believers encountered. Many felt that because Jesus came to God's Chosen People and was himself a Jew that new members must follow Jewish law. In fact, the early Church was considered a sect of Judaism for several years after Jesus' resurrection. Peter and Paul were on opposite ends of this argument for a time. Then, Peter had a dream in which God told him he could not pronounce anything unclean. Shortly afterward, the Gentile, Cornelius, seeks Peter out and, as Peter tells him about the dream, the Holy Spirit takes up the matter and comes upon Cornelius and his whole family. The Spirit didn't wait for the baptism with water but made the will of God known to all. Cornelius and his family were baptized that very day. In truth, the Holy Spirit made them welcome even before that. Afterward, a meeting between the apostles and elders, accompanied by prayer and discussion, a formal declaration is made that Gentiles can become Christian.

God Is Love

Both John's epistle and his Gospel emphasize the command that we love one another. In the epistle, John continues to contrast the behavior of those that know God and those that don't. His method is simple. If we love, then we are of God; those who don't show love don't know God. John goes on to say that the love of God is revealed in the passion and death of his Son, Jesus. We can love because God first loved us. And we know him through the sacrifice of Jesus, which forgave our sins.

The Gospel is part of Jesus' final instruction to his disciples, which is why there is such an emphasis on obedience and the law of love. Jesus, as the Son of God, acknowledges that the Father loved him and so, in turn he loves the disciples. In this way, he illustrates that all love comes from God. Just as he passes it on to them, they must pass it on to others. The significant word, *abide*, is used again. Remember that abide means to live or dwell in Christ's love. Jesus also makes the connection between the love he passes on to them and the joy that is the result. "I tell you this so that…your joy may be complete."

No Longer Servants, but Friends

The second half of the Gospel begins with the command to love one another. Jesus tells the disciples to emulate his response to receiving the Father's love. But there is a surprise. He describes the ultimate sacrifice of laying down one's life for his friends and then tells the disciples they are in a new relationship with him. Now they are friends of Jesus. Friends freely do what a friend asks of them, especially when an explanation has been offered. Jesus says: "I have made known to you everything I have heard from my Father." And he affirms he chose them, and their mission is to bear fruit. The ultimate sign of that fruit is that they love one another.

Good News for All of Us

The Holy Spirit is alive in the Church. Even now, the Spirit guides the Church and fills believers with wisdom and grace to do the work that faith requires. Every day we have opportunities to show our love to the world wherever we are and with people we encounter. When we reach out to others in need, our motivation should extend beyond simply wanting to make them feel better. In obedience to Christ, we are required to be in a relationship of love with them. We show love by treating others with dignity, remembering they also are children of God and our brothers and sisters in Christ. They too can serve us, and we can learn from them. This isn't possible without grace, which is found in the love God has already given us.

Questions for Reflection and Discussion

➤ Who has shown you great love in your life? Did you ever consider this as an extension of God's love for you?

➤ Peter says all who fear God and do what is right are acceptable to him. If so, why should anyone be baptized? Why not just lead a good life?

Related Journey of Faith Lesson

M5, "Our Call to Holiness"

Themes

Unity
    M5, "Our Call to Holiness"
Universality
    M8, "Evangelization"

Seventh Sunday of Easter, Year B

READING 1, ACTS 1:15–17, 20A, 20C–26

Peter stood up in the midst of the brothers—there was a group of about one hundred and twenty persons in the one place. He said, "My brothers, the Scripture had to be fulfilled which the Holy Spirit spoke beforehand through the mouth of David, concerning Judas, who was the guide for those who arrested Jesus. He was numbered among us and was allotted a share in this ministry. "For it is written in the Book of Psalms: *May another take his office.* Therefore, it is necessary that one of the men who accompanied us the whole time the Lord Jesus came and went among us, beginning from the baptism of John until the day on which he was taken up from us, become with us a witness to his resurrection." So they proposed two, Judas called Barsabbas, who was also known as Justus, and Matthias. Then they prayed, "You, Lord, who know the hearts of all, show which one of these two you have chosen to take the place in this apostolic ministry from which Judas turned away to go to his own place." Then they gave lots to them, and the lot fell upon Matthias, and he was counted with the eleven apostles.

PSALM 103:1–2, 11–12, 19–20

READING 2, 1 JOHN 4:11–16

Beloved, if God so loved us, we also must love one another. No one has ever seen God. Yet, if we love one another, God remains in us, and his love is brought to perfection in us. This is how we know that we remain in him and he in us, that he has given us of his Spirit. Moreover, we have seen and testify that the Father sent his Son as savior of the world. Whoever acknowledges that Jesus is the Son of God, God remains in him and he in God. We have come to know and to believe in the love God has for us. God is love, and whoever remains in love remains in God and God in him.

GOSPEL, JOHN 17:11B–19

Lifting up his eyes to heaven, Jesus prayed saying: "Holy Father, keep them in your name that you have given me, so that they may be one just as we are one. When I was with them I protected them in your name that you gave me, and I guarded them, and none of them was lost except the son of destruction, in order that the Scripture might be fulfilled. But now I am coming to you. I speak this in the world so that they may share my joy completely. I gave them your word, and the world hated them, because they do not belong to the world any more than I belong to the world. I do not ask that you take them out of the world but that you keep them from the evil one. They do not belong to the world any more than I belong to the world. Consecrate them in the truth. Your word is truth. As you sent me into the world, And I consecrate myself for them, so that they also may be consecrated in truth."

That They May Be One

In Genesis, we learn about the creation of the world and the estrangement that took place after the sin of Adam and Eve. They became estranged from God, one another, and the rest of creation. Through Jesus, we've been reconciled to God and invited into a new and loving relationship with him. The early Church did its best to live out that relationship by loving, serving, learning, and sharing the Good News. They celebrated the Eucharist in house churches, they listened to the teachings of the apostles, and they cared for those who were less fortunate.

Jesus chose twelve apostles because one of the signs that the Messiah had come was the gathering of the twelve tribes of Israel. The apostles served as a sign of these tribes. When Judas betrayed Jesus and left the Twelve, they knew they would have to replace him to have the fullness of the symbol.

Here's the wonderful thing. They looked for Judas' replacement among those who had been traveling with them from the beginning. The apostles engage in discernment, which invites God into the process of making a decision, then they pray to God. Ultimately, they choose Matthias. We never hear about Matthias again. Presumably he goes back to his place and preaches the Gospel to all he meets. Many who serve the Lord forego promotion or notoriety. They just do what they are called to do every day and make the world a little better place.

The Gospel continues the theme as Jesus prays fervently to the Father before his death. His wish is that the disciples might have as close a relationship with each other as Jesus has with the Father. He prays for God's protection and that they will become one.

Sent into the World

The Gospel presents an ominous view of the world from a Christian perspective. The disciples have already seen some of the hatred that Jesus' teachings have stirred up. They have witnessed the anger that has made the authorities want to arrest Jesus. Part of Jesus' prayer is one of protection for the disciples who will face the same kind of persecution Jesus did. Jesus also prays that his joy might be complete in them. And he prays that they might be made holy (sanctified) in the truth of Jesus. In the Hebrew Scriptures, the word for holy means "set apart." The disciples are set apart from the world by their faith. Another way to say it is that they are in the world but not of it. Thus, they will be sent into the world as living witnesses of the love of God.

John's epistle continues to echo the theme of love. This time he emphasizes God's love for us because he sent his Son as the Savior of the world. But his last line makes it clear that the disciples are also to approach the world with love. "God is love, and those who abide in love abide in God, and God abides in them."

Good News for All of Us

The world today seems more polarized than ever. Voices on the extremes of politics, religion, and society shout endlessly about how bad opposing views are. Many have withdrawn into their own little world to avoid the negativity and disparity. If ever we needed voices of peace and love, this is the time. As disciples of Christ, we have been sent into the world to serve as witnesses of God in our own lives. How often do we invite conversation that allows one person to speak respectfully and ask questions of the other? We may be afraid of being yelled at or ignored. And while that might happen, Jesus himself prayed for his joy to be in us, for the Father's protection and for the truth to surround us. That should give us the courage to speak and act with justice and love.

Questions for Reflection and Discussion

➤ *As a disciple in the world, where do you think you can best witness to God's love in your life?*

➤ *Have you ever witnessed someone standing up to discrimination or hatred? What was the result?*

Related Journey of Faith Lesson

M8, "Evangelization"

Themes

Jesus
    Q7, "Your Prayer Life"
Mission
    M8, "Evangelization"
Vocation
    M2, "The Role of the Laity"

Pentecost Sunday, Year B

READING 1, ACTS 2:1–11

When the time for Pentecost was fulfilled, they were all in one place together. And suddenly there came from the sky a noise like a strong driving wind, and it filled the entire house in which they were. Then there appeared to them tongues as of fire, which parted and came to rest on each one of them. And they were all filled with the Holy Spirit and began to speak in different tongues, as the Spirit enabled them to proclaim. Now there were devout Jews from every nation under heaven staying in Jerusalem. At this sound, they gathered in a large crowd, but they were confused because each one heard them speaking in his own language. They were astounded, and in amazement they asked, "Are not all these people who are speaking Galileans? Then how does each of us hear them in his native language? We are Parthians, Medes, and Elamites, inhabitants of Mesopotamia, Judea and Cappadocia, Pontus and Asia, Phrygia and Pamphylia, Egypt and the districts of Libya near Cyrene, as well as travelers from Rome, both Jews and converts to Judaism, Cretans and Arabs, yet we hear them speaking in our own tongues of the mighty acts of God."

PSALM 104:1, 24, 29–30, 31, 34

READING 2, 1 CORINTHIANS 12:3B–7, 12–13

Brothers and sisters: No one can say, "Jesus is Lord," except by the Holy Spirit. There are different kinds of spiritual gifts but the same Spirit; there are different forms of service but the same Lord; there are different workings but the same God who produces all of them in everyone. To each individual the manifestation of the Spirit is given for some benefit. As a body is one though it has many parts, and all the parts of the body, though many, are one body, so also Christ. For in one Spirit we were all baptized into one body, whether Jews or Greeks, slaves or free persons, and we were all given to drink of one Spirit.

GOSPEL, JOHN 20:19–23

On the evening of that first day of the week, when the doors were locked, where the disciples were, for fear of the Jews, Jesus came and stood in their midst and said to them, "Peace be with you." When he had said this, he showed them his hands and his side. The disciples rejoiced when they saw the Lord Jesus said to them again, "Peace be with you. As the Father has sent me, so I send you." And when he had said this, he breathed on them and said to them, "Receive the Holy Spirit. Whose sins you forgive are forgiven them, and whose sins you retain are retained."

The Gift of the Spirit

Today's readings are all about gifts—the amazing gift of the Holy Spirit to the Church as a whole and the gifts the Holy Spirit gives to us individually. All are intended to build up the faith community. In service to this theme, we hear the story of Pentecost, which shows the Spirit coming down on the gathered disciples in the form of wind, fire, and a strange new language.

Paul uses his image of the body of Christ in reference to the Church. The gifts given to its members are all of one Spirit because we are baptized into one body. The Gospel of John is a second hearing of the Gospel for the second Sunday of Easter. Here, the reading gives special emphasis to the gift of forgiveness of sins, which is the reason Jesus—out of love—came to us in the first place.

A Mighty Wind

The prophet Joel spoke about the day that the Lord would pour out his Spirit on the sons and daughters of Israel, indeed on the whole world (Joel 2:28). The prophecy comes true in the passage from Acts. Three things stand out. The first is the sound of a mighty wind. In both Greek and Hebrew, the word for Spirit is the same as "breath" or "wind." God breathes his Spirit into us at creation. We also know that wind blows freely, as does the Spirit. Second, tongues as of fire appear. Fire is a purifying element that refines metal, provides warmth and also has the ability to destroy what it touches. So, too, the Holy Spirit. Finally, the disciples begin to speak in a strange language, and they are compelled to preach in it. We refer to this today as speaking in tongues; this was the first gift of the Spirit.

Genesis 11 tells the story of all the inhabitants of the earth who had one language building a great tower to heaven. Seeing their impudence, God confuses their language, so that they could not understand each other. The nations that are named in Genesis are largely included here. God reverses his punishment so that every person who hears the disciples preach in this strange tongue understands it as if it is spoken in his or her own language. Remembering Joel's prophecy that God's Spirit would be poured out to all flesh, we might call this the other gift of the Spirit. Is it any wonder that the disciples preach about God's deeds of power?

God's mercy is evident here as well as in the gift of forgiveness that Jesus hands over to the disciples for the benefit of the whole world. Had Christ not died, we would not have been reconciled to God. Forgiveness brings the peace of Christ to our hearts. The Spirit continues to pour out that peace on us now.

Many Gifts, One Body

It's human nature to want to compare ourselves to others. The Corinthians fought among one another about whose gifts were more important and who had the greater claim on God's promise. Paul provides a corrective. All gifts come from the same Spirit; all activities come from the same God. For Paul the important thing is that gifts are used for the common good. Clearly fighting about them did not contribute to that end.

Good News for All of Us

The Spirit was poured out on the whole world. That means every person has a share of the Spirit's gifts. Paul lists many of them in his letters: pastor, preacher, teacher, and so on. We have a tendency in the Church to think that gifts only belong to those in authority, like priests or deacons. In truth, we all have something to contribute. The catechist teaching Sunday school is as valuable as the bishop watching over his diocese. It's important for us to encourage gifts that we see in others and invite them to contribute these to our parishes and prayer groups. In turn, we should use our own for the common good of the faith community.

Questions for Reflection and Discussion

➤ Consider what gifts you have that others may have brought to your attention. Are you using your gift(s) today?

➤ How does the Church welcome and reflect diversity in your parish, city, or in the world?

Related Journey of Faith Lesson

M3, "Your Spiritual Gifts"

Themes

Church
    M2, "The Role of the Laity"
Holy Spirit
    M3, "Your Spiritual Gifts"

Trinity Sunday, Year B

READING 1, DEUTERONOMY 4:32–34, 39–40

Moses said to the people: "Ask now of the days of old, before your time, ever since God created man upon the earth; ask from one end of the sky to the other: Did anything so great ever happen before? Was it ever heard of? Did a people ever hear the voice of God speaking from the midst of fire, as you did, and live? Or did any god venture to go and take a nation for himself from the midst of another nation, by testings, by signs and wonders, by war, with strong hand and outstretched arm, and by great terrors, all of which the LORD, your God, did for you in Egypt before your very eyes? This is why you must now know, and fix in your heart, that the LORD is God in the heavens above and on earth below, and that there is no other. You must keep his statutes and commandments that I enjoin on you today, that you and your children after you may prosper, and that you may have long life on the land which the LORD, your God, is giving you forever."

PSALM 33:4–5, 6, 9, 18–19, 20, 22

READING 2, ROMANS 8:14–17

Brothers and sisters: For those who are led by the Spirit of God are sons of God. For you did not receive a spirit of slavery to fall back into fear, but you received a Spirit of adoption, through whom we cry, "Abba, Father!" The Spirit himself bears witness with our spirit that we are children of God, and if children, then heirs, heirs of God and joint heirs with Christ, if only we suffer with him so that we may also be glorified with him.

GOSPEL MATTHEW 28:16–20

The eleven disciples went to Galilee, to the mountain to which Jesus had ordered them. When they all saw him, they worshiped, but they doubted. Then Jesus approached and said to them, "All power in heaven and on earth has been given to me. Go, therefore, and make disciples of all nations, baptizing them in the name of the Father, and of the Son, and of the Holy Spirit, teaching them to observe all that I have commanded you. And behold, I am with you always, until the end of the age."

A Relationship Like No Other

Trinity Sunday provides the bridge from the Easter season back into Ordinary Time. Let's take time to reflect on what being an Easter people is all about. Our lives have changed; our relationship with God has changed. How will we live into this new reality? Of course, the Trinity is a mystery. We know that Father, Son, and Holy Spirit are three ways we understand God; and our faith also tells us that our God is one God. God is in a relationship with himself. Contemporary models of Trinity use the images of Lover (Father), Beloved (Son), and the love between them (Spirit) or Source, Wellspring, and Fountain of Life. Both sets capture something of the oneness of God in three entities, but none of them fully describe the mystery. Our language is poor at best for such a task. And so, we bless ourselves in the name of the Father, Son, and Holy Spirit, as our ancestors did and remember that God is more than we can imagine.

A God Like No Other

Moses begins our reflection with his words to the Israelites as they are about to cross into the Promised Land. "Did anything so great ever happen before?" he asks them. "Did a people ever hear the voice of God speaking from the midst of fire, as you did, and live?" The gods of the neighboring nations didn't do this. Those gods seemed fickle, creating human beings to be their slaves on earth and demanding sacrifice. This God is different, Moses says. How are the Israelites to live in relationship with this God? They are to observe all of his laws and commandments "that you and your children after you may prosper, and that you may have long life on the land which the LORD, your God, is giving you forever." Throughout Deuteronomy, Moses reminds the people that God intervened in their history and loved them. Their response of obedience is out of gratitude for so great a mercy.

Paul's Letter to the Romans comes to the same conclusion. This God is like no other. His Spirit freed us. We are no longer slaves, but God's adopted children and heirs with Christ to God's promise. What we do out of gratitude for God's mercy is suffer with Christ in whatever way that comes upon us, knowing that we will also be glorified with him. Like the Israelites, God has freed us from slavery that we might serve freely as his children.

Make Disciples of All Nations

In our Gospel, when Jesus appears after the resurrection, the disciples worship him, but not all are convinced that it is Jesus. Remarkably, Jesus does not address that. Rather, he claims his authority and commissions all of them to do three things: make disciples of everyone; baptize in the name of the Father, Son, and Holy Spirit; and teach them to obey everything Jesus has commanded. The disciples become, in effect, new versions of Moses. They give witness to what God has done through Christ and they invite people to follow Christ by obeying his commandments. Jesus promises them he will be there always just as God promised to go before the Israelites into the Promised Land. We aren't alone. God will never forsake us.

Good News for All of Us

This bears repeating. The Bible is not just a story of people who lived long ago and far away. The Bible is the living word for us now. We are in a period of new evangelization for the Church. Many Catholics have simply stopped practicing their faith, whether because of hectic lifestyles, disillusion with the scandals of the Church, or lack of faith. Still others never had an opportunity to learn faith in their families. Jesus calls us, even if we have doubts, to share the stories of what God has done for us and to invite others to experience God's mercy and grace for themselves. We may never see the result; sometimes all we can do is plant a seed. We know, though, that the Father, Son, and Holy Spirit—this great Trinity—watches over all we encounter.

Questions for Reflection and Discussion

➤ What are some ways you spread the Good News in your own life? If you don't, how can you start?

➤ Name some high or low points in your life where God might have been present, but you may not have realized it.

Related Journey of Faith Lesson

Q3, "The Holy Trinity"

Themes

Call
    Q2, "What Is Faith?"
    M1, "Conversion: A Lifelong Process"
Family
    M7, "Family Life"
Name
    Q3, "The Holy Trinity"
    Q12, "Who Shepherds the Church?"
    M3, "Your Spiritual Gifts"

Body and Blood of Christ, Year B

READING 1, EXODUS 24:3–8

When Moses came to the people and related all the words and ordinances of the LORD, they all answered with one voice,
"We will do everything that the Lord has told us." Moses then wrote down all the words of the Lord and, rising early the next day, he erected at the foot of the mountain an altar and twelve pillars for the twelve tribes of Israel. Then, having sent certain young men of the Israelites to offer holocausts and sacrifice young bulls as peace offerings to the Lord, Moses took half of the blood and put it in large bowls; the other half he splashed on the altar. Taking the book of the covenant, he read it aloud to the people, who answered, "All that the Lord has said, we will heed and do." Then he took the blood and sprinkled it on the people, saying, "This is the blood of the covenant that the Lord has made with you in accordance with all these words of his."

PSALM 116:12–13, 15–16, 17–18

READING 2, HEBREWS 9:11–15

Brothers and sisters: When Christ came as high priest of the good things that have come to be, passing through the greater and more perfect tabernacle not made by hands, that is, not belonging to this creation, he entered once for all into the sanctuary, not with the blood of goats and calves but with his own blood, thus obtaining eternal redemption. For if the blood of goats and bulls and the sprinkling of a heifer's ashes can sanctify those who are defiled so that their flesh is cleansed, how much more will the blood of Christ, who through the eternal Spirit offered himself unblemished to God, cleanse our consciences from dead works to worship the living God. For this reason he is mediator of a new covenant: since a death has taken place for deliverance from transgressions under the first covenant, those who are called may receive the promised eternal inheritance.

GOSPEL, MARK 14:12–16, 22–26

On the first day of the feast of Unleavened Bread, when they sacrificed the Passover lamb, Jesus' disciples said to him, "Where do you want us to go and prepare for you to eat the Passover?" He sent two of his disciples and said to them, "Go into the city and a man will meet you, carrying a jar of water. Follow him. Wherever he enters, say to the master of the house, 'The Teacher says, "Where is my guest room where I may eat the Passover with my disciples?"' Then he will show you a large upper room furnished and ready. Make the preparations for us there." The disciples then went off, entered the city, and found it just as he had told them; and they prepared the Passover. While they were eating, he took bread, said the blessing, broke it, gave it to them, and said, "Take it; this is my body." Then he took a cup, gave thanks, and gave it to them, and they all drank from it. He said to them, "This is my blood of the covenant, which will be shed for many. Amen, I say to you, I shall not drink again the fruit of the vine until the day when I drink it new in the kingdom of God." Then, after singing a hymn, they went out to the Mount of Olives.

Blood and Covenant

Today we celebrate another mystery. How do we understand the Body and Blood of Christ to be an atoning sacrifice? Each reading for the day speaks about blood and sacrifice in reference to the covenant God made with his people. In Deuteronomy, after God presents the Ten Commandments, the people give their assent to obedience and Moses slaughters a young bull to offer as sacrifice. The blood that Moses spills on the altar and on the people is a bond between them and the Lord. Such an oath was taken very seriously and signaled commitment by both parties. God promised to love and care for his people and the people promised to obey the commandments of God. The Mosaic Covenant reminded people that the Laws of God were to be obeyed. Later in the Old Testament, God would make the Davidic Covenant, which was the reminder that God also loved his people even in their sinfulness. We need both covenants to balance our understanding of God's mercy and judgment.

Our High Priest in Heaven

In the Mosaic Covenant, the high priest alone could enter the Holy of Holies once a year to offer sacrifice for the sins of the Israelites. This was known as Yom Kippur, or the Day of Atonement. Jews today still observe the feast. While they do not offer sacrifice, they follow other rituals, including fasting, confession of sins, and asking forgiveness. In the time of Exodus, the sacrifice of a young bull and a goat were accepted as sin offerings for the high priest and the people. Thus, the blood covenant first received on Mount Sinai was continued.

The early Christian community recognized the sacrifice of Christ (the Lamb of God) as the atoning sacrifice for all time. The Letter to the Hebrews expands on this theology, calling Jesus our High Priest who is in heaven. His blood purifies us so we might worship God. Jesus, the High Priest, is also called the mediator of the New Covenant, which, for Christians, replaces the Mosaic Covenant. In the next chapter of Hebrews, the writer tells us that since we have a great high priest in heaven, we can also approach the sanctuary "with a sincere heart and in absolute trust" (Hebrews 10:22).

The New Covenant in My Blood

Mark's sparse narration of the Last Supper might leave out some well-known details, but it maintains all the highlights. We hear Jesus say, "This is my body," over the bread and "This is my blood of the covenant which will be shed on behalf of many" over the cup of wine. In the vision of the New Covenant (see Jeremiah 31:31–34), God says he will write the covenant on our heart. The blood is not sprinkled on our bodies as Moses did in Deuteronomy; rather, we drink the blood. Figuratively, it is sprinkled on our hearts and we recommit ourselves to God's New Covenant every time we receive the Body and Blood of Christ in Communion.

Good News for All of Us

It's hard to believe that God continues to make his covenant with us, especially when we don't always uphold our end of the agreement. And yet, through Jesus, God continually offers forgiveness, justice, mercy, and salvation to all who earnestly seek it. We also have a wonderful gift in the bread and wine that are offered in the Mass, each element becomes the Body and Blood, soul and divinity of Christ offered once and for all through his passion, death, and resurrection. Every time we receive Communion, we assent to the covenant again and pledge ourselves to obedience to the Lord.

Questions for Reflection and Discussion

> *Is there anyone with whom you have made a solemn agreement or oath to do something? How did it feel to make such a promise?*

> *Knowing the solemnity of a blood covenant, what can you do to better prepare yourself to receive Communion?*

Related Journey of Faith Lesson

C5, "The Sacrament of the Eucharist"

Themes

Covenant
  E4, "The Creed"
Eucharist
  Q9, "The Mass"
  C5, "The Sacrament of the Eucharist"
  M5, "Our Call to Holiness"
Liturgy
  Q7, "Your Prayer Life"
  Q13, "The Church as Community"

Ninth Sunday in Ordinary Time, Year B

READING 1, DEUTERONOMY 5:12–15

Thus says the LORD: "Take care to keep holy the sabbath day as the LORD, your God, commanded you. Six days you may labor and do all your work; but the seventh day is the sabbath of the LORD, your God. No work may be done then, whether by you, or your son or daughter, or your male or female slave, or your ox or ass or any of your beasts, or the alien who lives with you. Your male and female slave should rest as you do. For remember that you too were once a slave in Egypt, and the LORD, your God, brought you from there with his strong hand and outstretched arm. That is why the LORD, your God, has commanded you to observe the sabbath day."

PSALM 81:3–4, 5–6, 6–8, 10–11

READING 2, 2 CORINTHIANS 4:6–11

Brothers and sisters: God who said, Let light shine out of darkness, has shone in our hearts to bring to light the knowledge of the glory of God on the face of Jesus Christ. But we hold this treasure in earthen vessels, that the surpassing power may be of God and not from us. We are afflicted in every way, but not constrained; perplexed, but not driven to despair; persecuted, but not abandoned; struck down, but not destroyed; always carrying about in the body the dying of Jesus, so that the life of Jesus may also be manifested in our body. For we who live are constantly being given up to death for the sake of Jesus, so that the life of Jesus may be manifested in our mortal flesh.

GOSPEL, MARK 2:23—3:6

As Jesus was passing through a field of grain on the sabbath, his disciples began to make a path while picking the heads of grain. At this the Pharisees said to him, "Look, why are they doing what is unlawful on the sabbath?" He said to them, "Have you never read what David did when he was in need and he and his companions were hungry? How he went into the house of God when Abiathar was high priest and ate the bread of offering that only the priests could lawfully eat, and shared it with his companions?" Then he said to them, "The sabbath was made for man, not man for the sabbath. That is why the Son of Man is lord even of the sabbath." Again he entered the synagogue. There was a man there who had a withered hand. They watched him closely to see if he would cure him on the Sabbath so that they might accuse him. He said to the man with the withered hand, "Come up here before us." Then he said to them, "Is it lawful to do good on the sabbath rather than to do evil, to save life rather than to destroy it?" But they remained silent. Looking around at them with anger and grieved at their hardness of heart, he said to the man, "Stretch out your hand." He stretched it out and his hand was restored. The Pharisees went out and immediately took counsel with the Herodians against him to put him to death.

A Sabbath to the Lord

I remember in my childhood that stores were closed on Sunday, presumably so people could attend church and visit family. Gradually, the culture changed so that Sunday doesn't appear to be different than any other day. The command to keep the Sabbath holy is a command to set apart one day of the week where the relationship with God and community takes precedence over everything else. There are two places the command is given as part of the Ten Commandments. In Exodus, we keep the Sabbath because God rested on the seventh day from the work of creation. In today's reading from Deuteronomy, the Sabbath is kept because we were once slaves in Egypt and God freed us. We also keep the Sabbath to remember and give thanks for all God has created and given us and for the wondrous deeds that God has done on our behalf. It is a re-creation for the world and for us.

Our Jewish brothers and sisters mark Saturday as their Sabbath. Christians gradually accepted Sunday, which they called the Lord's day, as theirs. Done right, the Sabbath allows us to reconnect with God and the faith community in prayer during Mass, and with our families over Sunday dinner. There are some who have begun to set their own Sabbath rules. They don't use their cell phones or computers, and they don't watch TV. They prefer instead to unplug and pay attention to the signs of God's presence all around them in people, church, and in the lives they lead.

A Light Not of Our Making

When the songwriter Leonard Cohen died, the internet took to quoting some of his lyrics. A popular one talks about how everything has a crack in it; that's how the light gets in. Paul's Letter to the Corinthians would seem to be the forerunner of Cohen's words. If people see the glory of God shining from us, it is because of the power of God who chose us, despite our being broken vessels.

Paul is encouraging Christian believers who are being taunted and persecuted every day. He may also be encouraging himself. Paul sees such suffering as a way of carrying the death of Jesus in the body so that the life of Christ might be visible to all who see the peace and joy of the Christians as they witness to the resurrection of Christ and God's saving power.

In Mark's Gospel, Jesus has already demonstrated his authority over demons, illness, and sin. Here he moves back to the synagogue to show he also has authority over the Sabbath. Is Jesus contradicting the Father, whose command to keep the Sabbath was part of the Mosaic covenant? If we look closely, what Jesus rails against is the Pharisees' letter-of-the-law interpretation of the commandment. He points out the exception to the rule in Scripture where David ate the holy bread on the Sabbath as he was fleeing from Saul (1 Samuel 21:1–11). God's law was to keep the Sabbath. The Pharisees themselves made the subsequent laws about what it meant to keep the Sabbath holy. Exceptions could be made, and Jesus claims his authority as the Son of Man to make them.

As if to underscore the point, Jesus enters the synagogue, sees the man with the withered hand, and pauses simply to ask if it is lawful to do good or do harm on the Sabbath. They have no answer, and he heals the hand. In doing so, he took authority from the Pharisees, which they felt belonged to them. They were not pleased.

Good News for All of Us

We can reclaim the Sabbath for ourselves. More and more people are looking for rest and quiet in the midst of daily demands, which seem overwhelming at times. Remember, we are merely clay vessels that can break easily. Observing the Sabbath can provide the rest we need to live out Jesus' call in the week ahead. This Sunday, try to let go of the mentality that you need to do something and just be. Embrace the quiet with the Lord and your family.

Questions for Reflection and Discussion

➤ *What do you do on your typical Sunday? Is it a day of rest, prayer, and visiting friends or family, or do you work on the Sabbath?*

➤ *What part of your "earthen vessel" is cracked or broken? Do you realize God chose you to shine his light anyway?*

Related Journey of Faith Lesson

C10, "The People of God"

Themes

Law
    Q4, "Who Is Jesus Christ"
    E4, "The Creed"
Rest
    Q7, "Your Prayer Life"
    Q8, "Catholic Prayers and Practices"
Sabbath
    Q9, "The Mass"
    M5, "Our Call to Holiness"

READING 1, GENESIS 3:9–15

After the man, Adam, had eaten of the tree, the LORD God called to the man and asked him, "Where are you?" He answered, "I heard you in the garden; but I was afraid, because I was naked, so I hid myself." Then he asked, "Who told you that you were naked? You have eaten, then, from the tree of which I had forbidden you to eat!" The man replied, "The woman whom you put here with me—she gave me fruit from the tree, and so I ate it." The LORD God then asked the woman, "Why did you do such a thing?" The woman answered, "The serpent tricked me into it, so I ate it." Then the LORD God said to the serpent: "Because you have done this, you shall be banned from all the animals and from all the wild creatures; on your belly shall you crawl, and dirt shall you eat all the days of your life. I will put enmity between you and the woman, and between your offspring and hers; he will strike at your head, while you strike at his heel."

PSALM 130:1–2, 3–4, 5–6, 7–8

READING 2, 2 CORINTHIANS 4:13—5:1

Brothers and sisters: Since we have the same spirit of faith, according to what is written, *I believed, therefore I spoke,* we too believe and therefore we speak, knowing that the one who raised the Lord Jesus will raise us also with Jesus and place us with you in his presence. Everything indeed is for you, so that the grace bestowed in abundance on more and more people may cause the thanksgiving to overflow for the glory of God. Therefore, we are not discouraged; rather, although our outer self is wasting away, our inner self is being renewed day by day. For this momentary light affliction is producing for us an eternal weight of glory beyond all comparison, as we look not to what is seen but to what is unseen; for what is seen is transitory, but what is unseen is eternal. For we know that if our earthly dwelling, a tent, should be destroyed, we have a building from God, a dwelling not made with hands, eternal in heaven.

GOSPEL, MARK3:20–35

Jesus came home with his disciples. Again the crowd gathered, making it impossible for them even to eat. When his relatives heard of this they set out to seize him, for they said, "He is out of his mind." The scribes who had come from Jerusalem said, "He is possessed by Beelzebul," and "By the prince of demons he drives out demons." Summoning them, he began to speak to them in parables, "How can Satan drive out Satan? If a kingdom is divided against itself, that kingdom cannot stand. And if a house is divided against itself, that house will not be able to stand. And if Satan has risen up against himself and is divided, he cannot stand; that is the end of him. But no one can enter a strong man's house to plunder his property unless he first ties up the strong man. Then he can plunder the house. Amen, I say to you, all sins and all blasphemies that people utter will be forgiven them. But whoever blasphemes against the Holy Spirit will never have forgiveness, but is guilty of an everlasting sin." For they had said, "He has an unclean spirit." His mother and his brothers arrived. Standing outside they sent word to him and called him. A crowd seated around him told him, "Your mother and your brothers and your sisters are outside asking for you." But he said to them in reply, "Who are my mother and my brothers?" And looking around at those seated in the circle he said, "Here are my mother and my brothers. For whoever does the will of God is my brother and sister and mother."

A House Divided

As we move further into Ordinary Time, our readings help us reflect on the cause of division in God's house. The Genesis story picks up just after Adam and Eve eat the fruit of the tree of knowledge. In that moment, something changed, and we see it as soon as God appears in the Garden of Eden. God created Adam out of the dust; now Adam is afraid to be seen because he's naked. When God finds out Adam's shame, he addresses Adam with curiosity. The division of this house has already begun as the excuses are given. Adam blames God; Eve blames the serpent. God starts with the serpent in meting out punishment, but God knows that all are responsible. Ultimately Adam and Eve must leave the house God has provided for them.

In the responsorial psalm, we cry in despair: "Out of the depths, I cry to you, O Lord." This is a sinner who seeks forgiveness and doesn't want to be cast away from God. Jesus asks what happens if a kingdom is divided against itself and answers his own question: "It cannot stand." The answer to all this division is one thing: God.

A House Not Made with Hands

For Paul, the imprisonment and persecution of Christians created great stress within the community. It was not sin that divided them; it was the fear of death. Paul uses his own life as an example: "I believe," he says. Paul cannot help but preach the Good News and give witness. Paul's faith is very strong as he reminds them of God's promise to raise them up just as Jesus was raised up. Then they will be in his presence. Paul sees this "momentary affliction" as an opportunity to share in Christ's suffering so we can be prepared for an even greater joy—to see God face to face. This house of God is united in God's eternal home in heaven.

A House Open to the World

Though he had many followers, Jesus was also the cause of skepticism and anger by those who did not believe him. When he returns home, he is accused by some of being crazy; the scribes claim he is possessed. What Jesus says makes sense. "How can Satan cast out Satan?" Everyone knows that a house divided can't withstand attacks or disasters. Then Jesus gets to the heart of the issue. Sinners do divide the house, but they can be forgiven. It is the scribes themselves who have sinned against the Holy Spirit by ascribing to the devil what is the work of God. Jesus calls their sin eternal, for they refuse to see him as he is. Then Jesus shows the antidote to division; it is to include more in the house. "Who are my mother, brothers, and sisters? Anyone who does the will of God." Those who obey God are the children of God. Everyone is invited in.

Good News for All of Us

In God's house, we are all part of the family. All are counted among us: the poor and rich, sinner and saint, and those who doubt and are sure. Our unity in Christ is what binds us together. It is our own sinfulness that can divide us. Jesus assures us of forgiveness if we repent and try to do better. What we cannot do is forget that it is God's grace and bounty that gathered us here in the first place. Who else might we help gather into God's house? How can we be the ones who offer love, mercy, and comfort to the stranger who comes to the door?

Questions for Reflection and Discussion

➤ *Is there any division in your family? If so, what is the consequence?*

➤ *Think back on your faith journey. Did you ever question your faith? How do you respond to those who think religion is a source of evil in the world or who don't understand why you believe in God?*

Related Journey of Faith Lesson

Q8, "Catholic Prayers and Practices"

Themes

Family
    M7, "Family Life"
Forgiveness
    Q6, "Divine Revelation"
    Q7, "Your Prayer Life"
    Q8, "Catholic Prayers and Practices"
Sin
    E4, "The Creed"
    M5, "Our Call to Holiness

Eleventh Sunday in Ordinary Time, Year B

READING 1, EZEKIEL 17:22–24

Thus says the Lord God: I, too, will take from the crest of the cedar, from its topmost branches tear off a tender shoot, and plant it on a high and lofty mountain; on the mountain heights of Israel I will plant it. It shall put forth branches and bear fruit, and become a majestic cedar. Birds of every kind shall dwell beneath it, every winged thing in the shade of its boughs. And all the trees of the field shall know that I, the Lord, bring low the high tree, lift high the lowly tree, wither up the green tree, and make the withered tree bloom. As I, the Lord, have spoken, so will I do.

PSALM 92:2–3, 13–14, 15–16

READING 2, 2 CORINTHIANS 5:6–10

Brothers and sisters: We are always courageous, although we know that while we are at home in the body we are away from the Lord, for we walk by faith, not by sight. Yet we are courageous, and we would rather leave the body and go home to the Lord. Therefore, we aspire to please him, whether we are at home or away. For we must all appear before the judgment seat of Christ, so that each may receive recompense, according to what he did in the body, whether good or evil.

GOSPEL, MARK 4:26–34

Jesus said to the crowds: "This is how it is with the kingdom of God; it is as if a man were to scatter seed on the land and would sleep and rise night and day and through it all the seed would sprout and grow, he knows not how. Of its own accord the land yields fruit, first the blade, then the ear, then the full grain in the ear. And when the grain is ripe, he wields the sickle at once, for the harvest has come." He said, "To what shall we compare the kingdom of God, or what parable can we use for it? It is like a mustard seed that, when it is sown in the ground, is the smallest of all the seeds on the earth. But once it is sown, it springs up and becomes the largest of plants and puts forth large branches, so that the birds of the sky can dwell in its shade." With many such parables he spoke the word to them as they were able to understand it. Without parables he did not speak to them, but to his own disciples he explained everything in private.

A God Who Plants and Harvests

Some people have a green thumb. When they plant, transplant, or graft one branch on another, the plant flourishes, bearing fruit or growing blossoms in abundance. Some of us don't have that gift and are, perhaps, a little jealous of those who do, but we certainly have an appreciation of the beauty of gardens, farms, and forests. And all of us, planters and nonplanters alike, can see the presence of God in the beauty of and variety in creation.

Our readings today give us two such examples. The first, from Ezekiel, describes the care God takes to plant a cutting from the cedar tree and plant it in the mountains of Israel. In ancient Israel, the cedar symbolized strength and wisdom. Solomon built the first Temple out of cedar wood, and righteous people were often compared to the cedars of Lebanon. The cedar God plants will provide shade for every bird and will be a sign to the trees of the field that the Lord has spoken. For Ezekiel, this is a word of hope for a people that have seen war and the destruction of the Temple. God will restore Israel, and all will know the Lord.

Parables of the Kingdom That's Here and to Come

Complementing Ezekiel's prophecy are the two parables Jesus tells in Mark's Gospel. The interpretation of the kingdom parables rests on the commonplace analogy Jesus uses to talk about God's kingdom. In the first parable, the kingdom of God is the sower (God) who scatters seed on the ground and watches in wonder as it sprouts and grows to maturity. God's ground is the human heart, and he watches for signs of growth. When the time is right, God harvests the bountiful yield that the seed produces.

In the second parable, the kingdom is the smallest seed that gets sown but grows large enough for all the birds of the air to make a nest. In Christian theology, we speak about the kingdom of God being here, but it has not yet come to completion. When Jesus came, he had a few followers; he taught them, by planting seeds in their hearts and nurtured them until they came to believe fully in him. After his death, the number of believers multiplied because of the witness of the first followers. They found life in the community of faith, which continues to grow. In the end, the Father himself will harvest the growth when the kingdom comes in its fullness.

As we continue with Paul's Second Letter to the Corinthians, Paul explains that we are not fully with Jesus and the Father in this world. But he also believed that those who were baptized were transformed and, by the power of grace, could live as children of God, not influenced by worldly temptations. His famous line: "We walk by faith, and not by sight," indicates a maturing in belief. (Remember that Jesus told Thomas, "Blessed are those who have not seen and yet believe.") Those who were baptized had the confidence to follow the words that Jesus taught and to wait for Christ to come again. At the end of our Creed, we acknowledge this as we acclaim: "We wait in joyful hope for the coming of our Savior, Jesus Christ."

Good News for All of Us

We are made in the image of God. Just as God planted a garden and us in it, so also we are responsible for the figurative gardens we plant. Whether we are dealing with family members, neighbors, colleagues, or people in our faith communities, the words we say and actions we take are seeds planted in the hearts of those we encounter. How will they grow? If they are words and actions that demean someone, the plant will be stunted and fail to thrive. If they are words of encouragement, love, and faith, the plant will yield far more than we can imagine. Ask God, the heavenly gardener, to help you plant seeds that will grow.

Questions for Reflection and Discussion

➤ Talk about something you have planted, whether it's a garden, an idea, or a plan to surprise someone. How did you feel when it came to fruition?

➤ When was the seed of faith first planted in you? How was it nurtured? How can you keep it growing?

Related Journey of Faith Lessons

Q1, "Welcome to OCIA"; and Q2, "What Is the Faith?"

Themes

Growth
    Q2, "What Is Faith?"
    M1, "Conversion: A Lifelong Process"
Hope
    Q2, "What Is Faith?"
    Q4, "Who Is Jesus Christ?"
Praise
    Q7, "Your Prayer Life"
    Q8, "The Sacrament of Matrimony"

Twelfth Sunday in Ordinary Time, Year B

READING 1, JOB 38:1, 8–11

The LORD addressed Job out of the storm and said: Who shut within doors the sea, when it burst forth from the womb; when I made the clouds its garment and thick darkness its swaddling bands? When I set limits for it and fastened the bar of its door, and said: Thus far shall you come but no farther, and here shall your proud waves be stilled!

PSALM 107:23–24, 25–26, 28–29, 30–31

READING 2, 2 CORINTHIANS 5:14–17

Brothers and sisters: The love of Christ impels us, once we have come to the conviction that one died for all; therefore, all have died. He indeed died for all, so that those who live might no longer live for themselves but for him who for their sake died and was raised. Consequently, from now on we regard no one according to the flesh; even if we once knew Christ according to the flesh, yet now we know him so no longer. So whoever is in Christ is a new creation: the old things have passed away; behold, new things have come.

GOSPEL, MARK 4:35–41

On that day, as evening drew on, Jesus said to his disciples: "Let us cross to the other side." Leaving the crowd, they took Jesus with them in the boat just as he was. And other boats were with him. A violent squall came up and waves were breaking over the boat, so that it was already filling up. Jesus was in the stern, asleep on a cushion. They woke him and said to him, "Teacher, do you not care that we are perishing?" He woke up, rebuked the wind, and said to the sea, "Quiet! Be still!" The wind ceased and there was great calm. Then he asked them, "Why are you terrified? Do you not yet have faith?" They were filled with great awe and said to one another, "Who then is this whom even wind and sea obey?"

The Power of God for Us

The power of nature holds a certain fascination for us. Videos of hurricanes, tornadoes, tidal waves, and volcanoes draw our attention as we stand in awe of the destructive force of such phenomena. We are also keenly aware of how small and weak we seem in the face of these forces. The Jews of both the Old and New Testaments understood that God who had created these things could control them if he chose to do so. In the first reading, the Lord asks Job whom he thinks shut in the sea. The question is rhetorical. In the Gospel, the authority of Jesus to control the wind and sea awes and surprises the disciples. It is also not entirely comfortable for them.

A Tale of Woe

Job's life had been comfortable, but a series of unfortunate events had robbed him of his family and his riches. In his anguish, he continually asks God why this is happening. In God's only speech in the entire book (and in the whole of Wisdom literature), the Lord asks Job if he was there at the beginning of the universe or if he has control over the creatures in it. The answer is, of course, no. Both Job and we learn that sometimes, bad things happen to good people. God lets him know that he may never have the answer to the question: Why? What he does have is the assurance that God hears his cry and is with him.

The responsorial psalm celebrates both God's power over nature and his mercy toward his people. God, who can raise the violent winds and waves, can also calm them again. Because of this, the psalmist calls on all to give thanks.

Who Is This?

Mark continues to expand on the scope of Jesus' authority. As the wind and the waves pound the ship, the disciples seek out Jesus, who is asleep, and beg him to wake up. The text reads that he rebuked the wind. "Rebuke" is the same word used when Jesus casts out demons and tells them to be quiet. The wind ceases immediately and Jesus wonders why the disciples were afraid. "Do you not yet have faith," he asks. The disciples have forgotten the many times in which God saved the people (see Psalm 107). Their question is more immediate. Who is this that has such authority? They would not immediately find the answer.

Good News for All of Us

At the end of the nineteenth century, John Dalberg-Acton observed, "All power tends to corrupt and absolute power tends to corrupt absolutely." Such is the nature of power in human hands. Without grace and guidance, those with authority over others can be tempted to use that power to destroy. By contrast, God's power is infused with love and mercy. We may sometimes wonder why the power of nature or human sin sometimes overwhelms us. Why doesn't God intervene to stop natural disasters or corrupt leaders? We may never know the answer to that question. But we do know that as creatures we are not perfect and we have free will to obey God or not; to do good or evil. God promises that he will never abandon us. Through the Incarnation, God entered the reality of human suffering, showing us that God's weakness is greater than any human power and his love for us more than anything we have ever experienced.

Questions for Reflection and Discussion

➤ *What do you think Paul meant when he said if we are in Christ, we no longer see with a human point of view?*

➤ *Think about a time when someone offered you comfort. How did the person help you?*

Related Journey of Faith Lesson

Q2, "What Is Faith?"

Themes

Power
    Q5, "The Bible"
    M2, "The Role of the Laity"
Service
    Q15, "The Saints"
    M3, "Your Spiritual Gifts"
Water
    Q8, "Catholic Prayers and Practices"
    M1, "Conversion: A Lifelong Process"

Thirteenth Sunday in Ordinary Time, Year B

READING 1, WISDOM 1:13–15; 2:23–24

God did not make death, nor does he rejoice in the destruction of the living. For he fashioned all things that they might have being; and the creatures of the world are wholesome, and there is not a destructive drug among them nor any domain of the netherworld on earth, for justice is undying. For God formed man to be imperishable; the image of his own nature he made him. But by the envy of the devil, death entered the world, and they who belong to his company experience it.

PSALM 30:2, 4, 5–6, 11, 12, 13

READING 2, 2 CORINTHIANS 8:7, 9, 13–15

Brothers and sisters: As you excel in every respect, in faith, discourse, knowledge, all earnestness, and in the love we have for you, may you excel in this gracious act also. For you know the gracious act of our Lord Jesus Christ, that though he was rich, for your sake he became poor, so that by his poverty you might become rich. Not that others should have relief while you are burdened, but that as a matter of equality your abundance at the present time should supply their needs, so that their abundance may also supply your needs, that there may be equality. As it is written: *Whoever had much did not have more, and whoever had little did not have less.*

GOSPEL, MARK 5:21–43

When Jesus had crossed again in the boat to the other side, a large crowd gathered around him, and he stayed close to the sea. One of the synagogue officials, named Jairus, came forward. Seeing him he fell at his feet and pleaded earnestly with him, saying, "My daughter is at the point of death. Please, come lay your hands on her that she may get well and live." He went off with him, and a large crowd followed him and pressed upon him. There was a woman afflicted with hemorrhages for twelve years. She had suffered greatly at the hands of many doctors and had spent all that she had. Yet she was not helped but only grew worse. She had heard about Jesus and came up behind him in the crowd and touched his cloak. She said, "If I but touch his clothes, I shall be cured." Immediately her flow of blood dried up. She felt in her body that she was healed of her affliction. Jesus, aware at once that power had gone out from him, turned around in the crowd and asked, "Who has touched my clothes?" But his disciples said to Jesus, "You see how the crowd is pressing upon you, and yet you ask, 'Who touched me?'" And he looked around to see who had done it. The woman, realizing what had happened to her, approached in fear and trembling. She fell down before Jesus and told him the whole truth. He said to her, "Daughter, your faith has saved you. Go in peace and be cured of your affliction." While he was still speaking, people from the synagogue official's house arrived and said, "Your daughter has died; why trouble the teacher any longer?" Disregarding the message that was reported, Jesus said to the synagogue official, "Do not be afraid; just have faith." He did not allow anyone to accompany him inside except Peter, James, and John, the brother of James. When they arrived at the house of the synagogue official, he caught sight of a commotion, people weeping and wailing loudly. So he went in and said to them, "Why this commotion and weeping? The child is not dead but asleep." And they ridiculed him. Then he put them all out. He took along the child's father and mother and those who were with him and entered the room where the child was. He took the child by the hand and said to her, *Talitha koum,*" which means, "Little girl, I say to you, arise!" The girl, a child of twelve, arose immediately and walked around. At that they were utterly astounded. He gave strict orders that no one should know this and said that she should be given something to eat.

The Power that Conquers Death

In the first few chapters of Mark's Gospel, Jesus displays his authority over demons, illness, sin, physical impairment, and storms. In the Gospel today, he encounters someone who is dying and someone who is dead, and he helps both. Centuries before Christ, the Book of Wisdom described God's creative power. Where God is, there is life. God created us for life, not for death.

We also know we were created in the image of God, but we are not God. We are not perfect. Whether we ascribed what happened in the Garden of Eden to our own sinfulness or the devil's envy—or both—we know our free will sometimes means that we choose to sin rather than follow God's will. Thus, death enters the world. Sin doesn't always kill our bodies, but it can and does kill our souls either gradually (in the case of venial sin), or all at once (in mortal sin). Sin separates us from the love of God.

Praise the Lord Who Saves Us

Both our responsorial psalm and epistle today express further thoughts about God's power over death. The psalmist celebrates God who saved him from his enemies and "brought him up from the pit." Enemies can have quite a broad interpretation—physical enemies, sin, the devil, or our own temptations. When we are delivered from any of these, it is God who gets the glory. Paul revels in the excellent faith of the Corinthians, and then exhorts them to further good deeds as they consider helping those who are less fortunate. Paul advocates balance between rich and poor so that everyone is taken care of. His example is Jesus, who became poor so that we might become rich in grace. Surely for his sake, we can give out of our abundance to those who have less.

Rise Up

Mark's story within a story is the culmination of the healings Jesus provides, which brings him to the depths of human experience and shows his authority over all things. There is an encounter with a woman who has had a hemorrhage for twelve years. Blood is life; as far as the village is concerned, this woman has been dying for twelve years. The woman shouldn't have been out (she was considered unclean), but, desperate, she manages to touch Jesus' cloak, believing that this holy man can cure her. The power of healing, indeed of life, goes out from Jesus immediately. Both he and she know it. The disciples are, of course, uncomprehending. When she comes before Jesus, she fears she has done something wrong. But her faith in the power of God for life saves her and makes her whole.

Meanwhile, Jairus' daughter has died. Jesus enters the house, takes her hand, and tells her to get up. When she does, her parents, Peter, James, and John are all amazed. Jesus' response is practical—he tells them to give her something to eat. Jesus meets these two women in their most vulnerable and hopeless time and brings life.

Thirteenth Sunday in Ordinary Time, Year B

Good News for All of Us

In the healing stories of Mark's Gospel, we watch Jesus enter deeply into the human experience, bringing us to wholeness through word, touch, and divine life itself. One thing is immediately clear. We are limited. We get sick; we fall into temptation; and sometimes under the influence of evil. In every instance, Jesus brings new life and a second chance. His power to forgive sins makes us whole again. In the Gospels, the proof of wholeness is often the physical healing that follows. We may not always see physical healing, but we know that wholeness in our hearts and spirits does not depend on that either. God created us so that he could dwell within us. Jesus died so that we might share eternity with God. How will you open yourself up to God today?

Questions for Reflection and Discussion

➤ *Have you ever personally experienced healing in mind, body, and spirit in your own life or witnessed it in someone else's life?*

➤ *Our faith encourages us to strive to be "perfect as our heavenly Father is perfect" (Matthew 5:48). Why is that important in our faith journey? Where is the good news when you fall short of perfection?*

Related Journey of Faith Lesson

Q4, "Who Is Jesus Christ?"

Themes

Death
> Q2, "What Is Faith?"
> Q16, "Eschatology: The 'Last Things'"
> M1, "Conversion: A Lifelong Process"

Life
> Q10, "The Church Year"
> M3, "Your Spiritual Gifts"

Popularity
> Q15, "The Saints"
> M2, "The Role of the Laity"

Fourteenth Sunday in Ordinary Time, Year B

READING 1, EZEKIEL 2:2–5

As the LORD spoke to me, the spirit entered into me and set me on my feet, and I heard the one who was speaking say to me: Son of man, I am sending you to the Israelites, rebels who have rebelled against me; they and their ancestors have revolted against me to this very day. Hard of face and obstinate of heart are they to whom I am sending you. But you shall say to them: Thus says the LORD GOD! And whether they heed or resist—for they are a rebellious house—they shall know that a prophet has been among them.

PSALM 123:1–2, 2, 3–4

READING 2, 2 CORINTHIANS 12:7–10

Brothers and sisters: That I, Paul, might not become too elated, because of the abundance of the revelations, a thorn in the flesh was given to me, an angel of Satan, to beat me, to keep me from being too elated. Three times I begged the Lord about this, that it might leave me, but he said to me, "My grace is sufficient for you, for power is made perfect in weakness." I will rather boast most gladly of my weaknesses, in order that the power of Christ may dwell with me. Therefore, I am content with weaknesses, insults, hardships, persecutions, and constraints, for the sake of Christ; for when I am weak, then I am strong.

GOSPEL, MARK 6:1–6

Jesus departed from there and came to his native place, accompanied by his disciples. When the sabbath came he began to teach in the synagogue, and many who heard him were astonished. They said, "Where did this man get all this? What kind of wisdom has been given him? What mighty deeds are wrought by his hands! Is he not the carpenter, the son of Mary, and the brother of James and Joses and Judas and Simon? And are not his sisters here with us?" And they took offense at him. Jesus said to them, "A prophet is not without honor except in his native place and among his own kin and in his own house." So he was not able to perform any mighty deed there, apart from curing a few sick people by laying his hands on them. He was amazed at their lack of faith.

When I Am Weak, I Am Strong

In today's culture, strength is often equated with power, and it comes in many disguises. Wealth, education, weapons, material goods, and position in society can give an individual power over others and not always in a good way. Today's readings propose the opposite of societal values. Paul says, "When I am weak, then I am strong." For many people, that statement would seem odd. How can we be strong in weakness? In fact, this is the paradox of the Christian life. At the point of his greatest weakness in the crucifixion, Jesus was at his greatest strength. He gave his life that we might live.

Today's readings illustrate the theme. The Lord sends Ezekiel to the people of Israel who may or may not listen to him. Paul, the great evangelist and theologian of the early Church was given a thorn in his flesh to keep him from being too elated at his success. And Jesus returns to his hometown only to find that the people's familiarity with his family prevented them from hearing what he had to say. Jesus was just the kid who grew up in their midst. He seemed to have learned a lot, but what could he possibly teach them?

Prophet with a Mission

Ezekiel's task seems impossible. Go and speak to a people who likely will reject you. God needs his voice to be heard whether the people accept it or not. It will get worse for Ezekiel. In the next chapter, he will be told that if he doesn't go and the people continue to sin, he will be held responsible. The prophet's task is to point to God's presence in the world and call everyone to faithfulness to God's law. God assures the prophet that the people will know that a prophet has been among them. Whether that will happen immediately or eventually is unclear.

Jesus, Son of God and prophetic figure, understands his own mission well. He returns to his hometown to teach the people about the Good News—that the kingdom of God is at hand. Despite the amazing things he has done in the surrounding area, the people are skeptical of anything he has to say. They note that he has a lot of wisdom, but "isn't this the carpenter, the son of Mary?" Jesus' family didn't have enough influence and power to convince their neighbors about who Jesus was. The result was immediate. Their lack of faith prevented Jesus from doing the powerful deeds he was known for in the surrounding towns. Only a few sick people saw him for who he was and what he could do. This is one of the few places where we hear about Jesus being amazed at the people's unbelief. They couldn't believe that anyone coming from Nazareth could be powerful, perhaps because they felt so powerless themselves.

My Grace Is Sufficient

We know Paul was imprisoned and probably tortured to some extent. He rarely talks about it. In his Second Letter to the Corinthians, we don't know what the thorn in his side is, but he gives a glimpse into the life of someone who is suffering. Like many in that situation, he prayed to God multiple times. Perhaps he wondered why God didn't answer him and take the suffering away. What he finally understands is that God answers prayer but not always in the way we expect. For Paul, the message was, "My grace is sufficient for you, for power is made perfect in weakness." The power of God working through Paul made him strong.

Good News for All of Us

The Bible is filled with stories of people who felt powerless (Leah), outcast (Rahab), slow of speech (Moses), sinful (Isaiah and Peter), or suffering (Paul). God's response to each was the same: *But you are the one I want...you are the one through whom I will make my presence known.* It is pure grace to know that God can enter our weakness and use it for strength, even when we are doubtful. That is good news indeed!

Questions for Reflection and Discussion

➤ *What are your weaknesses? Have they ever been sources of strength for someone else?*

➤ *Why do you think the people's lack of faith prevented Jesus from accomplishing powerful deeds? What is the link between faith and miracles?*

Related Journey of Faith Lesson

Q5, "The Bible"

Themes

Opposition
    Q2, "What Is Faith?"
    M2, "The Role of the Laity"
Strength
    Q8, "Catholic Prayers and Practices"
    M3, "Your Spiritual Gifts"
    M8, "Evangelization"
Weakness
    Q8, "Catholic Prayers and Practices"
    M4, "Discernment"

Fifteenth Sunday in Ordinary Time, Year B

READING 1, AMOS 7:12–15

Amaziah, priest of Bethel, said to Amos, "Off with you, visionary, flee to the land of Judah! There earn your bread by prophesying, but never again prophesy in Bethel; for it is the king's sanctuary and a royal temple." Amos answered Amaziah, "I was no prophet, nor have I belonged to a company of prophets; I was a shepherd and a dresser of sycamores. The LORD took me from following the flock, and said to me, Go, prophesy to my people Israel."

PSALM 85:9–10, 11–12, 13–14

READING 2, EPHESIANS 1:3–14

Blessed be the God and Father of our Lord Jesus Christ, who has blessed us in Christ with every spiritual blessing in the heavens, as he chose us in him, before the foundation of the world, to be holy and without blemish before him. In love he destined us for adoption to himself through Jesus Christ, in accord with the favor of his will, for the praise of the glory of his grace that he granted us in the beloved. In him we have redemption by his blood, the forgiveness of transgressions, in accord with the riches of his grace that he lavished upon us. In all wisdom and insight, he has made known to us the mystery of his will in accord with his favor that he set forth in him as a plan for the fullness of times, to sum up all things in Christ, in heaven and on earth. In him we were also chosen, destined in accord with the purpose of the One who accomplishes all things according to the intention of his will, so that we might exist for the praise of his glory, we who first hoped in Christ. In him you also, who have heard the word of truth, the gospel of your salvation, and have believed in him, were sealed with the promised holy Spirit, which is the first installment of our inheritance toward redemption as God's possession, to the praise of his glory.

GOSPEL, MARK 6:7–13

Jesus summoned the Twelve and began to send them out two by two and gave them authority over unclean spirits. He instructed them to take nothing for the journey but a walking stick—no food, no sack, no money in their belts. They were, however, to wear sandals but not a second tunic. He said to them, "Wherever you enter a house, stay there until you leave. Whatever place does not welcome you or listen to you, leave there and shake the dust off your feet in testimony against them." So they went off and preached repentance. The Twelve drove out many demons, and they anointed with oil many who were sick and cured them.

Here I Am; Send Me

The Ordinary Time that follows Easter gives us a chance to reflect on what it means to follow Jesus. Today's readings give us three examples of lives changed because the Lord's call to go out was so compelling that people left their homes and jobs to do it. The short reading from Amos recounts his version of that story. Amos prophesied to the northern kingdom of Israel in the years before Assyria conquered and destroyed it in the eighth century. Amos didn't go looking for the job. He experienced the call of God as he herded sheep and tended sycamore trees. God didn't ask if he wanted to go, but for Amos, God's command was enough. His message of God's displeasure at Israel's sin was not universally well received. That didn't stop him. God's command had to be obeyed.

Here We Are; Send Us

Not long after Jesus began his public ministry, Jesus went away to pray. His disciples came and told him, "Everyone is looking for you…" Jesus tells them, "Let us go on to the nearby villages…" (Mark 1:29–39). The Twelve learned quickly that Jesus' mission was also theirs. He begins to share his power with them, sending them out two by two to preach, call for repentance, cast out demons, and heal the sick. The catch was that they could take only the bare minimum with them. They would have to rely on the kindness of strangers and their trust in God to get them through. Jesus advises them to enter the lives of the people to whom they preached and to shake the dust from their feet of any place that didn't welcome them or hear what they had to say. Jesus was telling the disciples they shouldn't let themselves be weighed down by disappointment, anger, or envy. They should simply move on to the next destination to do what Jesus has told them.

Chosen in Christ

Why would we respond so readily to God's call? Why would we trust God to deliver us from sin and death? In the long history of Israel and the early Christian Church, the Lord has never failed to come through. In the Old Testament, he constantly reaches out to his people to welcome them into covenant and protect them. In the New Testament, he sends his Son to show us the presence of God in the depths of our lives and, ultimately, to lead us back to God through his suffering and death. When Paul reflects on God's action in human history, he uses the only terms that make sense to him. God is a loving parent who has adopted us as his children and wants only what is best for us. God has also revealed that in the fullness of time, he will "sum up all things in Christ, in heaven and on earth." God, who accomplishes all things, can use even us. We are called to participate in his great plan. How can we say anything but yes?

Good News for All of Us

In the process of their training to become members of the order, Jesuit novices are sent on pilgrimage, taking only a minimum amount of money and possessions. They are expected to trust in God and the kindness of strangers to make their way from beginning to end. When I first heard about this, I was fascinated. It seemed like such a concrete way to experience what the apostles did in Mark's Gospel. I'm not sure how many of us would have the courage to do that, but Paul is convinced that God watches over us and can do more than we can possibly imagine. Trusting God means believing that God holds us in his hand even if we are being called to do something that seems unfamiliar, odd, or even a little scary. Do we have the courage to follow?

Questions for Reflection and Discussion

➤ *How recently have you responded to a change in life direction or job? Where was the hand of God in that change?*

➤ *How did you prepare to make the most recent decision of significance in your life? How was God involved?*

Related Journey of Faith Lesson

Q6, "Divine Revelation"

Themes

Chosen
    Q2, "What Do Catholics Believe?"
    M2, "The Role of the Laity"
Discipleship
    Q2, "What Is Faith?"
    M3, "Your Spiritual Gifts"
Service
    Q13, "The Church as Community"
    M8, "Evangelization"

Sixteenth Sunday in Ordinary Time, Year B

READING 1, JEREMIAH 23:1–6

Woe to the shepherds who mislead and scatter the flock of my pasture, says the LORD. Therefore, thus says the LORD, the God of Israel, against the shepherds who shepherd my people: You have scattered my sheep and driven them away. You have not cared for them, but I will take care to punish your evil deeds. I myself will gather the remnant of my flock from all the lands to which I have driven them and bring them back to their meadow; there they shall increase and multiply. I will appoint shepherds for them who will shepherd them so that they need no longer fear and tremble; and none shall be missing, says the LORD. Behold, the days are coming, says the LORD, when I will raise up a righteous shoot to David; as king he shall reign and govern wisely, he shall do what is just and right in the land. In his days Judah shall be saved, Israel shall dwell in security. This is the name they give him: "The LORD our justice."

PSALM 23:1–3, 3–4, 5, 6

READING 2, EPHESIANS 2:13–18

Brothers and sisters: In Christ Jesus you who once were far off have become near by the blood of Christ. For he is our peace, he who made both one and broke down the dividing wall of enmity, through his flesh, abolishing the law with its commandments and legal claims, that he might create in himself one new person in place of the two, thus establishing peace, and might reconcile both with God, in one body, through the cross, putting that enmity to death by it. He came and preached peace to you who were far off and peace to those who were near, for through him we both have access in one Spirit to the Father.

GOSPEL, MARK 6:30–34

The apostles gathered together with Jesus and reported all they had done and taught. He said to them, "Come away by yourselves to a deserted place and rest a while." People were coming and going in great numbers, and they had no opportunity even to eat. So they went off in the boat by themselves to a deserted place. People saw them leaving and many came to know about it. They hastened there on foot from all the towns and arrived at the place before them. When he disembarked and saw the vast crowd, his heart was moved with pity for them, for they were like sheep without a shepherd; and he began to teach them many things.

A Shepherd for the Sheep

Shepherds were big business in ancient Israel and early Christianity. Those who were wealthy enough to own flocks of sheep had a ready source of food, clothing, and barter. Those who owned sheep would hire the best shepherds to care for their flocks, fend off hungry wolves, and bring the sheep safely home to pasture. In Jeremiah's vision, God himself takes the role of shepherd because the teachers and leaders of Israel, who were supposed to be doing the job, failed miserably. In Jeremiah's vision, God will gather the flock and care for their wounds. God then gives his promise that he will raise up a shepherd-king who will bring justice to the land so that Israel might live secure. While Jeremiah might not have had Jesus in mind, Christians can't help but think about Jesus when they hear this passage. In the Gospels, multiple passages use the analogy of shepherd and sheep to refer to Jesus and the people. In John's Gospel, Jesus calls himself the Good Shepherd (see John 10). Many of us don't have direct experience with sheep or shepherds, but the image brings to mind care and affection.

The Peace of God

Tying the Old and New Testament readings together, we recite the familiar Psalm 23, acknowledging that the Lord is our shepherd. This psalm expresses trust in God. The images of still waters and green pastures suggest a peace that can't be disturbed, even in times of trouble. That same sentiment is echoed in Paul's Letter to the Ephesians. With the coming of Christ, God has made two people (Gentiles and Jews) into one people of God. For Paul, Christ is the promised shepherd-king and the Son of God sent by the Father to save us. His message of peace is not the peace the world gives but the eternal peace we find when God rules both heaven and earth.

The Shepherd Teacher

Mark's short Gospel passage is a transition with a hint of what is to come. The disciples have returned from mission (see last week's readings), and Jesus rightly invites them to rest and pray. Jesus knows that all missions must be grounded in prayer as he himself has demonstrated. But even the best-laid plans are sometimes thwarted. The people who see them go hasten so quickly that they arrive in the deserted place before the disciples. Mark immediately writes of the image of the shepherd. Jesus sees a crowd hungry for the truth and for a leader, much like sheep without a shepherd. What he teaches them is food for their spirits.

Good News for All of Us

I have heard a few excellent teachers and preachers in my life. When that has happened, I have found myself eager for the next meeting. Preachers, who are so attuned to the living Scripture and the needs of the community, offer a message that has meaning for almost every individual in the congregation. While we are not always so fortunate to have such dynamic preachers, we can be sure of one thing. God never stops speaking to us. God speaks through Scripture, conversations, art, music, creation, stories, and homilies. It's important to remember that we are made new every day and what we didn't understand in a particular context a year ago might be made crystal clear today when put in the context of an alternate person or situation. Pay attention, listen to Scripture, learn from others. We never know what shepherd God will send to guide us to the true Shepherd, Jesus.

Questions for Reflection and Discussion

➤ Is there a story either from Scripture or another source that speaks to you about your relationship with God?

➤ Who have been your mentors? What did they say or do that made you look up to them as examples?

Related Journey of Faith Lesson

Q7, "Your Prayer Life"

Themes

Leadership
    Q12, "Who Shepherds the Church?"
    M3, "Your Spiritual Gifts"
Ministry
    Q10, "The Church Year"
    M4, "Discernment"
Refreshment
    Q7, "Your Prayer Life"
    Q8, "Catholic Prayers and Practices"

Seventeenth Sunday in Ordinary Time, Year B

READING 1, 2 KINGS 4:42–44

A man came from Baal-shalishah bringing to Elisha, the man of God, twenty barley loaves made from the firstfruits, and fresh grain in the ear. Elisha said, "Give it to the people to eat." But his servant objected, "How can I set this before a hundred people?" Elisha insisted, "Give it to the people to eat." "For thus says the LORD, 'They shall eat and there shall be some left over.'" And when they had eaten, there was some left over, as the LORD had said.

PSALM 145:10–11, 15–16, 17–18

READING 2, EPHESIANS 4:1–6

Brothers and sisters: I, a prisoner for the Lord, urge you to live in a manner worthy of the call you have received, with all humility and gentleness, with patience, bearing with one another through love, striving to preserve the unity of the spirit through the bond of peace: one body and one Spirit, as you were also called to the one hope of your call; one Lord, one faith, one baptism; one God and Father of all, who is over all and through all and in all.

GOSPEL, JOHN 6:1–15

Jesus went across the Sea of Galilee. A large crowd followed him, because they saw the signs he was performing on the sick. Jesus went up on the mountain, and there he sat down with his disciples. The Jewish feast of Passover was near. When Jesus raised his eyes and saw that a large crowd was coming to him, he said to Philip, "Where can we buy enough food for them to eat?" He said this to test him, because he himself knew what he was going to do. Philip answered him, "Two hundred days' wages worth of food would not be enough for each of them to have a little." One of his disciples, Andrew, the brother of Simon Peter, said to him, "There is a boy here who has five barley loaves and two fish; but what good are these for so many?" Jesus said, "Have the people recline." Now there was a great deal of grass in that place. So the men reclined, about five thousand in number. Then Jesus took the loaves, gave thanks, and distributed them to those who were reclining, and also as much of the fish as they wanted. When they had had their fill, he said to his disciples, "Gather the fragments left over, so that nothing will be wasted." So they collected them, and filled twelve wicker baskets with fragments from the five barley loaves that had been more than they could eat. When the people saw the sign he had done, they said, "This is truly the Prophet, the one who is to come into the world." Since Jesus knew that they were going to come and carry him off to make him king, he withdrew again to the mountain alone.

A Life Worthy of Your Call

As we continue to read Paul's Letter to the Ephesians, we hear his exhortation to honor God's call to the early Christians to live in unity and harmony with one another. The call echoes Jesus' words in John's Gospel: "they may all be one" (John 17:21). It was a call to unity for the Jews and Gentiles who had been baptized into Christ. Among the characteristics necessary to live as one were humility, patience, and love. We struggle with each of these, maybe more often than we would wish. Paul was convinced, however, that the grace of baptism and the Holy Spirit would enable every person to live as Christ would have desired.

Giving What We Have

Part of living in harmony with each other is sharing the gifts we have been given and recognizing from whom they originated. The Old Testament and Gospel readings that bookend Paul's letter tell of a miraculous feeding. In the reading from 2 Kings, the twenty barley loaves seem minuscule compared to the hundred people who would eat it. However, the prophet Elisha has confidence in God. Not only are the people fed, but there are also leftovers.

Our psalm response acts as a reminder of the story and what will follow. It is a psalm of praise for what God has done. The last verse we hear speaks the truth the psalmist knows about God: "You open wide your hand / and satisfy the desire of every living thing" (Psalm 145:16).

In John's familiar Gospel story, the disciples have forgotten Elisha's story and express their own doubt about feeding the multitudes. A young child (the only miracle story in which a child plays a critical part) gives his offering of five loaves and two fish. Jesus accepts the child's offering, blesses it, portions it out, and feeds the crowd. For John this is the eucharistic meal. Jesus' actions of taking, blessing, breaking, and giving are the same ones we read about in the Last Supper stories. God takes what is ordinary and makes it extraordinary. He feeds everyone with the food the child brought forth. You may wonder why Jesus doesn't say, "This is my body…" which we hear in the other Gospels. Don't worry. For the next few weeks, we will hear Jesus talk about himself as the Bread of Life that gives eternal life.

Two things are worthy of note in this story. The first is that Jesus gives us the food of God, and it is everything we need. The second is that this child gave everything he had, just as the man did in Elisha's story, and it was enough for Jesus to use. God, who created us, wants us to use what he has given to build up the community of faith and give witness to his goodness. Even if we think we don't have much to give, we trust that God can use it for good and everyone will be satisfied. Giving all we have is the way we will live a life worthy of God's call.

Good News for All of Us

Catholics believe that the Eucharist is the Body and Blood, soul and divinity of Jesus Christ. It's interesting that we have not always seen the importance of receiving it regularly. In ages past, holy Communion was considered a rare privilege unfit for any but the most holy. So few people received it that the Church felt it necessary to include among its precepts that the Eucharist must be received at least once a year during the Easter season. Much of that changed after Vatican II, when the Eucharist was named as the "source and summit of our lives." It is recognized as the place where we encounter Christ most intimately. We have been given the opportunity—and are encouraged—to receive Communion every day if we desire it. Of course, one of our responsibilities is to live a life worthy of reception of such a great gift. We do this in part by using the gifts God gives us, praying regularly for God's grace to live in his light, and by being aware and confessing those times when we fail and turn away from God's commandments.

Questions for Discussion and Reflection

> *How have you used your God-given gifts to serve others?*

> *What would a life worthy of God's calling look like based on the circumstances you find yourself in today?*

Related Journey of Faith Lesson

E6, "The Lord's Prayer"

Themes

Hunger
    Q2, "What Is Faith?"
    M8, "Evangelization"
Signs
    Q10, "The Church Year"
    M4, "Discernment"
Thanksgiving
    Q7, "Your Prayer Life"
    Q8, "Catholic Prayers and Practices"

READING 1, EXODUS 16:2–4, 12–15

The whole Israelite community grumbled against Moses and Aaron. The Israelites said to them, "Would that we had died at the LORD's hand in the land of Egypt, as we sat by our fleshpots and ate our fill of bread! But you had to lead us into this desert to make the whole community die of famine!" Then the LORD said to Moses, "I will now rain down bread from heaven for you. Each day the people are to go out and gather their daily portion; thus will I test them, to see whether they follow my instructions or not. "I have heard the grumbling of the Israelites. Tell them: In the evening twilight you shall eat flesh, and in the morning you shall have your fill of bread, so that you may know that I, the LORD, am your God." In the evening quail came up and covered the camp. In the morning a dew lay all about the camp, and when the dew evaporated, there on the surface of the desert were fine flakes like hoarfrost on the ground. On seeing it, the Israelites asked one another, "What is this?" for they did not know what it was. But Moses told them, "This is the bread that the LORD has given you to eat."

PSALM 78:3–4, 23–24, 25, 54

READING 2, EPHESIANS 4:17, 20–24

Brothers and sisters: I declare and testify in the Lord that you must no longer live as the Gentiles do, in the futility of their minds; that is not how you learned Christ, assuming that you have heard of him and were taught in him, as truth is in Jesus, that you should put away the old self of your former way of life, corrupted through deceitful desires, and be renewed in the spirit of your minds, and put on the new self, created in God's way in righteousness and holiness of truth.

GOSPEL, JOHN 6:24–35

When the crowd saw that neither Jesus nor his disciples were there, they themselves got into boats and came to Capernaum looking for Jesus. And when they found him across the sea they said to him, "Rabbi, when did you get here?" Jesus answered them and said, "Amen, amen, I say to you, you are looking for me not because you saw signs but because you ate the loaves and were filled. Do not work for food that perishes but for the food that endures for eternal life, which the Son of Man will give you. For on him the Father, God, has set his seal." So they said to him, "What can we do to accomplish the works of God?" Jesus answered and said to them, "This is the work of God, that you believe in the one he sent." So they said to him, "What sign can you do, that we may see and believe in you? What can you do? Our ancestors ate manna in the desert, as it is written: *He gave them bread from heaven to eat.*" So Jesus said to them, "Amen, amen, I say to you, it was not Moses who gave the bread from heaven; my Father gives you the true bread from heaven. For the bread of God is that which comes down from heaven and gives life to the world." So they said to him, "Sir, give us this bread always." Jesus said to them, "I am the bread of life; whoever comes to me will never hunger, and whoever believes in me will never thirst."

Bread of Angels

We might be surprised to learn that many people do not have access to adequate food or clean drinking water. Few things are more distressing than seeing those who are victims of famine and drought in the world. We feel compelled to help them in some way. Economic policies, political realities, and discrimination all impact the availability of basic resources for various populations. Those of us who are not affected may take this reality for granted.

In their journey from Egypt to the Promised Land, the Israelites suffered the same problems as migrants do today. They were in a desert without access to adequate food and water. They worried for their survival and wondered if they had done the right thing. They didn't always trust that God would provide for them. The story of their survival includes a miracle. As it was remembered, God told Moses that he would rain down bread from heaven. The bread resembled frost. The name for it—manna—means, "man" in Hebrew. Moses instructed them to gather only what they needed daily. This story teaches us that we depend on God every day. We remind ourselves of that dependency when we pray the Lord's Prayer: "Give us this day our daily bread."

The Bread of Life

As Jesus tries to teach them after feeding the 5,000, the Jews recount the powerful experience their ancestors shared about God's miracle in the desert. For them it was a reminder of God's bounty. When Jesus spoke of working for the food that endures for eternal life, they could not imagine something greater than the manna their ancestors had. They might be forgiven for demanding a sign that they should believe in him. Jesus gently reminds them that the manna, which came to their ancestors, was from God, but it wasn't the true bread of heaven. The true bread of heaven brings life to the entire world. When they ask for this bread, Jesus'

response is no doubt puzzling to those listening: "I am the bread of life; whoever comes to me will never hunger, and whoever believes in me will never thirst."

Jesus makes seven "I am" statements in John's Gospel; this is the first. The "I am" reminds readers of God's self-identification to Moses in Exodus 3:14. Each of the other statements follows the pattern of this one, though with a different description at the end. For a group of people that are poor and marginalized under Roman rule, Jesus' statement about never being hungry or thirsty must have seemed like an impossible reality. No doubt many of them heard it as a literal promise and wondered how it could be possible. As we continue to hear Jesus speak, we might do well to remember Paul's words to the Ephesians. We cannot hear Jesus simply with our minds; we must also hear him with our hearts and our spirits. In baptism, we were made a new creation. We are no longer bound solely by human logic but by grace which shows us the truth of God, renews our mind, and enables us to live a holy life.

Good News for All of Us

Jesus spoke to people who were oppressed by Roman rule and may well have been hungry themselves. Their belief in God was fed by the stories of God's bounty to their ancestors and their hope in God's promises. Many people today leave their homes because of famine, drought, or political unrest in search of a better life for themselves and their children. We have an opportunity to welcome them with shelter, food, and water and assist them in becoming productive citizens in our country. Why would we do this? We do it because God has made us a new creation in Christ. We do it because—though we are sinners— we have been given the Bread of Life and have been welcomed as citizens of God's kingdom. Surely, we can do the same for others.

Questions for Reflection and Discussion

➤ *How do you welcome guests into your house? How do you prepare and what do you do when they arrive?*

➤ *What can you do to help those who are less fortunate?*

Related Journey of Faith Lesson

Q13, "The Church as Community"

Themes

Bread
    Q7, "Your Prayer Life"
    Q9, "The Mass"
Life
    M5, "Our Call to Holiness"
Values
    Q13, "The Church as Community"
    M4, "Discernment"

Nineteenth Sunday in Ordinary Time, Year B

READING 1, 1 KINGS 19:4–8

Elijah went a day's journey into the desert, until he came to a broom tree and sat beneath it. He prayed for death saying: "This is enough, O LORD! Take my life, for I am no better than my fathers." He lay down and fell asleep under the broom tree, but then an angel touched him and ordered him to get up and eat. Elijah looked and there at his head was a hearth cake and a jug of water. After he ate and drank, he lay down again, but the angel of the LORD came back a second time, touched him, and ordered, "Get up and eat, else the journey will be too long for you!" He got up, ate, and drank; then strengthened by that food, he walked forty days and forty nights to the mountain of God, Horeb.

PSALM 34:2–3, 4–5, 6–7, 8–9

READING 2, EPHESIANS 4:30—5:2

Brothers and sisters: Do not grieve the Holy Spirit of God, with which you were sealed for the day of redemption. All bitterness, fury, anger, shouting, and reviling must be removed from you, along with all malice. And be kind to one another, compassionate, forgiving one another as God has forgiven you in Christ. So be imitators of God, as beloved children, and live in love, as Christ loved us and handed himself over for us as a sacrificial offering to God for a fragrant aroma.

GOSPEL, JOHN 6:41–51

The Jews murmured about Jesus because he said, "I am the bread that came down from heaven," and they said, "Is this not Jesus, the son of Joseph? Do we not know his father and mother? Then how can he say, 'I have come down from heaven'?" Jesus answered and said to them, "Stop murmuring among yourselves. No one can come to me unless the Father who sent me draw him, and I will raise him on the last day. It is written in the prophets: *They shall all be taught by God.* Everyone who listens to my Father and learns from him comes to me. Not that anyone has seen the Father except the one who is from God; he has seen the Father. Amen, amen, I say to you, whoever believes has eternal life. I am the bread of life. Your ancestors ate the manna in the desert, but they died; this is the bread that comes down from heaven so that one may eat it and not die. I am the living bread that came down from heaven; whoever eats this bread will live forever; and the bread that I will give is my flesh for the life of the world."

Food for the Journey

Whenever we went on a trip as a family, we always made sure that we packed an assortment of snacks and drinks or a picnic lunch so we could eat and drink when we had the opportunity. It was also cheaper (and probably better) than food that we could have bought on the way. The readings today approach the idea of food for the journey from slightly different angles. For Elijah, the food miraculously appeared when he was fleeing from Ahab and Jezebel, who threatened to kill him after he bested her prophets. Wandering in the wilderness, he was sure that he was doomed. The cake and water were a gift from God that allowed him to continue traveling for forty days and nights to Mount Horeb. This was no accident. Mount Horeb was where God gave Moses the Ten Commandments and made a covenant with the people.

The number forty should sound familiar. God made it rain for forty days and nights before the great Flood. The Israelites wandered forty years in the desert. Jesus was tempted in the desert for forty days and nights. The number means a substantial length of time. Forty years was a generation in Israel. Forty days frequently represented a period of chastisement or discipline.

Food for Thought

Paul was serious when he said, "Whoever is in Christ is a new creation" (2 Corinthians 5:17). He often includes a section in his letters that tells people how they must behave in the light of baptism. In this section of the Letter to the Ephesians, Paul exhorts them to be kind, compassionate, and forgiving—loving as Christ loved them. Paul is giving them food for thought, reminding them that Jesus came to bring forgiveness and life to the world. If we are to do anything, it is to become like him.

Food for Life

Jesus continues his discourse on the Bread of Life and experiences the same skepticism that Mark detailed when Jesus first preached in Nazareth. The people listening know his family. They remember him as a child. How can he have come down from heaven? It seems utterly unbelievable.

Jesus' long discourses (teaching sections) in John's Gospel often repeat words and phrases and can be confusing to hear the first time. The Israelites (and even the disciples) frequently didn't understand what he was saying. His message here has five important areas of focus: (1) No one comes to me unless the Father draws him. (2) I will raise him up on the last day. (3) Whoever believes [in me] will have eternal life. (4) Whoever eats of this bread will live forever. (5) The bread I give is my flesh.

In these five areas, Jesus defends those who follow him as doing the will of God. He references their resurrection on the last day (remember, resurrection was not widely believed among the Jews). Jesus also claims that those who believe already have eternal life (they will not die like their ancestors who ate manna). Eternal life is something they possessed immediately if they believe in him. Finally, Jesus again claims his identity as the bread of life and adds one piece of additional information. The bread of life is his flesh.

Next week, we will see how people reacted to this claim. We can imagine how the audience grappled with the idea that the manna in the desert was somehow less than the food Jesus offered. His was a promise of eternal life for the whole world. How would you react?

Good News for All of Us

We take Jesus at his word. The bread and wine of Eucharist is not a symbol or a sign. When consecrated at Mass, it becomes the Body and Blood of Jesus Christ given for us. We receive the host and chalice from the hands of the priest or minister and know that Christ is present to us in a way unlike any other. This is our food for the journey, which gives us the strength to be a disciple who loves as Jesus did and follows the road to God.

Questions for Reflection and Discussion

➤ *What foods do you eat for strength? For comfort? For nutrition? How do you feel when you indulge in junk food?*

➤ *Catholics call the belief that the bread and wine become the Body and Blood of Christ at Mass "transubstantiation." How is this belief significant to your faith life?*

Related Journey of Faith Lesson

Q9, "The Mass"

Themes

Eucharist
    Q7, "Your Prayer Life"
    Q9, "The Mass"
Roots
    Q1, "Welcome to OCIA!"
    M1, "Conversion: A Lifelong Process"
Trinity
    Q5, "The Bible"
    M5, "Our Call to Holiness"

Twentieth Sunday in Ordinary Time, Year B

READING 1, PROVERBS 9:1–6

Wisdom has built her house, she has set up her seven columns; she has dressed her meat, mixed her wine, yes, she has spread her table. She has sent out her maidens; she calls from the heights out over the city: "Let whoever is simple turn in here; To the one who lacks understanding, she says, Come, eat of my food, and drink of the wine I have mixed! Forsake foolishness that you may live; advance in the way of understanding."

PSALM 34:2–3, 4–5, 6–7

READING 2, EPHESIANS 5:15–20

Brothers and sisters: Watch carefully how you live, not as foolish persons but as wise, making the most of the opportunity, because the days are evil. Therefore, do not continue in ignorance, but try to understand what is the will of the Lord. And do not get drunk on wine, in which lies debauchery, but be filled with the Spirit, addressing one another in psalms and hymns and spiritual songs, singing and playing to the Lord in your hearts, giving thanks always and for everything in the name of our Lord Jesus Christ to God the Father.

GOSPEL, JOHN 6:51–58

Jesus said to the crowds: "I am the living bread that came down from heaven; whoever eats this bread will live forever; and the bread that I will give is my flesh for the life of the world." The Jews quarreled among themselves, saying, "How can this man give us his flesh to eat?" Jesus said to them, "Amen, amen, I say to you, unless you eat the flesh of the Son of Man and drink his blood, you do not have life within you. Whoever eats my flesh and drinks my blood has eternal life, and I will raise him on the last day. For my flesh is true food, and my blood is true drink. Whoever eats my flesh and drinks my blood remains in me and I in him. Just as the living Father sent me and I have life because of the Father, so also the one who feeds on me will have life because of me. This is the bread that came down from heaven. Unlike your ancestors who ate and still died, whoever eats this bread will live forever."

A Communion of Knowledge and Understanding

As Jesus continues his discourse on the bread of life, the Old Testament reading moves us away from Elijah and Elisha into the books of Kings and gives us a glimpse of Wisdom as she is shown in the Book of Proverbs. The Wisdom literature belongs to the group of biblical books the Jews call "The Writings." These are books that do not tell the stories of God's great deeds or prophetic utterances. Rather, these books reflect the human experience of the writers and force us to remember what God has said and done. Catholics consider seven books to be part of the Wisdom literature: Psalms, Proverbs, Job, Wisdom, Ecclesiastes, Song of Songs, and Sirach.

Wisdom is a female figure. The word in Hebrew is *hokmah* and in Greek, *Sophia*. She is presented here as a master teacher who will give understanding and knowledge to the foolish or naïve. In Proverbs, she uses the same imagery of bread and wine that Jesus does. The one who eats at this table will have the insight that only wisdom can give. Wisdom is begotten of God (Proverbs 8:22) and God's master worker (Proverbs 8:29). If these phrases sound familiar, it is because they were appropriated to help people articulate how they thought about Jesus.

Drunk on the Spirit

When the apostles preached the Good News after Pentecost, many observers thought they were drunk (Acts 2:13). Peter quickly dispels that rumor, but the idea that belief in Christ could make people say and do incredible things has not been entirely dismissed. We have only to look at the saints: for love of Christ, they serve the poor, free the imprisoned, welcome the immigrant and the oppressed, and do extraordinary things in ordinary circumstances. Paul's admonition not to drink wine but to be filled with the Spirit is an appeal to live in such a way that people notice something different. Some may think you are drunk. But what they are seeing is the joy and thanksgiving that comes from being a child of God.

Communion with the Lord

Jesus' announcement that the bread he gives is his flesh for the life of the world was not received well. The Jews who heard him started arguing about what he meant. Jesus doubled down, saying: "Unless you eat the flesh of the Son of Man and drink his blood, you do not have life within you." We learned a few weeks ago that blood is life and anyone who touches blood is unclean for a time. Jewish dietary laws state clearly that animals must be butchered in such a way that no blood remains in the meat. For the Jews, what Jesus is saying seems absurd. How are they to understand it?

Jesus gives one clue. If we eat his flesh and drink his blood, he abides (dwells) in us and we in him. The act of eating makes us one, just as Jesus and the Father are one. This is the ultimate in "we become what we eat." It's hard to comprehend, but Christ not only gave his body on the cross for us, he gives himself to us every time we receive Communion. We come to that Last Supper table to be fed by the only one who can give us eternal life. That life is Christ dwelling within us.

Good News for All of Us

People may not know that the theological term for bread and wine becoming the Body and Blood of Christ is transubstantiation. But they know that a life lived in holiness includes reaching out to care for others; it exudes a sense of profound joy, and seems grounded in faith. Something has happened to that person. Our faith tells us it's the encounter with the living Christ. God stirs our hearts in the presence of such people. We wonder how can we be more like them. Come to Mass every week—or even every day—and you may be surprised by what people see in you.

Questions for Reflection and Discussion

> *How do you "get wisdom?" Where would you go to find it?*

> *Paul urges us to give thanks to the Father all the time. What are you thankful to God for today?*

Related Journey of Faith Lesson

C5, "The Sacrament of the Eucharist"

Themes

Living
    Q2, "What Is Faith?"
    M1, "Conversion: A Lifelong Process"
Sacrament
    Q7, "Your Prayer Life"
    Q10, "The Church Year"
Wisdom
    Q5, "Your Prayer Life"
    Q13, "The Church as Community"

Twenty-first Sunday in Ordinary Time, Year B

READING 1, JOSHUA 24:1–2A, 15–17, 18B

Joshua gathered together all the tribes of Israel at Shechem, summoning their elders, their leaders, their judges, and their officers. When they stood in ranks before God, Joshua addressed all the people: "If it does not please you to serve the LORD, decide today whom you will serve, the gods your fathers served beyond the River or the gods of the Amorites in whose country you are now dwelling. As for me and my household, we will serve the LORD." But the people answered, "Far be it from us to forsake the LORD for the service of other gods. For it was the LORD, our God, who brought us and our fathers up out of the land of Egypt, out of a state of slavery. He performed those great miracles before our very eyes and protected us along our entire journey and among the peoples through whom we passed. Therefore we also will serve the LORD, for he is our God."

PSALM 34:2–3, 16–17, 18–19, 20–21

READING 2, EPHESIANS 5:21–32

Brothers and sisters: Be subordinate to one another out of reverence for Christ. Wives should be subordinate to their husbands as to the Lord. For the husband is head of his wife just as Christ is head of the church, he himself the savior of the body. As the church is subordinate to Christ, so wives should be subordinate to their husbands in everything. Husbands, love your wives, even as Christ loved the church and handed himself over for her to sanctify her, cleansing her by the bath of water with the word, that he might present to himself the church in splendor, without spot or wrinkle or any such thing, that she might be holy and without blemish. So also husbands should love their wives as their own bodies. He who loves his wife loves himself. For no one hates his own flesh but rather nourishes and cherishes it, even as Christ does the church, because we are members of his body. *For this reason a man shall leave his father and his mother and be joined to his wife, and the two shall become one flesh.* This is a great mystery, but I speak in reference to Christ and the church.

GOSPEL, JOHN 6:60–69

Many of Jesus' disciples who were listening said, "This saying is hard; who can accept it?" Since Jesus knew that his disciples were murmuring about this, he said to them, "Does this shock you? What if you were to see the Son of Man ascending to where he was before? It is the spirit that gives life, while the flesh is of no avail. The words I have spoken to you are Spirit and life. But there are some of you who do not believe." Jesus knew from the beginning the ones who would not believe and the one who would betray him. And he said, "For this reason I have told you that no one can come to me unless it is granted him by my Father." As a result of this, many of his disciples returned to their former way of life and no longer accompanied him. Jesus then said to the Twelve, "Do you also want to leave?" Simon Peter answered him, "Master, to whom shall we go? You have the words of eternal life. We have come to believe and are convinced that you are the Holy One of God."

I Pledge Allegiance

When I was a child, we began the school day with a prayer and the Pledge of Allegiance. The practice of reciting the pledge continues in many places today, a reminder that we are supposed to be loyal and faithful to the country in which we have our citizenship. The readings today ask to whom we owe our allegiance as faithful people. When Moses died just before the Israelites entered the Promised Land, he appointed Joshua as the leader. The entry into the land was not easy; there were many wars, and Joshua led the people to victory. At the end of his life, he gathers the elders and judges of Israel and invites them to renew their loyalty to the covenant God made with them at Mount Horeb when he gave them the Ten Commandments.

Joshua recognizes that true leadership does not force adherence but leads by example and persuasion. He is the first to pledge allegiance with his family. The others will make their own decision. But the experience of the Israelites in Egypt, in the desert, and in the battles in the promised land have convinced them that God has been faithful to them. They cannot imagine turning away to follow other gods in other places. "We will serve the Lord, for he is our God."

Be Subject to One Another

In our readings of the last few weeks, Paul has been writing about the way Christians should be in their day-to-day lives. If the priority was allegiance to Christ, then Christians were to guard against any behavior that took them away from Christ.

In this part of his Letter to the Ephesians, Paul tackles the institution of marriage, drawing an analogy with the relationship of Christ and the Church. Like all analogies, it isn't perfect, but we can learn from it. Pay attention to the opening line: "Be subordinate to one another...out of reverence for Christ." Jesus is always the first allegiance for both husbands and wives. Love is always other-directed. When we recall Paul's passages on love (as in 1 Corinthians 13), we see that in marriage, husbands and wives must build each other up as family. The "subordination" is mutual. Just as Christ laid down his life for the Church, we are to lay down our lives for one another.

This passage has often been used to demean women and force them into abusive relationships. It's challenging that Paul chose to use "subordinate" for wives in the first paragraph, and "love" for husbands in the second. Part of that comes from the Old Testament analogy of marriage for God's relationship with Israel. God is clearly the head of that relationship. In marriage relationships of the time, husbands were the heads of household; women had no rights of their own. That Paul begins by saying we are to be subordinate to one another is a step forward. Given all that Paul has said about Christian behavior and love, there is no interpretation that can support abuse, authoritarianism, or hatefulness in or out of marriage.

The Words of Eternal Life

The Gospel regarding the bread of life shook the belief of many. Last week, Jesus gave the command to eat his flesh and drink his blood to have eternal life. This week we hear the reaction: "This saying is hard; who can accept it?" The disciples didn't understand what Jesus meant, and Jesus himself knows that faith is a gift: "No one can come to me unless it is granted him by my Father." When they saw people leaving Jesus, I imagine that it became difficult for the disciples to stay. Peer pressure is amazingly persuasive. The Twelve had to decide to whom they would pledge allegiance. It took a lot of courage for Peter to say: "Master, to whom shall we go? You have the words of eternal life."

Good News for All of Us

As Christians, our first allegiance is always to Jesus Christ. We may be loyal to our families, country, sports teams, and brand names in varying degrees. These things may even influence what we decide to do in the world. But Christ should always be our first thought when making choices about life, love, and the way we will make a difference in the world. While Christ is our guide, we can trust that our decisions will help keep us on the right path.

Questions for Reflection and Discussion

➤ *Who do you feel loyal to? How do you express that loyalty?*

➤ *What would make you question your allegiance to something or someone?*

Related Journey of Faith Lesson

Q12, "Who Shepherds the Church?"

Themes

Covenant
    Q5, "The Bible"
    M2, "The Role of the Laity"
Friendship
    Q15, "The Saints"
    M8, "Evangelization"
Marriage
    M7, "Family Life"

Twenty-second Sunday in Ordinary Time, Year B

READING 1, DEUTERONOMY 4:1–2, 6–8

Moses said to the people: "Now, Israel, hear the statutes and decrees which I am teaching you to observe, that you may live, and may enter in and take possession of the land which the LORD, the God of your fathers, is giving you. In your observance of the commandments of the LORD, your God, which I enjoin upon you, you shall not add to what I command you nor subtract from it. Observe them carefully, for thus will you give evidence of your wisdom and intelligence to the nations, who will hear of all these statutes and say, 'This great nation is truly a wise and intelligent people.' For what great nation is there that has gods so close to it as the LORD, our God, is to us whenever we call upon him? Or what great nation has statutes and decrees that are as just as this whole law which I am setting before you today?"

PSALM 15:2–3, 3–4, 4–5

READING 2, JAMES 1:17–18, 21B–22, 27

Dearest brothers and sisters: All good giving and every perfect gift is from above, coming down from the Father of lights, with whom there is no alteration or shadow caused by change. He willed to give us birth by the word of truth that we may be a kind of firstfruits of his creatures. Humbly welcome the word that has been planted in you and is able to save your souls. Be doers of the word and not hearers only, deluding yourselves. Religion that is pure and undefiled before God and the Father is this: to care for orphans and widows in their affliction and to keep oneself unstained by the world.

GOSPEL, MARK 7:1–8, 14–15, 21–23

When the Pharisees with some scribes who had come from Jerusalem gathered around Jesus, they observed that some of his disciples ate their meals with unclean, that is, unwashed, hands. For the Pharisees and, in fact, all Jews, do not eat without carefully washing their hands, keeping the tradition of the elders. And on coming from the marketplace they do not eat without purifying themselves. And there are many other things

that they have traditionally observed, the purification of cups and jugs and kettles and beds. So the Pharisees and scribes questioned him, "Why do your disciples not follow the tradition of the elders but instead eat a meal with unclean hands?" He responded, "Well did Isaiah prophesy about you hypocrites, as it is written: *This people honors me with their lips, but their hearts are far from me; in vain do they worship me, teaching as doctrines human precepts.* You disregard God's commandment but cling to human tradition." He summoned the crowd again and said to them, "Hear me, all of you, and understand. Nothing that enters one from outside can defile that person; but the things that come out from within are what defile. "From within people, from their hearts, come evil thoughts, unchastity, theft, murder, adultery, greed, malice, deceit, licentiousness, envy, blasphemy, arrogance, folly. All these evils come from within and they defile."

The Gift of Law

In the Old Testament the verb "to hear" carried with it the connotation of obedience. To hear the word of God was to obey it. Conversely, if you didn't obey it, you didn't hear it. The one who believes acts on that belief. All the readings today suggest some element of "doing" the word that is heard. In the beginning of Deuteronomy, Moses tells the Israelites to keep the commandments so that other nations will see how wise and discerning they are. Moses reminds them that God is always near them and listens to them when they call to him. He also confirms that the laws he is giving them are a gift from God, which no other nation has. The laws set them apart.

Psalm 15 forms the perfect response to the first reading as it describes those who may dwell with the Lord. Among the many behaviors this group displays, the psalmist lists: doing right while refraining from slander, harm, and defame of neighbors. We might note the respect that is given to both God and neighbor by these laws. The psalm is a tribute to the wise and obedient servant of God's laws.

Be Doers and Not Just Hearers

We don't know exactly who wrote the Epistle of James. Some scholars attribute it to James, the brother of the Lord; others to one of the apostles named James. In any case, he identifies himself as a servant of God and the Lord, Jesus Christ, similar in some ways to Paul's self-identification. His letter is known for its practical theology and tells us how we are to act in the face of oppression and suffering. His answer indicates that some Christians have separated the connection between hearing and doing. For James, Christians are the first fruits of God's creatures. The word of God is the gift from which all other gifts come. It has been "planted" in the heart of all the baptized, who respond by obeying the laws God has given. In this passage, James names two immediate actions: the first comes straight from the Old Testament: care for orphans and widows in their affliction. The second is to keep oneself unstained by the world.

Doing from the Heart

Jesus' difficulty with the Pharisees comes not from their place in society or necessarily from their concern for right behavior. Rather, Jesus is concerned that their judgment and condemnation of others does not come from the genuine transformation of heart that comes from intimacy with God but from a very human desire to lord their position over others and to be in charge. He calls them hypocrites—the word in Greek means "actor" but comes from two words put together meaning "an interpreter from underneath," and makes sense when we remember that Greek actors wore large masks on stage. The suggestion is that the Pharisees were playing a part; they had a mask of religiosity but were not genuine. When Jesus speaks to the crowds, he is much clearer. When the heart is evil, then all manner of sin comes from it. The opposite is also true. When the heart is transformed by grace, the actions that follow are from God, for God dwells within that person.

Good News for All of Us

It's not always easy to know the right thing to do. That's why we read Scripture, listen to sermons, and pray for guidance, especially in difficult situations. Forming our conscience doesn't mean that all decisions will automatically be right, but if we keep the will of God before us, we will gradually conform our actions to God's will. We can start with the two great commandments to love God and neighbor. We have heard these. Are we doing them? How? Can we do more? The other question to ask is, "Have we allowed our hearts to be transformed by Christ?" And, do we look down on others and think we are better than they are? If that is at all the case, maybe we need to remove our masks and know ourselves as sinners who have been given a second chance.

Questions for Reflection and Discussion

➤ Has there ever been a situation in which you really didn't know the right thing to do? How did you decide?

➤ What do you consider the essential laws of God and his Church? Why do you think other rules were written?

Related Journey of Faith Lesson

Q10, "The Church Year"

Themes

Justice
    Q13, "The Church as Community"
    M8, "Evangelization"
Law
    Q12, "Who Shepherds the Church?"
    M4, "Discernment"
Service
    Q8, "Catholic Prayers and Practices"
    M2, "The Role of the Laity"

Twenty-third Sunday in Ordinary Time, Year B

READING 1, ISAIAH 35:4–7A

Thus says the LORD: Say to those whose hearts are frightened: Be strong, fear not! Here is your God, he comes with vindication; with divine recompense he comes to save you. Then will the eyes of the blind be opened, the ears of the deaf be cleared; then will the lame leap like a stag, then the tongue of the mute will sing. Streams will burst forth in the desert, and rivers in the steppe. The burning sands will become pools, and the thirsty ground, springs of water.

PSALM 146:7, 8–9, 9–10

READING 2, JAMES 2:1–5

My brothers and sisters, show no partiality as you adhere to the faith in our glorious Lord Jesus Christ. For if a man with gold rings and fine clothes comes into your assembly, and a poor person in shabby clothes also comes in, and you pay attention to the one wearing the fine clothes and say, "Sit here, please," while you say to the poor one, "Stand there," or "Sit at my feet," have you not made distinctions among yourselves and become judges with evil designs? Listen, my beloved brothers and sisters. Did not God choose those who are poor in the world to be rich in faith and heirs of the kingdom that he promised to those who love him?

GOSPEL, MARK 7:31–37

Again Jesus left the district of Tyre and went by way of Sidon to the Sea of Galilee, into the district of the Decapolis. And people brought to him a deaf man who had a speech impediment and begged him to lay his hand on him. He took him off by himself away from the crowd. He put his finger into the man's ears and, spitting, touched his tongue; then he looked up to heaven and groaned, and said to him, "Ephphatha!"— that is, "Be opened!"—And immediately the man's ears were opened, his speech impediment was removed, and he spoke plainly. He ordered them not to tell anyone. But the more he ordered them not to, the more they proclaimed it. They were exceedingly astonished and they said, "He has done all things well. He makes the deaf hear and the mute speak."

A Preferential Option for the Poor

How do we respond when we see someone begging on the sidewalk? Some of us walk by and pretend not to notice. Others may wonder why the person doesn't find work or question how he or she would spend any money we might give. Still others give a minimal amount and consider that good. Too often we don't spend time thinking about those who beg as having a place among us. What gifts could they bring to the community? What could they teach us? God loves the poor and those on the margins of society. Isaiah's prophecy is one of hope and redemption for those who are fearful, blind, and lame. In our society, those marginalized by disability are often the objects of pity. In God's hands, they see, hear, speak, and dance. God's salvation makes them whole. Isaiah pairs this with his vision of water in the wilderness and streams in the desert. The world is created new. What is broken will find healing.

The psalmist offers praise for the works of God who keeps faith forever and secures justice for the oppressed (146:6–7). It isn't that God doesn't care for the wealthy or important people; rather, God reaches out to those most in need first. The marginalized are often forgotten. God knows this and visits his grace on them first. Is that fair? Our idea of fairness is influenced greatly by our values. God judges by what he sees. All people are beloved children of God. Some may need to know that sooner rather than later. Theologians call this God's preferential option for the poor.

Recognizing Our Own Preferences

In his practical way of looking at faith, James has noticed that the wealthy are given places of honor in the Church and at the tables of other Christians, while the poor are regularly told to sit in the back or at the feet of the wealthy. James wastes no time in calling out such favoritism and reminds his brothers and sisters that God chose the poor to be rich in faith and heirs to the kingdom. Neither money, nor degrees, nor expertise, nor earthly authority guarantees a place in heaven. Doing the will of God and loving all people regardless of their status in society will help us on the way.

Be Opened

Throughout Mark's Gospel, people have brought friends and family to be healed. On this day in the Gospel, Jesus performs his healing in a different way. He takes the deaf man to a private place to heal him. Using both touch and commands, Jesus cures the man's deaf ears and mute tongue. As is common in Mark, Jesus orders the man and all who knew of the miracle to say nothing. And, as is common, they all proclaim it. The word used for "proclaim" is the same one that Mark uses for Jesus and the disciples when they preach the gospel. Jesus' concern is that they believe because of who he is and not solely because of what he does. When we hear Isaiah's prophecy together with the Gospel, we are reminded of exactly who Jesus is—God himself, the healer of the world.

Good News for All of Us

We often relate to the poor and marginalized by thinking about what we can do for them. This has led to an upturn in mission trips where the object is to come in, help with a few projects, and then return to our comfortable lives, feeling better about ourselves. We forget that Jesus commands us to be in a relationship of love with those we serve, just as God loves them. This means considering the ways in which we might learn from them, treating them as brothers and sisters, rejoicing in what they give to the community, and remembering them when we are no longer in their midst. Compassion (feeling with others) and solidarity (seeing others as part of a community of mutual support and contribution) are the watchwords for those who would adopt God's preferential option for the poor. God, give us the grace to do so.

Questions for Reflection and Discussion

> ➤ What are your honest reactions in thought and deed when you see someone panhandling on the sidewalk?

> ➤ Who are the marginalized in your church, town, or country? What can you do to welcome them in?

Related Journey of Faith Lesson

M4, "Discernment"

Themes

Compassion
    Q13, "The Church as Community"
    M8, "Evangelization"
Marginalized
    Q12, "Who Shepherds the Church?"
    M5, "Our Call to Holiness"
Prejudice
    Q2, "What Is Faith?"
    M1, "Conversion: A Lifelong Process"

Twenty-fourth Sunday in Ordinary Time, Year B

READING 1, ISAIAH 50:5–9A

The Lord GOD opens my ear that I may hear; and I have not rebelled, have not turned back. I gave my back to those who beat me, my cheeks to those who plucked my beard; my face I did not shield from buffets and spitting. The Lord GOD is my help, therefore I am not disgraced; I have set my face like flint, knowing that I shall not be put to shame. He is near who upholds my right; if anyone wishes to oppose me, let us appear together. Who disputes my right? Let that man confront me. See, the Lord GOD is my help; who will prove me wrong?

PSALM 114:1–2, 3–4, 5–6, 8–9

READING 2, JAMES 2:14–18

What good is it, my brothers and sisters, if someone says he has faith but does not have works? Can that faith save him? If a brother or sister has nothing to wear and has no food for the day, and one of you says to them, "Go in peace, keep warm, and eat well," but you do not give them the necessities of the body, what good is it? So also faith of itself, if it does not have works, is dead. Indeed someone might say, "You have faith and I have works." Demonstrate your faith to me without works, and I will demonstrate my faith to you from my works.

GOSPEL, MARK 8:27–35

Jesus and his disciples set out for the villages of Caesarea Philippi. Along the way he asked his disciples, "Who do people say that I am?" They said in reply, "John the Baptist, others Elijah, still others one of the prophets." And he asked them, "But who do you say that I am?" Peter said to him in reply, "You are the Christ." He warned them not to tell anyone about him. He began to teach them that the Son of Man must suffer greatly and be rejected by the elders, the chief priests, and the scribes, and be killed, and rise after

three days. Then Peter took him aside and began to rebuke him. At this he turned around and, looking at his disciples, rebuked Peter and said, "Get behind me, Satan. You are thinking not as God does, but as human beings do." He summoned the crowd with his disciples and said to them, "Whoever wishes to come after me must deny himself, take up his cross, and follow me. For whoever wishes to save his life will lose it, but whoever loses his life for my sake and that of the gospel will save it."

Finding Ourselves

In literature and in life, there are many stories of people who leave their homes to find out who they are, where they belong, and what's important to them. In *The Wizard of Oz* movie, Dorothy went in search of her heart's desire only to learn that it was back in Kansas all the time. The Celtic monks told of great pilgrimages to faraway places that served both to preach the gospel in foreign lands and to bear the suffering of leaving those they loved for a place they didn't know. For us as Christians, finding ourselves involves listening to the words of God, following his Son, Jesus, and doing as Jesus did. Today's readings show that the latter is not always an easy path. Finding ourselves almost always means losing the part of ourselves that gets in the way.

Courage in the Face of Evil

Our first reading is the third of four servant songs in Isaiah. As the songs unfold, the servant of God is sent to the nations to preach the word of God but is horribly abused in the process. In this particular song, the servant mentions he has opened his ear to God. Remember that if someone truly hears the word of God, he is compelled to obey it. In the face of taunts, insults, and spitting, this servant clings to his faith in God, almost daring his enemies to confront him. His trust in God is remarkable. It's the only thing that allows him to overcome fear and anger, and to keep going.

Finding Ourselves as People of Faith

How do you know you are a person of faith? James sees an intimate connection between faith and works. For him, true faith will compel a person to do good works. James can't help but believe that faith without works is dead. His example is particularly pointed. Who among us would see someone begging and simply say: "Good luck, stay warm...." In our society, a lot of us might do that—not necessarily out of malice, but simply because we don't know what to do at the time. If our faith is alive, we will do what we can. Such is the power of God in us.

Finding Ourselves on the Path of Jesus

"Who do you say that I am?" Jesus' question seems clear enough. Many people thought he was one of the great prophets or John the Baptist. It might have been easier to say that. If he was just another prophet, even a great one, he could be dismissed. The disciples must have looked at him silently until Peter said, "You are the Christ." That was the opening Jesus needed. He could not tell them about the suffering that he would go through. Peter forgot Isaiah's prophecy—that the servant would be spat on and tormented. When he protests, it becomes a temptation like the ones in the desert. Like Isaiah's servant, Jesus stands up to the temptation, "Get behind me, Satan." In one sense, he is telling Peter to get back in line. The reason soon becomes clear. Those who follow Jesus are bound to take up whatever individual cross is theirs and walk with Jesus to Calvary. They must be willing to lose part of themselves in order to find themselves again as a disciple of Christ.

Good News for All of Us

It's not easy to become a new creation. We have to change and grow. We have to lay aside childish things and self-focus and open ourselves to God's will and his plan for us. We are grounded in the fact that we are beloved children of God who wants us to be one with him. God calls us to use what we have been given in his service and with love for all of creation. God also knows that not everyone will welcome our identity as disciples or will tempt us to let go of any suffering that comes our way. With Isaiah's servant, we can stand firm in our trust and faith in God.

Questions for Reflection and Discussion

➤ *Have you had a cross to bear in your life? This could be any source of suffering that has made you a different person—even a better or stronger one.*

➤ *How does your faith express itself in works? What do you do that tells people you are a person of faith?*

Related Journey of Faith Lesson

Q15, "The Saints"

Themes

Discipleship
    Q14, "Mary"
    M2, "The Role of the Laity"
Identity
    Q2, "What Is Faith?"
    M1, "Conversion: A Lifelong Process"
Suffering
    Q8, "Catholic Prayers and Practices"
    M4, "Discernment"

Twenty-fifth Sunday in Ordinary Time, Year B

READING 1, WISDOM 2:12, 17–20

The wicked say: Let us beset the just one, because he is obnoxious to us; he sets himself against our doings, reproaches us for transgressions of the law and charges us with violations of our training. Let us see whether his words be true; let us find out what will happen to him. For if the just one be the son of God, God will defend him and deliver him from the hand of his foes. With revilement and torture let us put the just one to the test that we may have proof of his gentleness and try his patience. Let us condemn him to a shameful death; for according to his own words, God will take care of him.

PSALM 54:3–4, 5, 6, 8

READING 2, JAMES 3:16—4:3

Beloved: Where jealousy and selfish ambition exist, there is disorder and every foul practice. But the wisdom from above is first of all pure, then peaceable, gentle, compliant, full of mercy and good fruits, without inconstancy or insincerity. And the fruit of righteousness is sown in peace for those who cultivate peace. Where do the wars and where do the conflicts among you come from? Is it not from your passions that make war within your members? You covet but do not possess. You kill and envy but you cannot obtain; you fight and wage war. You do not possess because you do not ask. You ask but do not receive, because you ask wrongly, to spend it on your passions.

GOSPEL, MARK 9:30–37

Jesus and his disciples left from there and began a journey through Galilee, but he did not wish anyone to know about it. He was teaching his disciples and telling them, "The Son of Man is to be handed over to men and they will kill him, and three days after his death the Son of Man will rise." But they did not understand the saying, and they were afraid to question him. They came to Capernaum and, once inside the house, he began to ask them, "What were you arguing about on the way?" But they remained silent. They had been discussing among themselves on the way who was the greatest. Then he sat down, called the Twelve, and said to them, "If anyone wishes to be first, he shall be the last of all and the servant of all." Taking a child, he placed it in the their midst, and putting his arms around it, he said to them, "Whoever receives one child such as this in my name, receives me; and whoever receives me, receives not me but the One who sent me."

Wisdom from Above

All the families I know teach their children how to behave as soon as the little ones are able to learn. "Don't hit others...share your toys...be polite," are time-honored lessons we learned from our parents or trusted mentors. We recognize that without civility between persons and countries, the world can quickly become chaotic and disordered. Most of us have seen evidence of that in our own lives. The reading from James and the Gospel today revealed the truth about human passions. James reminds us that conflicts and disputes come from the jealousy that is in us. Wanting something is not inherently evil. Craving something someone else has until it's the only thing that matters makes people do some unspeakable things. Jealousy can lead to murder and war, theft, cheating, and power struggles—all because we want what someone else has and believe we are entitled to it.

James urges us to look for the wisdom from above. Just as the fruits of the Holy Spirit are the sign that the Holy Spirit dwells in us, God's wisdom is evident in the peace, gentleness, and mercy that are the characteristics of those who have found wisdom. This wisdom leads to righteousness.

In the Gospel, Jesus patiently tries to teach the disciples about the wisdom from above. They hadn't been paying attention to his prophecy about the crucifixion. Instead they argued about who was the greatest among them. This is exactly what James warns the early Christians against. The disciples seemingly knew their argument was wrong because they are silent when Jesus asks about it. In the face of their silence, Mark tells us that

Jesus sat down. This is the typical teaching position of the time. The master sits and the disciples stand around. Jesus' teaching confounds expectation. How can someone be first if he or she is last? How can a servant be the master? It will be some time before the disciples understand that teaching. Many of us are still trying to understand. We do know is that Jesus emptied himself on the cross so that we might live. As his disciples, we follow his example. His power didn't come from being the greatest in the eyes of the world.

The Test of Our Faith

The first reading minces no words in telling us we will be tested in our faith. The very presence of a righteous person is an inconvenience to the wicked because he or she gets in the way of whatever the wicked want to do. This is also the struggle between our own demons and better angels. The wicked are sure that under physical and emotional abuse, the righteous person's trust in God will waver. Of course, as Christians we read this passage and see the suffering of Jesus who challenged those in power to return to the fullness of God's law. We also know that we might be challenged in little ways every day. "How can you be Catholic when…" is a question I am often asked. Sometimes the person just wants information; sometimes they want to argue. I try to remember that gentleness, mercy, and peace may be better answers than argument and yelling. I am also aware that I can fall into the need to be right as easily as they can. That won't convince anyone.

Good News for All of Us

Human beings are born limited. Sometimes our emotions and passions get the better of us. Jesus doesn't say that our emotions are bad or being human is somehow evil. Rather, he invites us to experience the wonder of grace, which can help us do what seems impossible. We can choose not to fall victim to our passions. We can choose to let go of jealousy and anger. We can live in peace with all. That is the grace made available to us at baptism. It doesn't mean we will never sin; it does mean that we can follow the different path that Jesus lays out. We can become the servant that Jesus would have us be.

Questions for Reflection and Discussion

> *Have you experienced real jealousy in work, school, or life? How did you handle that?*

> *Can someone who is powerful and wealthy be the least of all? Can someone who is poor be the greatest of all, in human terms?*

Related Journey of Faith Lesson

Q8, "Catholic Prayers and Practices"

Themes

Justice
    Q15, "The Saints"
    M8, "Evangelization"
Leadership
    Q12, "Who Shepherds the Church?"
    M2, "The Role of the Laity"
Wisdom
    Q8, "Catholic Prayers and Practices"
    M5, "Our Call to Holiness"

READING 1, NUMBERS 11:25–29

The LORD came down in the cloud and spoke to Moses. Taking some of the spirit that was on Moses, the LORD bestowed it on the seventy elders; and as the spirit came to rest on them, they prophesied. Now two men, one named Eldad and the other Medad, were not in the gathering but had been left in the camp. They too had been on the list, but had not gone out to the tent; yet the spirit came to rest on them also, and they prophesied in the camp. So, when a young man quickly told Moses, "Eldad and Medad are prophesying in the camp," Joshua, son of Nun, who from his youth had been Moses' aide, said, "Moses, my lord, stop them." But Moses answered him, "Are you jealous for my sake? Would that all the people of the LORD were prophets! Would that the LORD might bestow his spirit on them all!"

PSALM 19:8, 10, 12–13, 14

READING 2, JAMES 5:1–6

Come now, you rich, weep and wail over your impending miseries. Your wealth has rotted away, your clothes have become moth-eaten, your gold and silver have corroded, and that corrosion will be a testimony against you; it will devour your flesh like a fire. You have stored up treasure for the last days. Behold, the wages you withheld from the workers who harvested your fields are crying aloud; and the cries of the harvesters have reached the ears of the Lord of hosts. You have lived on earth in luxury and pleasure; you have fattened your hearts for the day of slaughter. You have condemned; you have murdered the righteous one; he offers you no resistance.

GOSPEL, MARK 9:38–43, 45, 47–48

At that time, John said to Jesus, "Teacher, we saw someone driving out demons in your name, and we tried to prevent him because he does not follow us." Jesus replied, "Do not prevent him. There is no one who performs a mighty deed in my name who can at the same time speak ill of me. For whoever is not against us is for us. Anyone who gives you a cup of water to drink because you belong to Christ, amen, I say to you, will surely not lose his reward. "Whoever causes one of these little ones who believe in me to sin, it would be better for him if a great millstone were put around his neck and he were thrown into the sea. If your hand causes you to sin, cut it off. It is better for you to enter into life maimed than with two hands to go into Gehenna, into the unquenchable fire. And if your foot causes you to sin, cut if off. It is better for you to enter into life crippled than with two feet to be thrown into Gehenna. And if your eye causes you to sin, pluck it out. Better for you to enter into the kingdom of God with one eye than with two eyes to be thrown into Gehenna, where 'their worm does not die, and the fire is not quenched.'"

God's Gift for All People

Jesus' message isn't always easy to hear. In Mark's sparse storytelling style, Jesus is blunt in commanding his followers not to be a cause of sin for the "little ones." "If your hand causes you to sin, cut it off." We might shudder at such gruesomeness, but Jesus' lesson is an important one. Conflict, disputes, authoritarianism, clericalism, and just human pettiness can destroy a community of faith. The disciples try to prevent anyone they don't know from casting out demons. Their jealousy and intolerance threatened the whole community, as if to say they were the only ones worthy of God's great gifts. Jesus is quick to stop them: "Whoever is not against us is for us." We can interpret that to mean: Whoever does the smallest things in the name of Christ builds up the community of faith, whether or not he or she has earthly authority in that community.

Moses faced a similar situation in the desert. Overworked, Moses asked God for help and, in a beautiful description, God took some of the spirit he had given to Moses and gave it to seventy others. It's worth noting that Moses' authority was not diminished by this act; the seventy were helpers in his task. Eldad and Medad were not physically present at the tent meeting, but they also received some of that spirit of prophecy. Anxious to guard against interlopers, the young man and Joshua tell Moses to stop them. Both Joshua and the young man thought they knew the rules that God's spirit should follow and tried to get Moses and God to conform. The problem is, God does not abide by our rules. We are to abide by his. If God decides to give his Spirit to someone, no earthly rule can stop it. We can only hope that God will put a spirit of prophecy into everyone.

What You Sow, So Shall You Reap

James' practical theology takes square aim at the rich who make their wealth on the backs of the poor. His letter could have been written today. James touches on the treatment of workers, their wages, and the transient nature of worldly wealth. Every age sees those who enrich themselves at the expense of others and without regard to the impact on the poor. Many of the world's economic systems give an advantage to the rich and tend to disenfranchise the poor who can only trust that the rich will help them. Climbing out of poverty is increasingly difficult. In the United States, the gap between rich and poor continues to widen—today the top 1 percent of the people own more wealth than the bottom 90 percent. How do we give the poor an equal chance to get a fair wage, decent housing, and regular meals? The answer to that is something we all have to think about and act on, lest we "weep and wail over our impending miseries."

Good News for All of Us

It's easy to fall into the trap of assessing on our own who is and is not worthy of God's grace and mercy. It's easy to think we know what's best to keep the world, the Church, and our own lives in order. But the Spirit of God is free and falls on whomever God wills. Our task as disciples is to point to the Spirit and get out of the way, much like John the Baptist did for Jesus. Where and in whom can we notice the Spirit working in the world? How can we cooperate with that work? Are we willing to share what we have been given and humble ourselves to notice the gifts others have been given without becoming jealous or miserly. God's gifts are not ours to keep. They are to be given freely to the world.

Questions for Reflection and Discussion

➤ *Have you ever thought someone was unworthy to do something? How did you handle your feelings?*

➤ *Did you have any advantages growing up, like safe neighborhoods, good schools, parents who had decent jobs? If so, how did you think about or share those advantages with others? If not, how did you feel when you met others who did?*

Related Journey of Faith Lesson

Q13, "The Church as Community"

Themes

Judgment
    M4, "Discernment"
Personhood
    M3, "Your Spiritual Gifts"
Spirit
    M5, "Our Call to Holiness"

Twenty-seventh Sunday in Ordinary Time, Year B

READING 1, GENESIS 2:18–24

The LORD God said: "It is not good for the man to be alone. I will make a suitable partner for him." So the LORD God formed out of the ground various wild animals and various birds of the air, and he brought them to the man to see what he would call them; whatever the man called each of them would be its name. The man gave names to all the cattle, all the birds of the air, and all wild animals; but none proved to be the suitable partner for the man. So the LORD God cast a deep sleep on the man, and while he was asleep, he took out one of his ribs and closed up its place with flesh. The LORD God then built up into a woman the rib that he had taken from the man. When he brought her to the man, the man said: "This one, at last, is bone of my bones and flesh of my flesh; this one shall be called 'woman,' for out of 'her man' this one has been taken." That is why a man leaves his father and mother and clings to his wife, and the two of them become one flesh.

PSALM 128:1–2, 3, 4–5, 6

READING 2, HEBREWS 2:9–11

Brothers and sisters: He "for a little while" was made "lower than the angels," that by the grace of God he might taste death for everyone. For it was fitting that he, for whom and through whom all things exist, in bringing many children to glory, should make the leader to their salvation perfect through suffering. He who consecrates and those who are being consecrated all have one origin. Therefore, he is not ashamed to call them "brothers."

GOSPEL MARK 10:2–16

The Pharisees approached Jesus and asked, "Is it lawful for a husband to divorce his wife?" They were testing him. He said to them in reply, "What did Moses command you?" They replied, "Moses permitted a husband to write a bill of divorce and dismiss her." But Jesus told them, "Because of the hardness of your hearts he wrote you this commandment. But from the beginning of creation, God made them male and female. For this reason a man shall leave his father and mother and be joined to his wife, and the two shall become one flesh. So they are no longer two but one flesh. Therefore what God has joined together, no human being must separate." In the house the disciples again questioned Jesus about this. He said to them, "Whoever divorces his wife and marries another commits adultery against her; and if she divorces her husband and marries another, she commits adultery." And people were bringing children to him that he might touch them, but the disciples rebuked them. When Jesus saw this he became indignant and said to them, "Let the children come to me; do not prevent them, for the kingdom of God belongs to such as these. Amen, I say to you, whoever does not accept the kingdom of God like a child will not enter it." Then he embraced them and blessed them, placing his hands on them.

Commitment and Community

Today's young adults aren't—on a broad scale—thinking about getting married, entering the priesthood or religious life, or even seeing a position within a company as more than a steppingstone. The thought that they might work in the same place for forty years is utterly foreign to them. In an age when individualism is rampant and the next best thing is just over the horizon, committing oneself to a person, a community, or even a church seems challenging for many. At the same time adults, both young and old, yearn for community and friendship. They want to know they can count on others.

God's original plan for the creation of humankind recognized that people should not be alone. In Genesis, we hear the story of the creation of the woman, which is given as the reason that men and women marry and start their own families. The writer signals the closeness of the man and woman through a pun. Prior to the woman's creation, the man was *"ha-adam,"* the one created from dust, which is *"ha-ad'mah"* in Hebrew. We simply Anglicize it to say Adam. When God creates woman, she is *"isshah,"* for, as Adam says, she is taken from her "ish," which is the Hebrew word for man. Thus, the creation of human beings is not complete or differentiated until both male and female are created.

Though marriage and community were the ideal, divorce was permitted and by the time of Jesus, husbands could simply give a writ of divorce to their wives (the same was not true of Jewish women). In the Gentile world, both men and women could divorce and remarry. Jesus rails against this easy way of simply dismissing another person to whom a commitment had been made. This practice was particularly hard on women who did not have the same means of supporting themselves as men. In the same way, Jesus chastises those who saw children simply as a nuisance and burden. Children are a part of community life, and we make a commitment to them as well. They also provide a wonderful example of openness and innocence, which Jesus upholds as qualities we should all strive for.

Brothers and Sisters in Christ

The Epistle to the Hebrews reflects on the passion, death, and resurrection of Jesus not only as a means of salvation for all of us, but also as the means by which we become part of the family of God. Through his suffering, Jesus entered our suffering and made our unity with God possible. He tasted death as we all will, and God raised him from the dead. This is God's commitment to us. Jesus is the first fruit of that commitment. The last line of this reading points to God's continued commitment to us. We may be flawed and sinful, but Jesus is not ashamed to call us brothers and sisters. May we renew our commitment to him.

Good News for All of Us

Commitments, done right, help build the communities in which we live our lives. Commitments take courage, loyalty, hard work, and—in the case of another person—love. Certainly we should not rush into it. Nor are we obligated to stay in abusive or destructive relationships. But neither should we be distracted by the fear that we might miss something better. The Catholic spiritual life has many ways of helping people discern the path to follow and make decisions about important life changes. In addition, prayer and conversation with a trusted spiritual mentor can help when commitments become difficult. Remember that our brother, Jesus, stands ready to walk with us as he has all along.

Questions for Reflection and Discussion

➤ *Have you made a commitment to a person, a place, or a job? If so, what helped you decide? If not, what has stopped you?*

➤ *What is your understanding of the Church's teaching on divorce, remarriage, and annulment? Do you still have questions?*

Related Journey of Faith Lesson

C8, "The Sacrament of Marriage"

Themes

Family, Marriage, Relationships
 C8, "The Sacrament of Matrimony"
 Q12, "Who Shepherds the Church?"
 Q13, "The Church as Community"
 M7, "Family Life"

Twenty-eighth Sunday in Ordinary Time, Year B

READING 1, WISDOM 7:7–11

I prayed, and prudence was given me; I pleaded, and the spirit of wisdom came to me. I preferred her to scepter and throne, and deemed riches nothing in comparison with her, nor did I liken any priceless gem to her; because all gold, in view of her, is a little sand, and before her, silver is to be accounted mire. Beyond health and comeliness I loved her, and I chose to have her rather than the light, because the splendor of her never yields to sleep. Yet all good things together came to me in her company, and countless riches at her hands.

PSALM 90:12–13, 14–15, 16–17

READING 2, HEBREWS 4:12–13

Brothers and sisters: Indeed the word of God is living and effective, sharper than any two-edged sword, penetrating even between soul and spirit, joints and marrow, and able to discern reflections and thoughts of the heart. No creature is concealed from him, but everything is naked and exposed to the eyes of him to whom we must render an account.

GOSPEL, MARK 10:17–30

As Jesus was setting out on a journey, a man ran up, knelt down before him, and asked him, "Good teacher, what must I do to inherit eternal life?" Jesus answered him, "Why do you call me good? No one is good but God alone. You know the commandments: *You shall not kill; you shall not commit adultery; you shall not steal; you shall not bear false witness; you shall not defraud; honor your father and your mother.*" He replied and said to him, "Teacher, all of these I have observed from my youth." Jesus, looking at him, loved him and said to him, "You are lacking in one thing. Go, sell what you have, and give to the poor and you will have treasure in heaven; then come, follow me." At that statement his face fell, and he went away sad, for he had many possessions. Jesus looked around and said to his disciples, "How hard it is for those who have wealth to enter the kingdom of God!" The disciples were amazed at his words. So Jesus again said to them in reply, "Children, how hard it is to enter the kingdom of God! It is easier for a camel to pass through the eye of a needle than for one who is rich to enter the kingdom of God." They were exceedingly astonished and said among themselves, "Then who can be saved?" Jesus looked at them and said, "For human beings it is impossible, but not for God. All things are possible for God." Peter began to say to him, "We have given up everything and followed you." Jesus said, "Amen, I say to you, there is no one who has given up house or brothers or sisters or mother or father or children or lands for my sake and for the sake of the gospel who will not receive a hundred times more now in this present age: houses and brothers and sisters and mothers and children and lands, with persecutions, and eternal life in the age to come."

Loving Wisdom

It's hard to turn on the computer, TV, or radio without being barraged by endless commercials trying to convince us that we need to buy something in order to make our lives complete. Whether it's a new car, the latest fashion, or the next great self-help book, the sellers are sure that we will be happier or more fulfilled by additional possessions. It often works. Many of us have items we thought we needed taking up space in kitchen drawers and cabinets. Surely, there is more to life than belongings.

Today we learn about the "more" in our lives. Both main characters are wealthy; one recognizes that his wealth is transient and will fade away; the other never considered the possibility of giving up all he had. The first reading comes from the Wisdom literature, which draws its reflections from the lived experience of the people. In this case, the king (assumed to be King Solomon, to whom God gave wisdom—1 Kings 4:29) recognizes that wisdom is God's gift. He prefers her to his power and his riches. All his gold and silver is so much clay and dust before wisdom. It's hard to imagine someone saying that today when money, property, and power seem to be so much in demand. Still, those who have wisdom know the right thing to do in any situation. They seem attuned to the movement of culture and able to navigate it smoothly. Perhaps most importantly, Scripture portrays those with wisdom as having an ear for God's word in their hearts.

Practicing Wisdom

The man in the Gospel of Mark knew the rules and the law. His question was good—though admittedly a little self-serving: "What must I do to inherit eternal life?" For him, eternal life was just another thing to own. Jesus starts at the beginning and lists some of the Ten Commandments. The man's eager response to Jesus suggests that he hoped Jesus would tell him, "Congratulations! Eternal life is yours." Jesus suggests there is more. He asks him to let go of what he owns, give the money to the poor, and follow Jesus. For someone who may have seen wealth and possessions as a sign of status, this probably felt like an impossible task. We don't know what happened to the man. All we know is that he went away grieving over his many possessions.

Jesus' words invited the man to gain wisdom and come to know what's really important in life. He invited him to be like the king in the first reading. Possessions frequently get in the way of following Jesus and doing the right thing. The second reading reminds us that God will not look at what we own when judgment comes. Instead we will stand before him with our thoughts and hearts laid open.

Who can be saved? Jesus tells the disciples that, with God's grace, even a rich person can be saved. All of us, rich and poor, must transform our lives and refuse to love what we have more than God. Remember what Paul says: "For the love of money is the root of all evils, and some people in their desire for it have strayed from the faith and have pierced themselves with many pains" (1 Timothy 6:10).

Good News for All of Us

The Church celebrates wisdom figures. We call them saints. These are the ones who seem to hear God a little more clearly than the rest of us and follow where he leads them, even if it's not where they expected to go. Some were wealthy; many were poor. All of them had acquired the wisdom that comes from God. That same wisdom is available to us. The lives of saints can teach us much about wisdom and discipleship. Even in our own lives we may know a saint or two who models the behavior that comes from grace. Look for them and be inspired to transform your own life.

Questions for Reflection and Discussion

➤ *Have you ever given away something that was important to you? What were the challenges and rewards in that?*

➤ *Have you ever been wise in a situation? Do you recognize that as a gift from God?*

Related Journey of Faith Lesson

C15, "A Consistent Ethic of Life"

Themes

Community
    Q9, "The Mass"
    M2, "The Role of the Laity"
Gifts
    Q15, "The Saints"
    M3, "Your Spiritual Gifts"
Wisdom
    Q8, "Catholic Prayers and Practices"
    M4, "Discernment"

Twenty-ninth Sunday in Ordinary Time, Year B

READING 1, ISAIAH 53:10–11

The LORD was pleased to crush him in infirmity. If he gives his life as an offering for sin, he shall see his descendants in a long life, and the will of the LORD shall be accomplished through him. Because of his affliction he shall see the light in fullness of days; through his suffering, my servant shall justify many, and their guilt he shall bear.

PSALM 33:4–5, 18–19, 20, 22

READING 2, HEBREWS 4:14–16

Brothers and sisters: Since we have a great high priest who has passed through the heavens, Jesus, the Son of God, let us hold fast to our confession. For we do not have a high priest who is unable to sympathize with our weaknesses, but one who has similarly been tested in every way, yet without sin. So let us confidently approach the throne of grace to receive mercy and to find grace for timely help.

GOSPEL, MARK 10:35–45

James and John, the sons of Zebedee, came to Jesus and said to him, "Teacher, we want you to do for us whatever we ask of you." He replied, "What do you wish me to do for you?" They answered him, "Grant that in your glory we may sit one at your right and the other at your left." Jesus said to them, "You do not know what you are asking. Can you drink the cup that I drink or be baptized with the baptism with which I am baptized?" They said to him, "We can." Jesus said to them, "The cup that I drink, you will drink, and with the baptism with which I am baptized, you will be baptized; but to sit at my right or at my left is not mine to give but is for those for whom it has been prepared." When the ten heard this, they became indignant at James and John. Jesus summoned them and said to them, "You know that those who are recognized as rulers over the Gentiles lord it over them, and their great ones make their authority over them felt. But it shall not be so among you. Rather, whoever wishes to be great among you will be your servant; whoever wishes to be first among you will be the slave of all. For the Son of Man did not come to be served but to serve and to give his life as a ransom for many."

Jesus Was Like Us; Can We Be Like Him?

As we approach the end of the Church year, our reflection turns to lessons learned along the way. Have we changed this year? Have we grown a little closer to the Lord? Have the teachings of Jesus begun, to sink in and lead us toward conversion? In the progression of the readings today, we see a reminder that the servant of the Lord suffered on our behalf in Isaiah, we understand an identification between the servant and Jesus in the Letter to the Hebrews and we overhear Jesus tell James, John, and the rest of the disciples that following him isn't about fame and glory. It's about hard work and suffering. That may not have been the answer they were hoping for.

A Suffering Servant

We have heard the passage from Isaiah before. It's the first reading on Good Friday every year, and it details the anguish and suffering of the Lord's servant for the sake of the many. This passage comes from the end of the longer servant song and contains a word of hope. The servant's suffering is not in vain. Out of his anguish, he will see light, and his act of selflessness will justify many. The servant willingly bears the sins of all.

A Great High Priest

When the Letter to the Hebrews picks up the theme, the author identifies Jesus not only as the Son of God, but because he is fully God and fully human, he is the true high priest that the Aaronic priesthood foreshadowed. and who offered sacrifice for the transgressions of the people in ancient Israel. Jesus as High Priest is different, though. He knows our weaknesses; he has been tempted as we are tempted. Because of this, Jesus is filled with compassion and mercy for us and gives us grace to overcome temptation when it strikes. That grace is free to all who ask for it.

An Invitation to Be Like Jesus

James and John thought they would get to Jesus before anyone else. It was a simple request; the right and left hand of the master were the main places of honor. Those who sat there could be assured of the attention of all. Jesus refuses to answer them immediately, instead he asks if they can drink from the same cup as Jesus and be baptized as he is. As usual, they don't understand exactly what he is saying; their affirmative reply is a little too confident and eager. For us, we might remember that the Apostle Paul said: "...are you unaware that we who were baptized into Christ Jesus were baptized into his death?" (Romans 6:3). Jesus' cup is one of suffering; Jesus' baptism is a baptism of emptying oneself even to death for the sake of others. His final words bring us full circle: "whoever wishes to be great among you will be your servant" (Mark 10:43), just like the servant in Isaiah's prophecy.

Good News for All of Us

There are ample opportunities to serve others today. The Gospel provides a cautionary tale against allowing ambition to serve as a motive to follow Jesus. To follow Jesus and serve others means we must be willing to let go of ego, ambition, and the desire for fame. We are called to do one thing: love others without expectation of anything in return. It's sometimes harder than we may think, because we are not always aware of all the reasons we do something. Fortunately for us, Jesus gives us the grace to come closer to that ideal. Through prayer and reflection, we can serve more for love than for our own advantage.

Questions for Reflection and Discussion

➤ *Have you ever realized "mixed motives" for doing something good? Why did you act as you did?*

➤ *Were James and John bad people for asking what they did? Have you ever asked an important person for a favor?*

Related Journey of Faith Lesson

C14, "The Dignity of Life"

Themes

Servant
Q12, "Who Shepherds the Church?"
M2, "The Role of the Laity"
Status
Q14, "Mary"
M3, "Your Spiritual Gifts"
Suffering
Q15, "The Saints"
M8, "Evangelization"

Thirtieth Sunday in Ordinary Time, Year B

READING 1, JEREMIAH 31:7–9

Thus says the LORD: Shout with joy for Jacob, exult at the head of the nations; proclaim your praise and say: The LORD has delivered his people, the remnant of Israel. Behold, I will bring them back from the land of the north; I will gather them from the ends of the world, with the blind and the lame in their midst, the mothers and those with child; they shall return as an immense throng. They departed in tears, but I will console them and guide them; I will lead them to brooks of water, on a level road, so that none shall stumble. For I am a father to Israel, Ephraim is my first-born.

PSALM 126:1–2, 2–3, 4–5, 6

READING 2, HEBREWS 5:1–6

Brothers and sisters: Every high priest is taken from among men and made their representative before God, to offer gifts and sacrifices for sins. He is able to deal patiently with the ignorant and erring, for he himself is beset by weakness and so, for this reason, must make sin offerings for himself as well as for the people. No one takes this honor upon himself but only when called by God, just as Aaron was. In the same way, it was not Christ who glorified himself in becoming high priest, but rather the one who said to him: *You are my son: this day I have begotten you;* just as he says in another place: *You are a priest forever according to the order of Melchizedek.*

GOSPEL, MARK 10:46–52

As Jesus was leaving Jericho with his disciples and a sizable crowd, Bartimaeus, a blind man, the son of Timaeus, sat by the roadside begging. On hearing that it was Jesus of Nazareth, he began to cry out and say, "Jesus, son of David, have pity on me." And many rebuked him, telling him to be silent. But he kept calling out all the more, "Son of David, have pity on me." Jesus stopped and said, "Call him." So they called the blind man, saying to him, "Take courage; get up, Jesus is calling you." He threw aside his cloak, sprang up, and came to Jesus. Jesus said to him in reply, "What do you want me to do for you?"

The blind man replied to him, "Master, I want to see." Jesus told him, "Go your way; your faith has saved you." Immediately he received his sight and followed him.

What Do You Want Me to Do for You?

A single question ties together the Gospel stories for the last two weeks of readings. Jesus asks the same question of James and John that he asks of Bartimaeus. "What do you want me to do for you?" It's an invitation to share the desires of our heart with the Lord. We can almost imagine the fervent prayer in Jeremiah to which God responds: "What do you want me to do for you?" And the people reply, "Save us, O Lord." In response, God gives Jeremiah the vision of gathering all those who have been scattered, brings them back from exile and reestablishes his relationship with Israel as their father. We can only imagine the tears of joy, the laughter, and the celebration that came from the Israelites as they returned to their homes.

In the Letter to the Hebrews, the prayer of the people in response to God's question might have been: "Show us mercy, O Lord, in our sinfulness. Give us a true High Priest who stands before you." Once again, the passage gives God's response to this imagined prayer. Jesus, himself has been appointed as High Priest.

Unlike the Aaronic high priest referenced in Hebrews who must offer a sacrifice for himself "...for he himself is beset by weakness" (Hebrews 5:2). Jesus stands before God and offers himself as a sacrifice solely on our behalf. Because Jesus shares our human nature, he does however understand perfectly our weakness. The letter also suggests that Jesus didn't grasp this role out of ambition. Similar to Aaron, he was called by God. Christ did not glorify himself in becoming high priest, rather, he submitted himself to the Father and was appointed to be High Priest.

Answering Jesus from the Heart

The Gospel is the second of two stories about a blind man healed by Jesus. Sometimes in the Gospels, blindness indicates an unwillingness to understand Jesus and his teaching. When people see clearly, it means they gain understanding. Frequently, they also begin following Jesus. The story of Bartimaeus is the last healing before Jesus enters Jerusalem to be crucified. Bartimaeus is a marginalized person, forced into begging because of his blindness. He is not even allowed the dignity of his own name—Bartimaeus simply means the son of Timaeus, and he was tolerated because they probably knew Timaeus. The interchange between Jesus and Bartimaeus is a meeting of the hearts. Jesus asks from the fullness of who he is: "What do you want me to do for you?" Bartimaeus calls Jesus "my teacher," an unusual title for someone he has just met. He feels a personal connection to and trusts Jesus. Many would expect Bartimaeus to ask for money. Instead, he asks for his sight to be restored. Jesus answers with a miracle. I'm sure it caught everyone by surprise. Bartimaeus sees Jesus clearly and follows him into Jerusalem.

Good News for All of Us

Prayer is a meeting of the heart with God. We call on God, who listens even to our sighs and knows our needs. God asks us: "What do you want me to do for you?" Sometimes our prayer is for something that serves only us, like the request of James and John, which served their ambition and not God. Sometimes our request of God is simply to avoid the suffering that is part of the human condition. God doesn't promise that we won't suffer; God does promise he will walk with us in that suffering until we come into the light. Bartimaeus asked to see again. It was a prayer for physical healing, but even more, I think Bartimaeus was asking to understand clearly who Jesus was and what God could do. That's a good prayer for all of us.

Questions for Reflection and Discussion

> *How would you respond if God asked: "What do you want me to do for you?"*

> *A blind spot is an area, which keeps us from seeing clearly. What blind spots do you have in your life?*

Related Journey of Faith Lesson

C9, "The Sacrament of Holy Orders"

Themes

Faith
    Q2, "What Is Faith?"
    M4, "Discernment"
Healing
    Q10, "The Church Year"
    Q7, "Your Prayer Life"
Hope
    Q13, "The Church as Community"
    M5, "Our Call to Holiness"

Thirty-first Sunday in Ordinary Time, Year B

READING 1, DEUTERONOMY 6:2–6

Moses spoke to the people, saying: "Fear the Lord, your God, and keep, throughout the days of your lives, all his statutes and commandments which I enjoin on you, and thus have long life. Hear then, Israel, and be careful to observe them, that you may grow and prosper the more, in keeping with the promise of the Lord, the God of your fathers, to give you a land flowing with milk and honey. Hear, O Israel! The Lord is our God, the Lord alone! Therefore, you shall love the Lord, your God, with all your heart, and with all your soul, and with all your strength. Take to heart these words which I enjoin on you today."

PSALM 18:2–3, 3–4, 47, 51

READING 2, HEBREWS 7:23–28

Brothers and sisters: The levitical priests were many because they were prevented by death from remaining in office, but Jesus, because he remains forever, has a priesthood that does not pass away. Therefore, he is always able to save those who approach God through him, since he lives forever to make intercession for them. It was fitting that we should have such a high priest: holy, innocent, undefiled, separated from sinners, higher than the heavens. He has no need, as did the high priests, to offer sacrifice day after day, first for his own sins and then for those of the people; he did that once for all when he offered himself. For the law appoints men subject to weakness to be high priests, but the word of the oath, which was taken after the law, appoints a son, who has been made perfect forever.

GOSPEL, MARK 12:28B–34

One of the scribes came to Jesus and asked him, "Which is the first of all the commandments?" Jesus replied, "The first is this: Hear, O Israel! The Lord our God is Lord alone! You shall love the Lord your God with all your heart, with all your soul, with all your mind, and with all your strength. The second is this: You shall love your neighbor as yourself. There is no other commandment greater than these." The scribe said to him, "Well said, teacher. You are right in saying, 'He is One and there is no other than he.' And 'to love him with all your heart, with all your understanding, with all your strength, and to love your neighbor as yourself' is worth more than all burnt offerings and sacrifices." And when Jesus saw that he answered with understanding, he said to him, "You are not far from the kingdom of God." And no one dared to ask him any more questions.

Loving God with Your Whole Being

What is the greatest commandment? The answer was debated in Old and New Testament times and continues to be argued today, particularly in our political discourse.

In the first few chapters of Deuteronomy, Moses gives the Israelites his last words of wisdom before they enter the Promised Land. The commandments and decrees come from God himself and were presumably given to Moses on Mount Sinai and in the long conversations with God in the tent of meeting when the Israelites were wandering in the desert. In the previous chapter, Moses recounted the Ten Commandments (Deuteronomy 5:6–21). The first reading today boldly and clearly reworks the First Commandment (You shall have no other gods before me) into this command that Jews today still revere as the "Great Shema" (*shema* is the Hebrew command to "hear"). "The Lord is our God, the Lord alone! Therefore, you shall love the Lord, your God, with your whole heart, and with your whole being, and with your whole strength" (Deuteronomy 6:4–5).

The relationship of love between God and human beings is unique in the ancient Near East. Gods were to be feared, obeyed, bowed down before. Love didn't enter the picture; it was always more about power. God had it, human beings didn't. And yet, in Deuteronomy 4:7, Moses tells the people that it is out of love for their ancestors that God chose them. The command to love is a cementing of the relationship between God and his people. The listing of heart, whole being, and strength is Moses' way of talking about giving our all for God. When the scribes ask Jesus which commandment is the greatest, they are trying to goad him into joining the endless arguments among scholars about the relative importance of God's commandments. Jesus distills the whole of the law—613 commandments in total into two—those regarding our relationship with God and neighbor (Deuteronomy 6 and Leviticus 19:18). Every other commandment can be put under these categories. If we get these commandments right, almost everything else will fall into place. Evidently, Jesus' answer was satisfactory for the scribe, for even he recognized that without loving God and neighbor, sacrifices and burnt offerings mean very little. Jesus complements the scribe's understanding and stymies future critics with his wisdom.

God's Love for Us

The Letter to the Hebrews continues its discussion of Jesus as the great High Priest. Read in the context of the other two readings, though, we see that the Father sent Jesus to us out of love for us. In turn, Jesus willingly gave himself as a sacrifice for our sins so we could approach God through him in every age. That sacrifice was given once for all time. Because of Christ we can always pray to God; we can gather in community and experience the grace of salvation in every Eucharist; and we can go out again into the world sharing the love of God with others. The relationship of love between God and his people that was first described in the Old Testament has been brought to fulfillment in Jesus.

Good News for All of Us

As Christians, we live in a triangle of relationships. We have a relationship with ourselves, with God, and with our neighbor. Whenever one of those relationships is broken, it affects the other. One of my mentors said that loving your neighbor as yourself is sometimes not a good deal for the neighbor. This is especially true when we hold ourselves to unreasonable expectations or, conversely, never expect ourselves to accomplish anything. If my relationship with my neighbor is bad, my relationship with God can't be good. If I have sinned against God, it's a good bet I have also broken relationship with my neighbor. This is why reconciliation is so powerful. We mend our relationship with God, neighbor, and ourselves all at once and we are given the grace to strive to love God once more with our whole being.

Questions for Reflections and Discussion

➤ *If you only had current homilies and Church writings on which to base your response, what would you say is the greatest commandment?*

➤ *What are some of the best ways you can think to love God and neighbor today?*

Related Journey of Faith Lesson

C16, "Social Justice"

Themes

Forgiveness
    Q2, "What Is Faith?"
    M1, "Conversion: A Lifelong Process"
Love
    Q8, "Catholic Prayers and Practices"
    M5, "Our Call to Holiness"
Neighbors
    Q13, "The Church as Community"
    M7, "Family Life

Thirty-second Sunday in Ordinary Time, Year B

READING 1, 1 KINGS 17:10–16

In those days, Elijah the prophet went to Zarephath. As he arrived at the entrance of the city, a widow was gathering sticks there; he called out to her, "Please bring me a small cupful of water to drink." She left to get it, and he called out after her, "Please bring along a bit of bread." She answered, "As the LORD, your God, lives, I have nothing baked; there is only a handful of flour in my jar and a little oil in my jug. Just now I was collecting a couple of sticks, to go in and prepare something for myself and my son; when we have eaten it, we shall die." Elijah said to her, "Do not be afraid. Go and do as you propose. But first make me a little cake and bring it to me. Then you can prepare something for yourself and your son. For the LORD, the God of Israel, says, 'The jar of flour shall not go empty, nor the jug of oil run dry, until the day when the LORD sends rain upon the earth.'" She left and did as Elijah had said. She was able to eat for a year, and he and her son as well; the jar of flour did not go empty, nor the jug of oil run dry, as the LORD had foretold through Elijah.

PSALM 146:7, 8–9, 9–10

READING 2, HEBREWS 9:24–28

Christ did not enter into a sanctuary made by hands, a copy of the true one, but heaven itself, that he might now appear before God on our behalf. Not that he might offer himself repeatedly, as the high priest enters each year into the sanctuary with blood that is not his own; if that were so, he would have had to suffer repeatedly from the foundation of the world. But now once for all he has appeared at the end of the ages to take away sin by his sacrifice. Just as it is appointed that human beings die once, and after this the judgment, so also Christ, offered once to take away the sins of many, will appear a second time, not to take away sin but to bring salvation to those who eagerly await him.

GOSPEL, MARK 12:38–44

In the course of his teaching Jesus said to the crowds, "Beware of the scribes, who like to go around in long robes and accept greetings in the marketplaces, seats of honor in synagogues, and places of honor at banquets. They devour the houses of widows and, as a pretext recite lengthy prayers. They will receive a very severe condemnation." He sat down opposite the treasury and observed how the crowd put money into the treasury. Many rich people put in large sums. A poor widow also came and put in two small coins worth a few cents. Calling his disciples to himself, he said to them, "Amen, I say to you, this poor widow put in more than all the other contributors to the treasury. For they have all contributed from their surplus wealth, but she, from her poverty, has contributed all she had, her whole livelihood."

Sharing and Caring

The multiplication of the loaves and fish in the Gospels was not the first time that food had been miraculously increased. In the first reading today, the prophet Elijah encounters a widow who suffers from the drought that has gripped the land. Despite the precarious situation she and her son are in, she shares the little food she has with Elijah. Hospitality was an important value in the ancient Near East. Visitors were given something to eat and a place near the head of the table. The widow's care is rewarded; the flour and the oil are replenished, and there is enough for everyone. The miracle is remarkable, but the focus of this story rests on the woman and her response. She had very little to give, but she gave it freely, not knowing what the future would bring. She responded from the heart of a woman who knew that welcoming the stranger was the proper response of a gentile who had faith in the God of Israel. Her heart was attuned to the will of God and her faith was rewarded.

In Mark's Gospel, Jesus uses a scene near the Temple treasury to make a point about the conversion of heart necessary to be a faithful disciple. The scribes were teachers of the law and had great authority in the Israelite community at that time. From Jesus' comments in this story, some scribes seemed to revel in that power. They dressed to be noticed by others. They expected people to treat them with respect and honor. They prayed long prayers because they wanted to impress those around them. Their hearts were not turned to the Lord because their egos were in the way. They were among the wealthier people in part because they took advantage of the poor, particularly widows. In this, they contradicted the very law they pretended to uphold.

Jesus also invites our observation at the treasury. The people are paying the annual Temple tax that was required of everyone. The set amount of money was used for the sacrifices made for each person over the course of the year. Any additional funds were placed in a separate box as a voluntary contribution. Since women weren't allowed in the Temple, the treasury was in the Court of Women, and everyone could hear the coins being deposited and guess how much each person was giving. As Jesus points out, the rich made a show of how much they gave. And Jesus says that the rich give only after they have satisfied their own desires. They may even use money gained by oppressing the poor. In any case, they give out of ego, not out of love for God. But when the widow comes in quietly with the minimum amount necessary (and the only thing she can afford), it's clear that she gives all she has because her heart is turned to God and not because she wants to show off.

Caring for All Time

Between the first reading and the Gospel, the Letter to the Hebrews reflects more on Jesus as our great High Priest in heaven. The sacrifice Christ made in his passion and death continues to bring salvation to the world day after day and will continue to do so until he comes again. It will never run out. He gave all he had, including his life, out of love and care for us. The author makes a point to say that Christ was offered once to bear the sins of the world and comes again to save all who eagerly await his return.

Good News for All of Us

There are two lessons in today's readings. First: wealth and power don't mean that we have opened our hearts to God and one another. We may need to practice humility and gratitude a little more and become aware when our desires get in the way of helping those who have less. Second: we must trust that God will give us what we need, sometimes through divine intervention and often through other people who know, love, and serve him.

Questions for Reflection and Discussion

> *How do you respond when someone makes a request of you that requires sacrifice on your part?*

> *How do you feel about giving your time, talent, and treasure to the Church community? Do you budget for it?*

Related Journey of Faith Lesson

M6, "Living the Virtues"

Themes

Strength
    Q14, "Mary"
    M4, "Discernment"
Weakness
    Q2, "What Is Faith?"
    Q7, "Your Prayer Life"
Widowhood
    Q15, "The Saints"
    M7, "Family Life"

Thirty-third Sunday in Ordinary Time, Year B

READING 1, DANIEL 12:1–3

In those days, I Daniel, heard this word of the Lord: "At that time there shall arise Michael, the great prince, guardian of your people; it shall be a time unsurpassed in distress since nations began until that time. At that time your people shall escape, everyone who is found written in the book. "Many of those who sleep in the dust of the earth shall awake; some shall live forever, others shall be an everlasting horror and disgrace. "But the wise shall shine brightly like the splendor of the firmament, and those who lead the many to justice shall be like the stars forever."

PSALM 16:5, 8, 9–10, 11

READING 2, HEBREWS 10:11–14, 18

Brothers and sisters: Every priest stands daily at his ministry, offering frequently those same sacrifices that can never take away sins. But this one offered one sacrifice for sins, and took his seat forever at the right hand of God; now he waits until his enemies are made his footstool. For by one offering he has made perfect forever those who are being consecrated. Where there is forgiveness of these, there is no longer offering for sin.

GOSPEL, MARK 13:24–32

Jesus said to his disciples: "In those days after that tribulation the sun will be darkened, and the moon will not give its light, and the stars will be falling from the sky, and the powers in the heavens will be shaken. "And then they will see 'the Son of Man coming in the clouds' with great power and glory, and then he will send out the angels and gather his elect from the four winds, from the end of the earth to the end of the sky. "Learn a lesson from the fig tree. When its branch becomes tender and sprouts leaves, you know that summer is near. In the same way, when you see these things happening, know that he is near, at the gates. Amen, I say to you, this generation will not pass away until all these things have taken place. Heaven and earth will pass away, but my words will not pass away. "But of that day or hour, no one knows, neither the angels in heaven, nor the Son, but only the Father."

Behold, He Comes

At the end of the Church year, the readings turn our gaze to the future when Christ will come again both for judgment and salvation. Passages that depict this coming (or the coming of God in the Old Testament) are called *apocalyptic*, from the Greek word for revelation. Often, the appearance of God at the end of time is accompanied by conflict, death, and the reversal of what has gone before. In the Book of Revelation, there are multiple descriptions of the battle between God and the devil. The outcome is never in doubt. God will reign. Apocalyptic literature is usually written in a time of great persecution and upheaval to encourage believers to hold fast to the faith.

The last half of the Book of Daniel is an example of apocalyptic literature. His vision of Michael the archangel is associated both with anguish for the world and those who sin, and with everlasting life for those who lead people to righteousness. Earlier in the book, Daniel sees one *like* a Son of Man coming in the clouds (Daniel 7:13). For Daniel, that meant someone who looks like a human being (but may not be) and who is shown favor by God, for he is given dominion and glory.

In Mark's Gospel, Jesus describes the apocalyptic moment when the Son of Man will be revealed. Jesus' depiction of the world when that happens isn't a comforting one. Stars are falling and the heavens are shaken. But Jesus also says that the angels will gather all the believers together and they will know the Lord is coming. "Son of Man" in this passage is the way Jesus refers to himself in this Gospel, and it certainly means more than just looking human. Jesus, fully human and fully divine, is also given power and glory at the end. The Son of Man also promises that his words will not pass away. We hear this same promise of God's words in Isaiah 40:8.

The early Church believed that Christ would come very soon. Paul was so sure of this, so he did little to address the social injustices of his time. Instead, he encouraged Christians to be patient in their suffering and to live in expectation of the Second Coming. At the end of the year, we are urged to be expectant as well. No one knows when Christ will come, but our Creed says we live in joyful hope for the coming of our Savior. In this we are like all those who have come before us.

Waiting for the Right Time

The passage from Hebrews reminds us that we are not the only ones who wait. Christ waits as well for the fullness of time to reveal himself. Hebrews describes it as the time when his enemies are made into his footstool. We might use the Greek word *Kairos* as the right time, as opposed to *chronos*, which is the time our watches keep. Jesus will appear when he deems the world ready. We can't force that time to come, so it's fitting that we keep awake in heart and soul to watch for his coming.

Good News for All of Us

It's easy to get caught up in the mundane elements of our lives and forget that we are on a mission from God. In his command to love God and neighbor, Jesus Christ expects us to find as many ways as possible to express that love. Our Lord wants us to pray, share the Eucharist and care for those in need, not because we will be judged at the end for what we've done but because God first loved us into being and came to us as Jesus Christ, a sign of great love. That Christ will come again is our great hope, and we want to be ready.

Questions for Discussion and Reflection

➤ *War, famine, pestilence, and darkened skies are all biblical signs of the Last Judgment and the Second Coming of Christ. Many believe these are evident in today's world. What do you think?*

➤ *Some people find praying easy and serving others hard; others can pray and serve but don't like talking about faith. What do you find challenging about living out the Good News?*

Related Journey of Faith Lesson

Q16, "Eschatology: The 'Last Things'"

Themes

Confidence
    Q2, "What Is Faith?"
    Q7, "Your Prayer Life"
Revelation
    Q8, "Catholic Prayers and Practices"
    M4, "Discernment"
Second Coming
    E4, "The Creed"
    M1, "Conversion: A Lifelong Process"

Christma the King, Year B

READING 1, DANIEL 7:13–14

As the visions during the night continued, I saw one like a Son of man coming, on the clouds of heaven; when he reached the Ancient One and was presented before him, the one like a Son of man received dominion, glory, and kingship; all peoples, nations, and languages serve him. His dominion is an everlasting dominion that shall not be taken away, his kingship shall not be destroyed.

PSALM 93:1, 1–2, 5

READING 2, REVELATION 1:5–8

Jesus Christ is the faithful witness, the firstborn of the dead and ruler of the kings of the earth. To him who loves us and has freed us from our sins by his blood, who has made us into a kingdom, priests for his God and Father, to him be glory and power forever and ever. Amen. Behold, he is coming amid the clouds, and every eye will see him, even those who pierced him. All the peoples of the earth will lament him. Yes. Amen. "I am the Alpha and the Omega," says the Lord God, "the one who is and who was and who is to come, the almighty."

GOSPEL, JOHN 18:33B–37

Pilate said to Jesus, "Are you the King of the Jews?" Jesus answered, "Do you say this on your own or have others told you about me?" Pilate answered, "I am not a Jew, am I? Your own nation and the chief priests handed you over to me. What have you done?" Jesus answered, "My kingdom does not belong to this world. If my kingdom did belong to this world, my attendants would be fighting to keep me from being handed over to the Jews. But as it is, my kingdom is not here." So Pilate said to him, "Then you are a king?" Jesus answered, "You say I am a king. For this I was born and for this I came into the world, to testify to the truth. Everyone who belongs to the truth listens to my voice."

The Beginning and the End

If we look carefully at the descriptions of good kings in the Old Testament, we would find that the king had one job, and it wasn't to make laws or lead the people into battle. Rather, the king's job was to read and study the law and be obedient to God (Deuteronomy 17:18). On this basis he was judged righteous or not. When Pilate asked Jesus, "Are you the king of the Jews?" he was thinking of an earthly king who would rival Caesar for allegiance and go to battle against Rome. He didn't understand who Jesus was at all. Nor did he understand what Jesus told him. How could his kingdom not be from this world? Pilate thought he had trapped him and declares, "So you are a king." I am sure Jesus just shook his head. Pilate's own assumptions had blinded him to Jesus' true nature. Later, at the crucifixion, Pilate would inscribe "King of the Jews" on the cross. Pilate did it to mock Jesus, but those words were truer than he could have known. If a king's job was to be obedient to God, Jesus was truly that king, obedient to death, even death on a cross.

Our assumptions about people frequently get in the way of seeing them with clarity. Because Jesus was fully human, it took a long time to articulate his identity as God. Because they experienced his birth and death, others did not see that he was present at the beginning of creation and would be also at its end. That's one of the reasons the Book of Revelation begins by talking about who Jesus really is: first-born of the dead, ruler of kings, and the one who made us into a kingdom. The words are lofty. We might even think we are better than others until we read the description of that kingdom. We belong to a kingdom not of warriors but of priests who serve God and are themselves obedient to God's law of love. If we are disciples of Christ, we can be nothing else, for he is the High Priest and ruler of us all. As Christ was at our beginning, so he shall be at our end, "the Alpha and the Omega."

The King of Love

Last week we talked a little about the significance of the title Son of Man. In its use with Revelation and John's Gospel, the *Lectionary* leaves little doubt that the Church sees Jesus described in these words (whether Daniel meant to do that or not). Revelation borrows the language almost word for word, with one difference. Before he talks about the glory and dominion due to Christ, John describes him as the one who loved us and freed us from our sins by his blood. Just as his Father created us in love, so Christ makes us a new creation out of love. That obedience to his Father alone makes Christ worthy of dominion and glory. In the light of this day, says John, even those who crucified him will know him for who he truly is. Their assumptions will be cast away and they will finally recognize the one they killed. On that day, all the earth will cry over what they have done.

Good News for All of Us

According to Peter, we are a royal priesthood (1 Peter 2:9). In our baptism we are anointed into the mission of Jesus to be priest, prophet, and king, but we are to do so configured to Christ. As he was an example of obedience to God, so we also must be. As he served others and offered praise to God, so we must do. How can we best do that today? Every person has opportunities to serve others, to pray before the Lord, and to do what is right, even if that's hard. We can nurture our "royal" selves by praying to be like Christ at the beginning and end of our days. We can also form our conscience to follow God's will rather than our own and to joyfully give of ourselves.

Questions for Reflection and Discussion

> *Is there any leader in the world or in your life who tries to model the obedience to God that Christ does?*

> *What are some ways you can build the habit of making Christ the beginning and end of your day in prayer?*

Related Journey of Faith Lessons

Q4, "Who Is Jesus Christ?"
C1, "The OCIA Process and Rites"

Themes

Christianity
    E4, "The Creed"
    M1, "Conversion: A Lifelong Process"
Kingship/Queenship
    Q15, "The Saints"
    M2, "The Role of the Laity"
Service
    Q13, "The Church as Community"
    M3, "Your Spiritual Gifts"

Immaculate Conception of Mary, December 8, Year B

READING 1, GENESIS 3:9–15, 20

After the man, Adam, had eaten of the tree, the LORD God called to the man and asked him, "Where are you?" He answered, "I heard you in the garden; but I was afraid, because I was naked, so I hid myself." Then he asked, "Who told you that you were naked? You have eaten, then, from the tree of which I had forbidden you to eat!" The man replied, "The woman whom you put here with me, she gave me fruit from the tree, and so I ate it." The LORD God then asked the woman, "Why did you do such a thing?" The woman answered, "The serpent tricked me into it, so I ate it." Then the LORD God said to the serpent: "Because you have done this, you shall be banned from all the animals and from all the wild creatures; on your belly shall you crawl, and dirt shall you eat all the days of your life. I will put enmity between you and the woman, and between your offspring and hers; he will strike at your head, while you strike at his heel." The man called his wife Eve, because she became the mother of all the living.

PSALM 98:1, 2–3AB, 3CD–4

READING 2, EPHESIANS 1:3–6, 11–12

Brothers and sisters: Blessed be the God and Father of our Lord Jesus Christ, who has blessed us in Christ with every spiritual blessing in the heavens, as he chose us in him, before the foundation of the world, to be holy and without blemish before him. In love he destined us for adoption to himself through Jesus Christ, in accord with the favor of his will, for the praise of the glory of his grace that he granted us in the beloved. In him we were also chosen, destined in accord with the purpose of the One who accomplishes all things according to the intention of his will, so that we might exist for the praise of his glory, we who first hoped in Christ.

GOSPEL, LUKE 1:26–38

The angel Gabriel was sent from God to a town of Galilee called Nazareth, to a virgin betrothed to a man named Joseph, of the house of David, and the virgin's name was Mary. And coming to her, he said, "Hail, full of grace! The Lord is with you." But she was greatly troubled at what was said and pondered what sort of greeting this might be. Then the angel said to her, "Do not be afraid, Mary, for you have found favor with God. Behold, you will conceive in your womb and bear a son, and you shall name him Jesus. He will be great and will be called Son of the Most High, and the Lord God will give him the throne of David his father, and he will rule over the house of Jacob forever, and of his Kingdom there will be no end." But Mary said to the angel, "How can this be, since I have no relations with a man?" And the angel said to her in reply, "The Holy Spirit will come upon you, and the power of the Most High will overshadow you. Therefore the child to be born will be called holy, the Son of God. And behold, Elizabeth, your relative, has also conceived a son in her old age, and this is the sixth month for her who was called barren; for nothing will be impossible for God." Mary said, "Behold, I am the handmaid of the Lord. May it be done to me according to your word." Then the angel departed from her.

According to Your Word

When the Archangel came to Mary, she was told "the holy spirit would will come upon you, and the power of the Most High will overshadow you..." (Luke 1:35). This relates God's eagerness to dwell with us and bring us back to our first graced relationship with him. Given our long history of turning our backs and disobeying his commands, we might wonder why. It couldn't have been easy for God to watch us wander away time after time throughout the biblical story and even now. The answer, though, is found in today's readings.

In Genesis, God created us in love and seeks us out as he walks in the garden in the cool part of the day (Genesis 3:8). And while God punishes all the players—the serpent, the woman, and the man—his first curse is to the serpent who tempted the woman and man in the first place. Not only will he crawl on his belly for all time (we might wonder what he looked like before), but the woman's child will ultimately destroy him.

The story of that original sin and the inherent promise that evil would ultimately be destroyed that is found in God's words guided prophets and priests throughout Israel for centuries. Good and holy people spoke of God's commandments and prophesied in his name.

They did their best to follow what God said and urged others to do the same. Ultimately, wisdom and grace were embodied completely not in a king, priest, or prophet, but in a young Israelite woman named Mary. When Gabriel finds her, he calls her, "full of grace," and delivers his message. We celebrate the fullness of grace in her in this feast of the Immaculate Conception. The Church teaches that God sanctified Mary in the womb, keeping her free of original sin. Thus, she is the first among humans to experience the fruits of salvation. Because she is so attuned to God's words, Mary could give her wholehearted assent to God's plan for her life and the life of the world. It is her Son, Jesus, who will destroy evil forever.

Adopted Children of God

Because of Jesus Christ, born of Mary and Son of God, we have also become God's adopted children. We have been set free of original sin in baptism and have been given the grace to make decisions that turn us toward God, not toward evil. God's grace is a free gift to all who seek it and turn to Christ. How do we do that? We become more and more like Mary and say yes to God every chance we get. Just as we learn how to behave from our mothers and fathers in our childhood, so too we learn how to say yes to God from Mary, who is our mother in the Church. We also know that God continues to give us the grace to say yes through the sacraments and prayer of the Church so that we might live "for the praise of his glory" (Ephesians 1:12).

Good News for All of Us

We all sin because we are human, but we are not bound to sin. Rather, we are freed by grace to make decisions to do what is right and good. Blessed Mother Mary shows us what is possible when we allow grace to fill our hearts. She also gives us a foretaste of what is to come for those who are faithful to God. Mary was assumed bodily into heaven at the end of her life on earth. To come to God and be saved, we need to repent, have faith, and be baptized. If you commit mortal sin, you need to repent, have faith, and go to confession.

Questions for Reflection and Discussion

➤ *Has it ever been hard for you to do the right thing in a situation? What made you choose that thing in the end?*

➤ *Temptation comes in many forms. Name two or three things that you think are real temptations today.*

Related Journey of Faith Lesson

Q14, "Mary"

Themes

Immaculate Conception, Mary
    Q4, "Who Is Jesus Christ?"
    Q14, "Mary"
    C10, "The People of God"
Life
    C3, "The Sacrament of Baptism"
    C6, "The Sacrament of Penance and Reconciliation"
    C7, "The Sacrament of Anointing of the Sick"
    C14, "The Dignity of Life"
    C15, "A Consistent Ethic of Life"
Sin
    C6, "The Sacrament of Penance and Reconciliation"

READING 1 (ABC), ISAIAH 9:1–6

The people who walked in darkness have seen a great light; upon those who dwelt in the land of gloom a light has shone. You have brought them abundant joy and great rejoicing, as they rejoice before you as at the harvest, as people make merry when dividing spoils. For the yoke that burdened them, the pole on their shoulder, and the rod of their taskmaster you have smashed, as on the day of Midian. For every boot that tramped in battle, every cloak rolled in blood, will be burned as fuel for flames. For a child is born to us, a son is given us; upon his shoulder dominion rests. They name him Wonder-Counselor, God-Hero, Father-Forever, Prince of Peace. His dominion is vast and forever peaceful, from David's throne, and over his kingdom, which he confirms and sustains by judgment and justice, both now and forever. The zeal of the LORD of hosts will do this!

PSALM 96:1–2, 2–3, 11–12, 13

READING 2 (ABC), TITUS 2:11–14

Beloved: The grace of God has appeared, saving all and training us to reject godless ways and worldly desires and to live temperately, justly, and devoutly in this age, as we await the blessed hope, the appearance of the glory of our great God and savior Jesus Christ, who gave himself for us to deliver us from all lawlessness and to cleanse for himself a people as his own, eager to do what is good.

GOSPEL (ABC), LUKE 2:1–14

In those days a decree went out from Caesar Augustus that the whole world should be enrolled. This was the first enrollment, when Quirinius was governor of Syria. So all went to be enrolled, each to his own town. And Joseph too went up from Galilee from the town of Nazareth to Judea, to the city of David that is called Bethlehem, because he was of the house and family of David, to be enrolled with Mary, his betrothed, who was with child. While they were there, the time came for her to have her child, and she gave birth to her firstborn son. She wrapped him in swaddling clothes and laid him in a manger, because there was no room for them in the inn. Now there were shepherds in that region living in the fields and keeping the night watch over their flock. The angel of the Lord appeared to them and the glory of the Lord shone around them, and they were struck with great fear. The angel said to them, "Do not be afraid; for behold, I proclaim to you good news of great joy that will be for all the people. For today in the city of David a savior has been born for you who is Christ and Lord. And this will be a sign for you: you will find an infant wrapped in swaddling clothes and lying in a manger." And suddenly there was a multitude of the heavenly host with the angel, praising God and saying: "Glory to God in the highest and on earth peace to those on whom his favor rests."

A Promise Made and Kept

We have come to the day at last. The cards have been sent, the gifts have been acquired and wrapped, and Christmas traditions await sleeping children and tired parents. But we don't start there. We start with Isaiah's recognition that there have been dark times, if not for us, then for many others. We start with a proclamation of hope as light begins to break into darkness. Whatever has been weighing us down or making us weary is falling away because of an unlikely event—the birth of a child.

A Child of Paradox

When the Jews expected a Messiah, many had in mind a great warrior or king who would free them from the tyranny of others and vanquish their enemies. They longed for justice and the peace of a world in which God reigned and there was no more war. Some envisioned a great banquet on that day; others looked forward to a confirmation of their faith in God who had promised to send a prophet like Moses into their midst who would bring them to freedom by the grace of God. Isaiah's prophecy heralds the birth of royalty, a mighty God and an everlasting Father who will establish his kingdom with justice (Isaiah 9:6–7). One might imagine such a birth happening in a palace with royal attendants and the baby wrapped in the finest linen. That's not the birth we hear about in Luke.

Luke's Gospel tells us of Joseph traveling with his very pregnant wife because the census demanded their presence. While Joseph was of the house of David, he was by no means wealthy. They couldn't find a room in the town, and he clearly couldn't afford to outbid the few rooms that might have been available. His son was born in a cave used for animals. Mary swaddled him in whatever cloth she had and put him in the manger where the animals fed. Was this truly the king for whom they had waited for generations? It seems a far cry from Isaiah's prophecy.

But while Mary rested from her labor and Joseph kept watch over his family, something else was happening. Shepherds were shocked to see an angel appear to them in radiant light and announce to them the birth of a Messiah—the anointed one of God. The angel calls him "Lord," a term used for God in the Old Testament.

He points to the Child lying in a manger as proof. A multitude of angels praise God and proclaim peace. The Child in the manger is the wonder-counselor and God-hero of Isaiah, proof that our God is a God of surprises.

God's Grace on Our Lives

Early in the Church's life, Titus reflected on the gift God gave us in the Incarnation. It was nothing less than salvation, which allows us—indeed trains us—to live as Christ's disciples, in eager anticipation of his return. And it also points out the truth of Christian life. Jesus died that we might live. He gave himself for our redemption. Jesus calls us now to give witness to that Good News and walk with one another into his light.

Good News for All of Us

Christmas is a time of family and tradition. But there are many in our neighborhoods and church communities who have no family or are far away from their relatives. For them a phone call, an invitation to church or dinner, or a secret-Santa gift would be greatly appreciated. It's also a wonderful way to invite celebration into their lives while at the same time expressing our gratitude for the incredible gift of Christ in ours. Christ is the real gift that keeps on giving.

Questions for Reflection and Discussion

> *How will you show your gratitude (every day) for the gift of Jesus in your life?*

> *Reflect on an event or person in your life that turned out to be more important than you initially thought.*

Related Journey of Faith Lesson

Q4, "Jesus Christ"

Themes

Christmas, Savior
    Q4, "Who Is Jesus Christ"
    C5, "The Sacrament of the Eucharist"
    C14, "The Dignity of Life"
Commitment
    C4, "The Sacrament of Confirmation"
    C8, "The Sacrament of Matrimony"
    C9, "The Sacrament of Holy Orders"
    C10, "The People of God"
    C13, "Christian Moral Living"
    C16, "Social Justice"

Mary, Mother of God, January 1, Year B

READING 1, NUMBERS 6:22–27

The LORD said to Moses: "Speak to Aaron and his sons and tell them: This is how you shall bless the Israelites. Say to them: The LORD bless you and keep you! The LORD let his face shine upon you, and be gracious to you! The LORD look upon you kindly and give you peace! So shall they invoke my name upon the Israelites, and I will bless them."

PSALM 67:2–3, 5, 6, 8

READING 2, GALATIANS 4:4–7

Brothers and sisters: When the fullness of time had come, God sent his Son, born of a woman, born under the law, to ransom those under the law, so that we might receive adoption as sons. As proof that you are sons, God sent the Spirit of his Son into our hearts, crying out, "Abba, Father!" So you are no longer a slave but a son, and if a son then also an heir, through God.

GOSPEL, LUKE 2:16–21

The shepherds went in haste to Bethlehem and found Mary and Joseph, and the infant lying in the manger. When they saw this, they made known the message that had been told them about this child. All who heard it were amazed by what had been told them by the shepherds. And Mary kept all these things, reflecting on them in her heart. Then the shepherds returned, glorifying and praising God or all they had heard and seen, just as it had been told to them. When eight days were completed for his circumcision, he was named Jesus, the name given him by the angel before he was conceived in the womb.

God-Bearer

Many Catholics are surprised to learn that Mary is mentioned only a handful of times in the New Testament, and not always by name. Yet in the history of the Church, Mary occupies a place of honor as the woman who said yes to God and bore his Son. At the foot of the cross, Jesus gives her over to the care of the beloved disciple and tells John, "Behold, your mother" (John 19:27). When he did that, Mary became the Mother of the whole Church and is revered today under many names, including: Queen of Heaven, Queen of Peace, Immaculate Conception, Undoer of Knots, and many others. It is fitting that we should turn to Mary during the Christmas season and recognize that no human being was closer to Jesus. Mary carried him in her womb, she held the human and divine Christ in her arms. When she kissed his face, she kissed God.

Our readings today tell the story of God's favor on human beings in a few short passages. The Book of Numbers recounts the blessing that God gives to the people when they wander in the desert. Each pair of elements in this prayer enriches the other. To bless someone is to keep him or her safe. It relates the desire to sustain people in life and walk with them in times of trial. When God is gracious to us, his divine grace flows to everyone. Finally, the lifting of your countenance (facial expression) allows others to see you as you are. Those who hide their eyes don't want you to know what's going on with them. God wants us to see him, and when we do, we will be filled with peace. Such is God, who created us in love and who, when we seemed too far away to ever return, sent his Son to the world through Mary to show us the road back.

Kept in Her Heart

In this story of Jesus' birth from Luke's Gospel, God's gracious blessing was meant not only for the powerful, but also for the marginalized. Very few were in a lower class than the shepherds who kept the lambs for sacrifice, yet these were the first recipients of the Good News of peace on earth. They were the first to see Mary, Joseph, and the Baby in a manger. The lowly circumstances of Jesus' birth didn't bother Mary or the shepherds. They told her what the angels announced. A Savior was born, and his coming means peace for the world. Mary reflected on those words, keeping them close to her heart. I'm sure she wondered about the fullness of what they meant, but her immediate concern was the Child, and she tended to his needs before her own, calling him Jesus ("God saves").

In between the two readings, Galatians shows us who we are as a result of God's blessing to the world. We are no longer slaves but children; no longer strangers to God but beloved sons and daughters who cry out to the Father as our own. We are also heirs with Christ to the kingdom, brothers and sisters to the one who is our Master. And Mary is our Mother as well.

Good News for All of Us

The New Year is a time of hopes, dreams, and a new start. We make resolutions, light candles in the dark, and look eagerly for the first signs of spring. This Marian feast reminds us that God sent salvation, not because of anything we did but because he loved us. God didn't choose an important person to give birth to Jesus; he chose a fourteen-year-old peasant. He didn't announce the Good News to a king first, but to shepherds who wouldn't be last for the first time in their lives. From blessing to fulfillment, God has lifted his face to us and given us peace through Christ and a Mother who eagerly awaits us in heaven.

Questions for Reflection and Discussion

> *In your resolutions for the New Year, consider how you might get closer to God.*

> *Mary was the theotokos (Greek for "God-bearer"). How can we carry God into the world?*

Related Journey of Faith Lesson

Q14, "Mary"

Themes

Mary
    C10, "The People of God"
    Q4, "Who Is Jesus Christ?"
Parenthood
    C8, "The Sacrament of Matrimony"
    C14, "The Dignity of Life"
Shepherd
    C9, "The Sacrament of Holy Orders"
    C16, "Social Justice"

READING 1 (ABC), MALACHI 3:1–4

Thus says the Lord GOD: Lo, I am sending my messenger to prepare the way before me; And suddenly there will come to the temple the LORD whom you seek, And the messenger of the covenant whom you desire. Yes, he is coming, says the LORD of hosts. But who will endure the day of his coming? And who can stand when he appears? For he is like the refiner's fire, or like the fuller's lye. He will sit refining and purifying silver, and he will purify the sons of Levi, Refining them like gold or like silver that they may offer due sacrifice to the LORD. Then the sacrifice of Judah and Jerusalem will please the LORD, as in the days of old, as in years gone by.

PSALM 24:7, 8, 9, 10

READING 2 (ABC), HEBREWS 2:14–18

Since the children share in blood and flesh, Jesus likewise shared in them, that through death he might destroy the one who has the power of death, that is, the Devil, and free those who through fear of death had been subject to slavery all their life. Surely he did not help angels but rather the descendants of Abraham; therefore, he had to become like his brothers and sisters in every way, that he might be a merciful and faithful high priest before God to expiate the sins of the people. Because he himself was tested through what he suffered, he is able to help those who are being tested.

GOSPEL (ABC), LUKE 2:22–40

When the days were completed for their purification according to the law of Moses, Mary and Joseph took Jesus up to Jerusalem to present him to the Lord, just as it is written in the law of the Lord, *Every male that opens the womb shall be consecrated to the Lord*, and to offer the sacrifice of *a pair of turtledoves or two young pigeons*, in accordance with the dictate in the law of the Lord. Now there was a man in Jerusalem whose name was Simeon. This man was righteous and devout, awaiting the consolation of Israel, and the Holy Spirit was upon him. It had been revealed to him by the Holy Spirit that he should not see death before he had seen the Christ of the Lord. He came in the Spirit into the temple; and when the parents brought in the child Jesus to perform the custom of the law in regard to him, he took him into his arms and blessed God, saying: "Now, Master, you may let your servant go in peace, according to your word, for my eyes have seen your salvation, which you prepared in the sight of all the peoples: a light for revelation to the Gentiles, and glory for your people Israel."

The child's father and mother were amazed at what was said about him; and Simeon blessed them and said to Mary his mother, "Behold, this child is destined for the fall and rise of many in Israel, and to be a sign that will be contradicted and you yourself a sword will pierce so that the thoughts of many hearts may be revealed." There was also a prophetess, Anna, the daughter of Phanuel, of the tribe of Asher. She was advanced in years, having lived seven years with her husband after her marriage, and then as a widow until she was eighty-four. She never left the temple, but worshiped night and day with fasting and prayer. And coming forward at that very time, she gave thanks to God and spoke about the child to all who were awaiting the redemption of Jerusalem. When they had fulfilled all the prescriptions of the law of the Lord, they returned to Galilee, to their own town of Nazareth. The child grew and became strong, filled with wisdom; and the favor of God was upon him.

Presented to God and the World

Jewish law had a sense that, while a few people could visit a newborn at a time, the world would have to wait until the baby was presented. Today's Gospel combines two Jewish rituals into one celebration. The first is the purification of Mary. Women waited forty days after the birth of a son to be sure that they were not still bleeding (a state which would make them impure). In addition, the firstborn son is presented to a priest in the temple at least thirty days after his birth to give the customary offering (typically five shekels) by which the child is "redeemed." God is thus honored and the child is given back to his family. Luke's story marks the first public appearance of the family after the birth. On this occasion, the appearance of Jesus brings an old holy man and an elderly prophetic woman unimagined joy.

A Prophetic Witness

In the Christian Scriptures, the last book before the New Testament is Malachi ("my messenger"). It is Malachi who tells us that the prophet Elijah will appear before the day the Lord comes. And we might remember that John the Baptist appears in an appearance similar to that of Elijah. John also ate what Elijah was known to eat. Malachi speaks of the messenger who will prepare the way (see Isaiah 40), and then says clearly that the Lord "whom you seek" will suddenly come to the temple. The rest of Malachi's prophecy indicates that the coming of the Lord will include purification of the descendants of Levi, the priesthood of God. To describe this purification as a "refiner's fire" can't have been an entirely comforting image. Certainly, it would mean the fall of many and the raising up of others. No doubt Simeon remembered these words when he saw Jesus and his Mother in the Temple.

Both Simeon and Anna spoke of Jesus to those who heard them. Simeon declared to Mary and Joseph that the Child was a light to the Gentiles and that he would be opposed because he would reveal the hidden thoughts of many. Mary would remember those words for a long time to come. It was Anna's task to speak about the Child to all who were seeking salvation and redemption. Like prophets before her, she carried the word out to the world and encouraged their faithful obedience to God.

One Like Us

The Letter to the Hebrews continues to emphasize an important understanding: Jesus took flesh and blood and was made like us so that he might free us from the fear of death. The last line is powerful: "Because he himself was tested through what he suffered, he is able to help those who are being tested" (Hebrews 2:18). As Christians, our faith tells us that death is not the end. The Letter to the Hebrews reminds us that the devil uses the fear of death to lure us away from God, but Jesus conquered death so we don't have to be afraid anymore.

Good News for All of Us

Malachi, Simeon, Anna, and Mary each give us a model for how to think and behave today. Malachi reminds us to trust in the promise of God who has come into the world and will come again and who will purify us that we might see him if we are open to it. Simeon and Anna, our examples of patient hope and joyful proclamation, wait for the Lord's coming and proclaim it to the world. Mary is, of course, a symbol of obedience to God's will and thoughtful and prayerful reflection in troubled times. God has given us these guides as faithful companions on our way.

Questions for Reflection and Discussion

> What are some of the ways in which our fear of death, growing old, being poor, or just being human can tempt us away from the will of God?

> What life questions or "God answers" do you ponder in your heart?

Related Journey of Faith Lesson

C2, "The Sacraments: An Introduction"

Themes

Incarnation
    C2, "The Sacraments: An Introduction"
    C3, "The Sacrament of Baptism"
    C5, "The Eucharist"
    Q4, "Who Is Jesus Christ?"
Mary
    C8, "The Sacrament of Matrimony"
Prophecy
    C4, "The Sacrament of Confirmation"

St. Joseph, Husband of Mary, March 19

READING 1 (ABC), 2 SAMUEL 7:4–5A, 12–14A, 16

The LORD spoke to Nathan and said: "Go, tell my servant David, 'When your time comes and you rest with your ancestors, I will raise up your heir after you, sprung from your loins, and I will make his kingdom firm. It is he who shall build a house for my name. And I will make his royal throne firm forever. I will be a father to him, and he shall be a son to me. Your house and your kingdom shall endure forever before me; your throne shall stand firm forever.'"

PSALM 89:2–3, 4–5, 27, 29

READING 2 (ABC), ROMANS 4:13, 16–18, 22

Brothers and sisters: It was not through the law that the promise was made to Abraham and his descendants that he would inherit the world, but through the righteousness that comes from faith. For this reason, it depends on faith, that it may be a gift, and the promise may be guaranteed to all his descendants, not to those who only adhere to the law but to those who follow the faith of Abraham, who is the father of all of us, as it is written, *I have made you father of many nations.* He is our father in the sight of God, in whom he believed, who gives life to the dead and calls into being what does not exist. He believed, hoping against hope, that he would become *the father of many nations,* according to what was said, *Thus shall your descendants be.* That is why *it was credited to him as righteousness.*

GOSPEL, MATTHEW 1:16, 18–21, 24A

Jacob was the father of Joseph, the husband of Mary. Of her was born Jesus who is called the Christ. Now this is how the birth of Jesus Christ came about. When his mother Mary was betrothed to Joseph, but before they lived together, she was found with child through the Holy Spirit. Joseph her husband, since he was a righteous man, yet unwilling to expose her to shame, decided to divorce her quietly. Such was his intention when, behold, the angel of the Lord appeared to him in a dream and said, "Joseph, son of David, do not be afraid to take Mary your wife into your home. For it is through the Holy Spirit that this child has been conceived in her. She will bear a son and you are to name him Jesus, because he will save his people from their sins." When Joseph awoke, he did as the angel of the Lord had commanded him and took his wife into his home.

Faith in God's Future

Most of us like to be in control of our lives. We want to know what is happening and we like to think we have control over the future. Sometimes we may wish to control others in our family or at work. Such control can sometimes turn into tyranny and demand. Joseph, whose appearance in the Gospels is limited to a few stories in the Gospel of Matthew, is our best example of someone who submits to God's control of his life and attempts to follow it to the best of his ability. If we were to read all of the stories where Joseph is mentioned by name, we would learn that each one starts with him being awakened by an angel (Matthew 1:20; 2:13, 19). But we would also note that he was exceptionally attuned to God's command and obeyed it instantly. We often hold Mary up as the best example of obedience. But we could also look to Joseph, who heard God's messengers in his sleep and rose immediately to carry out their wishes, even if it wasn't what he originally planned. His faith in God embraced faith in the future God saw for him, Mary, and Jesus—a faith that was willing to let go of the need to control all things.

Faith in God's Promise

For Jews and Christians both, the stories of God's promise to make Abraham's descendants as numerous as the stars and to establish the house and kingdom of David, forever shaped how we thought of the promised Messiah and the reign of God at the end of time. For Jews, the triple promise of descendants, land, and blessings—which God gave to Abraham as well as the promise of a Messiah—is still coming into its fullness. For Christians, Jesus, heir of Abraham and Son of David as well as God's own Son, is the fulfillment of that promise whose fullness has not yet been realized.

In the reading from Samuel, God establishes the relationship he will have with David's descendants: "I will be a father to him, and he shall be a son to me." One of the reasons Jesus talks about God as Father is to claim his Davidic ancestry. Of course, Jesus will go on to tell his followers that they also are children of God. In times of trouble and of sinfulness, David and his descendants held on to faith that God's promise would not fail.

In the Letter to the Romans, Paul argues that Gentile Christians are heirs of Abraham not because they followed the law or were blood descendants. Rather, they were heirs by faith who believed that the promises of God made to a people long before they were born were brought to fulfillment by Jesus Christ. God's promises are fruitful no matter when and to whom they are given.

Good News for All of Us

While God may have revealed his plans to individuals, the fulfillment of those plans involved the whole community. We listen to God together; we await his coming as a community; and we recognize that together our faith is stronger than it is individually. When we come together to worship at Mass, we declare with one voice, "I believe..." There are times in our lives when we're held up by our neighbors standing next to us uttering those same words, sometimes giving voice for us when we're filled with doubt. We also know from the sacrifice of Christ that God's love for us has never failed. Let's hold fast to the faith Joseph showed and trust that we have a place in God's future.

Questions for Reflection and Discussion

➤ *What did you learn of faith from your family? Who was the primary example of faith?*

➤ *What is the place of faith in our society? How does/should it influence our choices and priorities?*

Related Journey of Faith Lesson

E1, "Election: Saying Yes to Jesus"

Themes

Faith
    E1, "Election: Saying Yes to Jesus"
    E3, "The Creed"
Family
    E7, "The Meaning of Holy Week"
    E8, "Easter Vigil Retreat"
Future
    E3, "Scrutinies: Looking Within"
    E5, "The Way of the Cross"

READING 1 (ABC), ISAIAH 7:10–14; 8:10

The LORD spoke to Ahaz, saying: Ask for a sign from the LORD, your God; let it be deep as the nether world, or high as the sky! But Ahaz answered, "I will not ask! I will not tempt the LORD!" Then Isaiah said: Listen, O house of David! Is it not enough for you to weary people, must you also weary my God? Therefore the Lord himself will give you this sign: the virgin shall be with child, and bear a son, and shall name him Emmanuel, which means "God is with us!"

PSALM 40:7–8A, 8B–9, 10, 11

READING 2 (ABC), HEBREWS 10:4–10

Brothers and sisters: It is impossible that the blood of bulls and goats take away sins. For this reason, when Christ came into the world, he said: "Sacrifice and offering you did not desire, but a body you prepared for me; in holocausts and sin offerings you took no delight. Then I said, 'As is written of me in the scroll, behold, I come to do your will, O God.'" First he says, "Sacrifices and offerings, holocausts and sin offerings, you neither desired nor delighted in." These are offered according to the law. Then he says, "Behold, I come to do your will." He takes away the first to establish the second. By this "will," we have been consecrated through the offering of the Body of Jesus Christ once for all.

GOSPEL (ABC), LUKE 1:26–38

The angel Gabriel was sent from God to a town of Galilee called Nazareth, to a virgin betrothed to a man named Joseph, of the house of David, and the virgin's name was Mary. And coming to her, he said, "Hail, full of grace! The Lord is with you." But she was greatly troubled at what was said and pondered what sort of greeting this might be. Then the angel said to her, "Do not be afraid, Mary, for you have found favor with God. Behold, you will conceive in your womb and bear a son, and you shall name him Jesus. He will be great and will be called Son of the Most High, and the Lord God will give him the throne of David his father, and he will rule over the house of Jacob forever, and of his Kingdom there will be no end." But Mary said to the angel, "How can this be, since I have no relations with a man?" And the angel said to her in reply, "The Holy Spirit will come upon you, and the power of the Most High will overshadow you. Therefore the child to be born will be called holy, the Son of God. And behold, Elizabeth, your relative, has also conceived a son in her old age, and this is the sixth month for her who was called barren; for nothing will be impossible for God." Mary said, "Behold, I am the handmaid of the Lord. May it be done to me according to your word." Then the angel departed from her.

An Offering of the Body

When the author of the Letter to the Hebrews reflected on the extraordinary impact of the Incarnation, the writer taught us to see Jesus as our great High Priest whose sacrifice on the cross opened the door to our reconciliation with God. Jesus freely submitted himself to the will of God, echoing Psalm 40:9 when he says, "Behold, I come to do your will, O God." In this passage, the author adds that it is the offering of the body of Jesus by which we have been consecrated (or sanctified).

The offering of the body is another way of talking about giving the whole self to God. In Deuteronomy, Moses tells us we are to love God with all our hearts, all our souls, and all our strength (Deuteronomy 6:5). Jesus made it clear that we give everything to the Lord and tell him wholeheartedly that we also have come to do his will.

The story of the annunciation presents us with another look at someone who willingly made an offering of her body to God. Mary understood that she was the servant of God, and answered the angel much the same way that Hebrews describes: "Here I am...." She then invites God to work his will through her. To give one's whole self to God—mind, heart, soul, body—is to say to God: "All you have given me is a gift; I freely give it back to you." It's an invitation for God's kingdom to come. Mary offers herself as an instrument of God's will.

God's Sign

In Isaiah's prophecy, King Ahaz is facing an attack on Jerusalem from two allied armies. Isaiah tells Ahaz not to fear because both Aram and Ephraim will be destroyed in a short time. God want to reassure Ahaz the prophecy is true, but Ahaz refuses to ask for a sign because he thinks Egypt will protect him from the invaders. Thus, he refuses to give his total confidence to God.

God tells Ahaz what to look for anyway. When the Jewish scribes translated the Hebrew Scriptures into Greek (the Septuagint, 200 BC), they chose the Greek word *Parthenos* (virgin) as the Greek word that best conveyed the meaning of the Hebrew word *almah* (young woman). This is the translation widely used at the time of Jesus and by the Gospel writers. The young woman shall bear a son, Isaiah says, and he shall be named Emmanuel. Literally translated, it means "with us is God." We shorten it to "God with us," and we see in Isaiah's prophecy the coming of the Messiah who will give himself for the salvation of the world.

Good News for All of Us

What are we willing to do for God? God calls us every day to serve him and use the gifts we have been given for his greater glory. Jesus told us he came that we might have life and have it abundantly (John 10:10). That life is all around us. We see it in the cycles of the seasons and in the hundreds of little deaths in our lives that give way to new life. That is the paschal mystery—signaled by our baptism when we are told that we die with Christ so we might rise with him to a new life. But perhaps this sign is particularly evident in pregnancy and childbirth. Every mother will bear witness that we don't think about the miracle of birth 24/7. Sometimes the back or the feet hurt, and we wonder if this child will ever come. But every now and then, the child kicks. That's amazing. And when that child is born, we know why we offered our bodies for this miracle. It's a sign of God's gift of life to us.

Questions for Reflection and Discussion

> *What are the signs—large and small—that God has been present in your life?*

> *How can you give your whole self to God on a daily basis?*

Related Journey of Faith Lesson

E1, "Election: Saying Yes to Jesus"

Themes

Annunciation, Discipleship, Mary
    E2, "Living Lent"
Redemption
    E1, "Election: Saying Yes to Jesus"
    E3, "Scrutinies: Looking Within"
    E5, "The Way of the Cross"
    E7, "The Meaning of Holy Week"

READING 1, EXODUS 17:3–7

In those days, in their thirst for water, the people grumbled against Moses, saying, "Why did you ever make us leave Egypt? Was it just to have us die here of thirst with our children and our livestock?" So Moses cried out to the LORD, "What shall I do with [these] people? [A] little more and they will stone me!" The LORD answered Moses, "Go over there in front of the people, along with some of the elders of Israel, holding in your hand, as you go, the staff with which you struck the river. I will be standing there in front of you on the rock in Horeb. Strike the rock, and the water will flow from it for the people to drink." This Moses did, in the presence of the elders of Israel. The place was called Massah and Meribah, because the Israelites quarreled there and tested the LORD, saying, "Is the LORD in our midst or not?"

PSALM 95:1–2, 6–7, 8–9

READING 2, ROMANS 5:1–2, 5–8

Brothers and sisters: Since we have been justified by faith, we have peace with God through our Lord Jesus Christ, through whom we have gained access by faith to this grace in which we stand, and we boast in hope of the glory of God. And hope does not disappoint, because the love of God has been poured out into our hearts through the Holy Spirit who has been given to us. For Christ, while we were still helpless, died at the appointed time for the ungodly. Indeed, only with difficulty does one die for a just person, though perhaps for a good person one might even find courage to die. But God proves his love for us in that while we were still sinners Christ died for us.

GOSPEL, LUKE 4:1–13

Filled with the Holy Spirit, Jesus returned from the Jordan and was led by the Spirit into the desert for forty days, to be tempted by the devil. He ate nothing during those days, and when they were over he was hungry. The devil said to him, "If you are the Son of God, command this stone to become bread." Jesus answered him, "It is written, *One does not live on bread alone.*" Then he took him up and showed him all the kingdoms of the world in a single instant. The devil said to him, "I shall give to you all this power and glory; for it has been handed over to me, and I may give it to whomever I wish. All this will be yours, if you worship me." Jesus said to him in reply, "It is written: *You shall worship the Lord, your God, and him alone shall you serve.*" Then he led him to Jerusalem, made him stand on the parapet of the Temple, and said to him, "If you are the Son of God, throw yourself down from here, for it is written: *He will command his angels concerning you, to guard you,* and: *With their hands they will support you, lest you dash your foot against a stone.*" Jesus said to him in reply, "It also says, *You shall not put the Lord, your God, to the test.*" When the devil had finished every temptation, he departed from him for a time.

Waters of Life

Whenever I teach a baptism class, we talk at length about the significance of water in Judeo-Christian history and in our own lives. The Spirit of God hovered over the waters at creation (Genesis 1:2), and forty days and nights of rain flooded the earth in the time of Noah (Genesis 7:4). The Israelites passed through the waters of the Red Sea (see Exodus 14:21 and following verses), and Jesus was baptized in the waters of the Jordan (Matthew 3:13). We need water to live and know that water can be a source of death for us.

In the first reading, the lack of water makes the Israelites fear death. They begin to doubt that they will make it through the wilderness and regret leaving Egypt (it won't be the first time such doubts creep in). When they complain to Moses, Moses complains to God. It's hard to trust that God will give you everything you need when you are hot and thirsty. The miraculous water from the hard rock reminds the Israelites that they must depend on God for everything. The responsorial psalm reminds us not to harden our hearts in difficult times. It's not a bad lesson for any of us.

Living Water

The ability to draw water from a deep well brings a Samaritan woman and Jesus to the same spot in the Gospel. Jews and Samaritans were different branches of the same ancestor. Jews looked down on Samaritans and did not consider them full members of Judaism. In any case, the Samaritan woman is surprised that Jesus would even speak to her and ask for a drink. Jews and Samaritans would never have taken a drink from the same bucket. But Jesus tells her if she just asks, he would give her living water. She doesn't understand at first, but after his description, she does ask: "Give me this water." Afterward, a remarkable exchange happens. The woman reveals her true self to Jesus as one who knows she is in an irregular relationship. She recognizes him as a prophet and confesses her belief in the coming Messiah. Jesus then reveals his true self as the Messiah who is to come. This is the living water for which she longed, and she leaves her water jar to proclaim the encounter in the village.

The last part of the Gospel alternates two scenes. The woman preaches to the villagers and the disciples return and question Jesus about talking to a woman (they are more surprised about that than about the fact she is a Samaritan). The woman's words are so powerful that the villagers go in search of Jesus. In the meantime, Jesus tells the disciples, "I sent you to reap that for which you did not labor." We can imagine the disciples looking up and seeing the crowd coming to Jesus ready for the harvesting, all because a Samaritan woman was filled with the living water that Jesus gave.

Good News for All of Us

How do we encounter the living water of God today? The reading from Romans gives us a clue. God pours out his love (like water) on us. The evidence is abundant in the people who love us and whom we love, in the beauty of creation, and in our own understanding that Jesus died for us even though we were (and are) sinners. In baptism we pour water on the heads of infants and adults. The symbol is unmistakable. We are being bathed in living water, which will take us home to God.

Questions for Reflection and Discussion

> *Who has reminded you of God's love and been a source of "life-giving water" to you?*

> *Is there someone for whom you would sacrifice your life? Can you imagine doing that for a stranger?*

Related Journey of Faith Lesson

E4, "The Creed"

Themes

Hope
    E2, "Living Lent"
Love
    E1, "Election: Saying Yes to Jesus"
Water
    E3, "Scrutinies: Looking Within"

Fourth Sunday of Lent, Year A

READING 1, 1 SAMUEL 16:1B, 6–7, 10–13A

The Lord said to Samuel: "Fill your horn with oil, and be on your way. I am sending you to Jesse of Bethlehem, for I have chosen my king from among his sons." As Jesse and his sons came to the sacrifice, Samuel looked at Eliab and thought, "Surely the Lord's anointed is here before him." But the Lord said to Samuel: "Do not judge from his appearance or from his lofty stature, because I have rejected him. Not as man sees does God see, because man sees the appearance but the Lord looks into the heart." In the same way Jesse presented seven sons before Samuel, but Samuel said to Jesse, "The Lord has not chosen any one of these." Then Samuel asked Jesse, "Are these all the sons you have?" Jesse replied, "There is still the youngest, who is tending the sheep." Samuel said to Jesse, "Send for him; we will not begin the sacrificial banquet until he arrives here." Jesse sent and had the young man brought to them. He was ruddy, a youth handsome to behold and making a splendid appearance. The Lord said, "There—anoint him, for this is the one!" Then Samuel, with the horn of oil in hand, anointed David in the presence of his brothers; and from that day on, the spirit of the Lord rushed upon David.

PSALM 23:1–3A, 3B–4, 5, 6

READING 2, EPHESIANS 5:8–14

Brothers and sisters: You were once darkness, but now you are light in the Lord. Live as children of light, for light produces every kind of goodness and righteousness and truth. Try to learn what is pleasing to the Lord. Take no part in the fruitless works of darkness; rather expose them, for it is shameful even to mention the things done by them in secret; but everything exposed by the light becomes visible, for everything that becomes visible is light. Therefore, it says: Awake, O sleeper, and arise from the dead, and Christ will give you light."

GOSPEL, JOHN 9:1–41

As Jesus passed by he saw a man blind from birth. His disciples asked him, "Rabbi, who sinned, this man or his parents, that he was born blind?" Jesus answered, "Neither he nor his parents sinned; it is so that the works of God might be made visible through him. We have to do the works of the one who sent me while it is day. Night is coming when no one can work. While I am in the world, I am the light of the world." When he had said this, he spat on the ground and made clay with the saliva, and smeared the clay on his eyes, and said to him, "Go wash in the Pool of Siloam" (which means "Sent"). So he went and washed, and came back able to see.

His neighbors and those who had seen him earlier as a beggar said, "Isn't this the one who used to sit and beg?" Some said, "It is," but others said, "No, he just looks like him." He said, "I am." So they said to him, "How were your eyes opened?" He replied, "The man called Jesus made clay and anointed my eyes and told me, 'Go to Siloam and wash.' So I went there and washed and was able to see." And they said to him, "Where is he?" He said, "I don't know."

They brought the one who was once blind to the Pharisees. Now Jesus had made clay and opened his eyes on a sabbath. So then the Pharisees also asked him how he was able to see. He said to them, "He put clay on my eyes, and I washed, and now I can see." So some of the Pharisees said, "This man is not from God, because he does not keep the sabbath." But others said, "How can a sinful man do such signs?" And there was a division among them. So they said to the blind man again, "What do you have to say about him, since he opened your eyes?" He said, "He is a prophet." Now the Jews did not believe that he had been blind and gained his sight until they summoned the parents of the one who had gained his sight. They asked them, "Is this your son, who you say was born blind? How does he now see?" His parents answered and said, "We know that this is our son and that he was born blind. We do not know how he sees now, nor do we know who opened his eyes. Ask him, he is of age; he can speak for himself." His parents said this because they were afraid of the Jews, for the Jews had already agreed that if anyone acknowledged him as the Christ, he would be expelled from the synagogue. For this reason his parents said, "He is of age; question him."

So a second time they called the man who had been blind and said to him, "Give God the praise! We know that this man is a sinner." He replied, "If he is a sinner, I do not know. One thing I do know is that I was blind and now I see." So they said to him, "What did he do to you? How did he open your eyes?" He answered them, "I told you already and you did not listen. Why do you want to hear it again? Do you want to become his disciples, too?" They ridiculed him and said, "You are that man's disciple; we are disciples of Moses! We know that God spoke to Moses, but we do not know where this one is from." The man answered and said to them, "This is what is so amazing, that you do not know where he is from, yet he opened my eyes. We know that God does not listen to sinners, but if one is devout and does his will, he listens to him. It is unheard of that anyone ever opened the eyes of a person born blind. If this man were not from God, he would not be able to do anything." They answered and said to him, "You were born totally in sin, and are you trying to teach us?" Then they threw him out.

When Jesus heard that they had thrown him out, he found him and said, "Do you believe in the Son of Man?" He answered and said, "Who is he, sir, that I may believe in him?" Jesus said to him, "You have seen him, and the one speaking with you is he." He said, "I do believe, Lord," and he worshiped him. Then Jesus said, "I came into this world for judgment, so that those who do not see might see, and those who do see might become blind."

Some of the Pharisees who were with him heard this and said to him, "Surely we are not also blind, are we?" Jesus said to them, "If you were blind, you would have no sin; but now you are saying, 'We see,' so your sin remains.

Seeing and Believing

In the Gospels, the healing of a blind person means more than enabling a person to see physically. It's also a metaphor for seeing who Jesus is and growing in faith. Today's readings present different examples of seeing. Samuel the prophet thinks he knows which of Jesse's sons God has chosen for king just by looking at them. God is quick to point out his mistake and even tells Samuel that God doesn't look at outward appearance. Rather, God looks into a person's heart. The chosen king is a mere boy, the shepherd of his father's sheep and the youngest of sons (a theme in the Old Testament). After the anointing, the Spirit of God comes on David and stays forever.

John's Gospel of the blind man shows the gradual growth of faith in the man who was healed and the growing stubbornness of the Pharisees who can see, but don't know what they are looking at. Where Jesus was Living Water last week, he is the Light of the World this week, and the curing of the man blind from birth is the living sign of that reality. As the man tells his story to the Pharisees and others, we witness to his growth. First he says: "The man called Jesus...made clay and anointed my eyes" (9:11). The second time, he calls Jesus a prophet (9:17). When he speaks to Jesus the third time, he calls Jesus "Lord" and worships him (9:38). The man born blind sees Jesus with the eyes of faith, a call for us to do the same.

By contrast, the Pharisees think they see everything and insist the man is wrong. Jesus can't be from God because he healed on the Sabbath (9:16). The second time they call Jesus a sinner to the man's face (9:23). When the man asks if they also want to become Jesus' disciples, they lash out. As disciples of Moses, they felt they had the upper hand: "We do not know where [he] is from!" (9:29). The third time, they run out of names to call Jesus and turn their anger on the man born blind, throwing him out of the Temple. Later the lesson is driven home when the Pharisees exclaim, "Surely we are not...blind..." (9:40). Jesus can only shake his head. They insist their human sight is greater than God's. They don't remember Samuel's teaching and thus are blind to Jesus' true identity.

Fourth Sunday of Lent, Year A

Good News for All of Us

Today, we are called to take these lessons to heart. We can't look only on appearances. We must realize that God's Spirit can fall on whomever God wills, whether we think they are worthy or not. The Bible is filled with stories of overlooked and marginalized people (like youngest sons or the poor) who are given the favor of God's attention to the surprise of those in charge. The Gospel also tells us that those in authority and the laws and policies of institutions don't always encourage us to see God working in other people and situations. Our refusal to see this is a kind of darkness. The Letter to the Ephesians tells us that we are now light in the Lord. The fruit of that light is an ability to see what is good and right in the Lord no matter where it appears. Paul urges us to look for that—to live as children of the light. We all have blind spots. Our faith makes us confident that God can heal our blindness and help us see him everywhere in the world.

Questions for Reflection and Discussion

➤ *Where do you make judgments about others based on assumptions or appearances? Have you ever been surprised when those judgments turned out to be false?*

➤ *Create a simple prayer that asks Jesus to heal your blind spots and share it with another person.*

Related *Journey of Faith* Lesson

E5, "The Way of the Cross"

Themes

Blindness
    E1, "Election: Saying Yes to Jesus"
Conversion
    E3, "Scrutinies: Looking Within"
Light
    E2, "Living Lent"

Fifth Sunday of Lent, Year A

READING 1, EZEKIEL 37:12–14

Thus says the Lord God: O my people, I will open your graves and have you rise from them, and bring you back to the land of Israel. Then you shall know that I am the Lord, when I open your graves and have you rise from them, O my people! I will put my spirit in you that you may live, and I will settle you upon your land; thus you shall know that I am the Lord. I have promised, and I will do it, says the Lord.

PSALM 130:1–2, 3–4, 5–6, 7–8

READING 2, ROMANS 8:8–11

Brothers and sisters: Those who are in the flesh cannot please God. But you are not in the flesh; on the contrary, you are in the spirit, if only the Spirit of God dwells in you. Whoever does not have the Spirit of Christ does not belong to him. But if Christ is in you, although the body is dead because of sin, the spirit is alive because of righteousness. If the Spirit of the one who raised Jesus from the dead dwells in you, the one who raised Christ from the dead will give life to your mortal bodies also, through his Spirit dwelling in you.

GOSPEL, JOHN 11:1–45

Now a man was ill, Lazarus from Bethany, the village of Mary and her sister Martha. Mary was the one who had anointed the Lord with perfumed oil and dried his feet with her hair; it was her brother Lazarus who was ill. So the sisters sent word to him saying, "Master, the one you love is ill." When Jesus heard this he said, "This illness is not to end in death, but is for the glory of God, that the Son of God may be glorified through it." Now Jesus loved Martha and her sister and Lazarus. So when he heard that he was ill, he remained for two days in the place where he was. Then after this he said to his disciples, "Let us go back to Judea." The disciples said to him, "Rabbi, the Jews were just trying to stone you, and you want to go back there?"

Jesus answered, "Are there not twelve hours in a day? If one walks during the day, he does not stumble, because he sees the light of this world. But if one walks at night, he stumbles, because the light is not in him." He said this, and then told them,

"Our friend Lazarus is asleep, but I am going to awaken him." So the disciples said to him, "Master, if he is asleep, he will be saved." But Jesus was talking about his death, while they thought that he meant ordinary sleep. So then Jesus said to them clearly, "Lazarus has died. And I am glad for you that I was not there, that you may believe. Let us go to him." So Thomas, called Didymus, said to his fellow disciples, "Let us also go to die with him."

When Jesus arrived, he found that Lazarus had already been in the tomb for four days. Now Bethany was near Jerusalem, only about two miles away. And many of the Jews had come to Martha and Mary to comfort them about their brother. When Martha heard that Jesus was coming, she went to meet him; but Mary sat at home. Martha said to Jesus, "Lord, if you had been here, my brother would not have died. But even now I know that whatever you ask of God, God will give you." Jesus said to her, "Your brother will rise." Martha said to him, "I know he will rise, in the resurrection on the last day."

Jesus told her, "I am the resurrection and the life; whoever believes in me, even if he dies, will live, and everyone who lives and believes in me will never die. Do you believe this?" She said to him, "Yes, Lord. I have come to believe that you are the Christ, the Son of God, the one who is coming into the world." When she had said this, she went and called her sister Mary secretly, saying, "The teacher is here and is asking for you."

As soon as she heard this, she rose quickly and went to him. For Jesus had not yet come into the village, but was still where Martha had met him. So when the Jews who were with her in the house comforting her saw Mary get up quickly and go out, they followed her, presuming that she was going to the tomb to weep there. When Mary came to where Jesus was and saw him, she fell at his feet and said to him, "Lord, if you had been here, my brother would not have died." When Jesus saw her weeping and the Jews who had come with her weeping, he became perturbed and deeply troubled, and said, "Where have you laid him?" They said to him, "Sir, come and see." And Jesus wept. So the Jews said, "See how he loved him." But some of them said,

"Could not the one who opened the eyes of the blind man have done something so that this man would not have died?"

So Jesus, perturbed again, came to the tomb. It was a cave, and a stone lay across it. Jesus said, "Take away the stone." Martha, the dead man's sister, said to him, "Lord, by now there will be a stench; he has been dead for four days." Jesus said to her, "Did I not tell you that if you believe you will see the glory of God?" So they took away the stone. And Jesus raised his eyes and said, Father, I thank you for hearing me. I know that you always hear me; but because of the crowd here I have said this, that they may believe that you sent me." And when he had said this, He cried out in a loud voice, "Lazarus, come out!"

The dead man came out, tied hand and foot with burial bands, and his face was wrapped in a cloth. So Jesus said to them, "Untie him and let him go."

Now many of the Jews who had come to Mary and seen what he had done began to believe in him.

The Spirit Is Life

A Bible we had when I was growing up had a disturbing picture of Lazarus. Jesus had called Lazarus to come out of the grave but the picture showed Lazarus still bound in his burial cloths with his face covered. I realize that what scared me was that I could not see his face. He didn't look human. Death separated us, and I did not yet understand Jesus' command to untie Lazarus, which was an act of restoration to the community. He who had been dead was now alive among us again and we could see him face to face.

Throughout Scripture, the Spirit of God gives life, wisdom, knowledge, piety, and courage. People who grow in the Spirit, grow in grace before God. When we find ourselves lost and near death physically, mentally, or spiritually, it is the Spirit of God that restores us to life...even from the grave.

Ezekiel gives his prophecy to people who have been in exile and feel dead inside. They have lost their homeland and live under foreign power. The promise that God will bring them back to Israel must have been incredible hope for weary souls. Ezekiel is not far off when he imagines this as a resurrection. God's own Spirit will inhabit the people and they shall live. When the people are restored to their land, they will know that God fulfills his promise.

When Jesus hears that his friend Lazarus died, he proposes going to Bethany of Judea. The disciples are afraid, and rightly so. The Jewish authorities threatened to stone Jesus on his last visit, and the disciples didn't want him to die. Jesus shows the depth of his love when he defies the authorities to return and comfort Mary and Martha. Martha's plaintive cry, "If you had been here, my brother would not have died," is one that might be familiar to us. It's a sign that we felt far away from God and from any miracle he might have done. Mary echoes the question. In the New Testament, we learn "Jesus wept." Compassion leads to the miracle. Jesus wants us to know that physical death is not the end for us. "I am the resurrection and the life," Jesus told Martha. He now makes good on that identity and calls Lazarus out of the grave. In Ezekiel, Israel is restored so that all will know the Lord. In the Gospel, the raising of Lazarus is done so all may believe that God sent Jesus to the world. The miracle had its desired effect since many came to believe in Jesus that day. Life begets life.

You Are in the Spirit

In the epistle, Paul plays on the theme of life and death. He contrasts those who live "in the flesh" and who follow the desires of the flesh with those who live "in the Spirit" and follow the law of God. Paul explains, belief in Christ is necessary to live in the Spirit, since it is Christ who conquers sin and death and dwells in us. Paul's contrast might make us believe that anything in the world is bad. That isn't the case. We recognize that the temptations of the world as well as those that stem from our own desires can lead us away from God. God's grace, through the Spirit, leads us home.

Fifth Sunday of Lent, Year A

Good News for All of Us

We believe that baptism begins to initiate us into life in the Spirit. But just as people had to untie Lazarus to release him, we also must participate in the Spirit's action by following Jesus' example. That might take the form of providing food and clothing for the poor or taking care of the elderly and marginalized. When we share our lives with others in service and love, we manifest the glory of God for all and share God's life.

Questions for Reflection and Discussion

> *What are some things you do to make the lives of others a little fuller?*

> *Has there been a time when you needed to be "untied" in order to come back to life? Who helped you with that?*

Related Journey of Faith Lesson

E6, "The Lord's Prayer"

Themes

Death
    E2, "Living Lent"
Spirit
    E7, "The Meaning of Holy Week"

The Lord's Supper (Holy Thursday), the Easter Triduum

READING 1 (ABC), EXODUS 12:1–8, 11–14

The LORD said to Moses and Aaron in the land of Egypt, "This month shall stand at the head of your calendar; you shall reckon it the first month of the year. Tell the whole community of Israel: On the tenth of this month every one of your families must procure for itself a lamb, one apiece for each household. If a family is too small for a whole lamb, it shall join the nearest household in procuring one and shall share in the lamb in proportion to the number of persons who partake of it. The lamb must be a year-old male and without blemish. You may take it from either the sheep or the goats. You shall keep it until the fourteenth day of this month, and then, with the whole assembly of Israel present, it shall be slaughtered during the evening twilight. They shall take some of its blood and apply it to the two doorposts and the lintel of every house in which they partake of the lamb. That same night they shall eat its roasted flesh with unleavened bread and bitter herbs. "This is how you are to eat it: with your loins girt, sandals on your feet and your staff in hand, you shall eat like those who are in flight. It is the Passover of the LORD. For on this same night I will go through Egypt, striking down every firstborn of the land, both man and beast, and executing judgment on all the gods of Egypt—I, the LORD! But the blood will mark the houses where you are. Seeing the blood, I will pass over you; thus, when I strike the land of Egypt, no destructive blow will come upon you. "This day shall be a memorial feast for you, which all your generations shall celebrate with pilgrimage to the LORD, as a perpetual institution."

PSALM 116:12–13, 15–16BC, 17–18

READING 2 (ABC), 1 CORINTHIANS 11:23–26

Brothers and sisters: I received from the Lord what I also handed on to you, that the Lord Jesus, on the night he was handed over, took bread, and, after he had given thanks, broke it and said, "This is my body that is for you. Do this in remembrance of me." In the same way also the cup, after supper, saying, "This cup is the new covenant in my blood. Do this, as often as you drink it, in remembrance of me." For as often as you eat this bread and drink the cup, you proclaim the death of the Lord until he comes.

GOSPEL (ABC), JOHN 13:1–15

Before the feast of Passover, Jesus knew that his hour had come to pass from this world to the Father. He loved his own in the world and he loved them to the end. The devil had already induced Judas, son of Simon the Iscariot, to hand him over. So, during supper, fully aware that the Father had put everything into his power and that he had come from God and was returning to God, he rose from supper and took off his outer garments. He took a towel and tied it around his waist. Then he poured water into a basin and began to wash the disciples' feet and dry them with the towel around his waist. He came to Simon Peter, who said to him, "Master, are you going to wash my feet?" Jesus answered and said to him, "What I am doing, you do not understand now, but you will understand later." Peter said to him, "You will never wash my feet." Jesus answered him, "Unless I wash you, you will have no inheritance with me." Simon Peter said to him, "Master, then not only my feet, but my hands and head as well." Jesus said to him, "Whoever has bathed has no need except to have his feet washed, for he is clean all over; so you are clean, but not all." For he knew who would betray him; for this reason, he said, "Not all of you are clean." So when he had washed their feet and put his garments back on and reclined at table again, he said to them, "Do you realize what I have done for you? You call me 'teacher' and 'master,' and rightly so, for indeed I am. If I, therefore, the master and teacher, have washed your feet, you ought to wash one another's feet. I have given you a model to follow, so that as I have done for you, you should also do."

Do This in Memory of Me

The evening Mass of the Lord's Supper on Holy Thursday marks the beginning of the sacred Triduum, three days in which we focus on the passion, death, and resurrection of Jesus Christ. These are our high holy days, for the events they remember are at the core of Christian belief. We believe that God came to us out of love, incarnated as Jesus Christ, and died for our sins so that we might be reconciled with him. That act of love alone is breathtaking and so important that we remember it every time we are together as a community at Mass. On Holy Thursday, we begin by remembering that Jesus shared his body with us and gave us an example of service to follow.

The Passover of the Lord

Christianity finds its roots in Judaism. The first reading from Exodus recounts the event of Passover, the last and hardest of the ten plagues in Egypt. Pharaoh was stubborn. God announced his plague and the Israelites were commanded to spread the blood of an unblemished lamb on their doorposts so that the angel of death would pass over their houses as he went about killing the firstborn of every family. In early Christian theology, Paul referred to Jesus as "Christ, our Passover lamb" (in Greek: *pascha,* from which we derive *paschal*), signifying that he understood that Christ destroyed death by his sacrifice. Death no longer has a hold over us.

Sharing More than Bread

Paul's narrative of the Last Supper is the story told at every Eucharist celebration as the bread and wine are consecrated and become the Body and Blood of Christ. The words are powerful and focus us on the actions taking place as the priest, in the person of Christ, stands at a table and does what he did. Someone once pointed out that Da Vinci's painting of the Last Supper only has figures on one side of the table. The other side, the person pointed out, is our place at the table so it is no accident that the words turn from third person (them and their) to second person (you). We are there at the table with Jesus and the disciples. We eat what they ate. And we follow his example.

Servants of the World

John's Gospel doesn't have the same Last Supper narrative that the other three Gospels do. Rather, John narrates a story of service. Jesus takes a basin and washes the disciples' feet. He washes the feet of one who will betray him, one who will deny him, and several who will hide in fear from his death. At the end of this service, he tells them plainly, "I have given you a model to follow, so that as I have done for you, you should also do" (John 13:15). In one action, Jesus forever links receiving the Eucharist with serving those around us, even those we may find unloving or unlovable. He gave his life for us. What can we do for others?

Good News for All of Us

In Scripture, when God remembers his people, God acts. The psalmist is comforted and even joyful when remembering God. Christ told us to remember how he gave us his Body and Blood in bread and wine. The sharing of that meal binds us to one another. If we truly remember it, it will lead us to act in service of one another. Washing feet, giving alms, praying for each other, and loving others as brothers and sisters all are a form of service, which we are all called to do. And we should do it gladly because Christ first loved and served us.

Questions for Reflection and Discussion

> ➤ *Many Christians are eager to serve, but often—like Peter—we aren't comfortable playing the good guest and being served. Why is it important to experience what it is like to be served?*

> ➤ *The Eucharist is the source and summit of our lives. How do you prepare? How can you deepen your preparation?*

Related Journey of Faith Lesson

C5, "The Sacrament of the Eucharist"

Themes

Community
  E4, "The Creed"
  E8, "Easter Vigil Retreat"
Eucharist
  E1, "Election: Saying Yes to Jesus"
  E7, "The Meaning of Holy Week"
Service
  E3, "Scrutinies: Looking Within"

The Lord's Passion (Good Friday), the Easter Triduum

READING 1 (ABC), ISAIAH 52:13—53:12

See, my servant shall prosper, he shall be raised high and greatly exalted. Even as many were amazed at him—so marred was his look beyond human semblance and his appearance beyond that of the sons of man—so shall he startle many nations, because of him kings shall stand speechless; for those who have not been told shall see, those who have not heard shall ponder it.

Who would believe what we have heard? To whom has the arm of the LORD been revealed? He grew up like a sapling before him, like a shoot from the parched earth; there was in him no stately bearing to make us look at him, nor appearance that would attract us to him. He was spurned and avoided by people, a man of suffering, accustomed to infirmity, one of those from whom people hide their faces, spurned, and we held him in no esteem.

Yet it was our infirmities that he bore, our sufferings that he endured, while we thought of him as stricken, as one smitten by God and afflicted. But he was pierced for our offenses, crushed for our sins; upon him was the chastisement that makes us whole, by his stripes we were healed. We had all gone astray like sheep, each following his own way; but the LORD laid upon him the guilt of us all.

Though he was harshly treated, he submitted and opened not his mouth; like a lamb led to the slaughter or a sheep before the shearers, he was silent and opened not his mouth. Oppressed and condemned, he was taken away, and who would have thought any more of his destiny? When he was cut off from the land of the living, and smitten for the sin of his people, a grave was assigned him among the wicked and a burial place with evildoers, though he had done no wrong nor spoken any falsehood. But the LORD was pleased to crush him in infirmity.

If he gives his life as an offering for sin, he shall see his descendants in a long life, and the will of the LORD shall be accomplished through him.

Because of his affliction he shall see the light in fullness of days; through his suffering, my servant shall justify many, and their guilt he shall bear. Therefore I will give him his portion among the great, and he shall divide the spoils with the mighty, because he surrendered himself to death and was counted among the wicked; and he shall take away the sins of many, and win pardon for their offenses.

PSALM 31:2, 6, 12–13, 15–16, 17, 25

READING 2 (ABC), HEBREWS 4:14–16; 5:7–9

Brothers and sisters: Since we have a great high priest who has passed through the heavens, Jesus, the Son of God, let us hold fast to our confession. For we do not have a high priest who is unable to sympathize with our weaknesses, but one who has similarly been tested in every way, yet without sin. So let us confidently approach the throne of grace to receive mercy and to find grace for timely help. In the days when Christ was in the flesh, he offered prayers and supplications with loud cries and tears to the one who was able to save him from death, and he was heard because of his reverence. Son though he was, he learned obedience from what he suffered; and when he was made perfect, he became the source of eternal salvation for all who obey him.

GOSPEL (ABC), JOHN 18:1—19:42

Jesus went out with his disciples across the Kidron valley to where there was a garden, into which he and his disciples entered. Judas his betrayer also knew the place, because Jesus had often met there with his disciples. So Judas got a band of soldiers and guards from the chief priests and the Pharisees and went there with lanterns, torches, and weapons. Jesus, knowing everything that was going to happen to him, went out and said to them, "Whom are you looking for?" They answered him, "Jesus the Nazorean." He said to them, "I AM." Judas his betrayer was also with them. When he said to them, "I AM," they turned away and fell to the ground. So he again asked them, "Whom are you looking for?" They said, "Jesus the Nazorean." Jesus answered, "I told you that I AM. So if you are looking for me, let these men go." This was to fulfill what he had said, "I have not lost any of those you gave me."

Then Simon Peter, who had a sword, drew it, struck the high priest's slave, and cut off his right ear. The slave's name was Malchus. Jesus said to Peter, "Put your sword into its scabbard. Shall I not drink the cup that the Father gave me?"

So the band of soldiers, the tribune, and the Jewish guards seized Jesus, bound him, and brought him to Annas first. He was the father-in-law of Caiaphas, who was high priest that year. It was Caiaphas who had counseled the Jews that it was better that one man should die rather than the people.

Simon Peter and another disciple followed Jesus. Now the other disciple was known to the high priest, and he entered the courtyard of the high priest with Jesus. But Peter stood at the gate outside. So the other disciple, the acquaintance of the high priest, went out and spoke to the gatekeeper and brought Peter in. Then the maid who was the gatekeeper said to Peter, "You are not one of this man's disciples, are you?" He said, "I am not." Now the slaves and the guards were standing around a charcoal fire that they had made, because it was cold, and were warming themselves. Peter was also standing there keeping warm.

The high priest questioned Jesus about his disciples and about his doctrine. Jesus answered him, "I have spoken publicly to the world. I have always taught in a synagogue or in the temple area where all the Jews gather, and in secret I have said nothing. Why ask me? Ask those who heard me what I said to them. They know what I said." When he had said this, one of the temple guards standing there struck Jesus and said, "Is this the way you answer the high priest?" Jesus answered him, "If I have spoken wrongly, testify to the wrong; but if I have spoken rightly, why do you strike me?" Then Annas sent him bound to Caiaphas the high priest.

Now Simon Peter was standing there keeping warm. And they said to him, "You are not one of his disciples, are you?" He denied it and said, "I am not." One of the slaves of the high priest, a relative of the one whose ear Peter had cut off, said, "Didn't I see you in the garden with him?" Again Peter denied it. And immediately the cock crowed.

Then they brought Jesus from Caiaphas to the praetorium. It was morning. And they themselves did not enter the praetorium, in order not to be defiled so that they could eat the Passover. So Pilate came out to them and said, "What charge do you bring against this man?" They answered and said to him, "If he were not a criminal, we would not have handed him over to you." At this, Pilate said to them, "Take him yourselves, and judge him according to your law." The Jews answered him, "We do not have the right to execute anyone," in order that the word of Jesus might be fulfilled that he said indicating the kind of death he would die. So Pilate went back into the praetorium and summoned Jesus and said to him, "Are you the King of the Jews?" Jesus answered, "Do you say this on your own or have others told you about me?" Pilate answered, "I am not a Jew, am I? Your own nation and the chief priests handed you over to me. What have you done?" Jesus answered, "My kingdom does not belong to this world. If my kingdom did belong to this world, my attendants would be fighting to keep me from being handed over to the Jews. But as it is, my kingdom is not here." So Pilate said to him, "Then you are a king?" Jesus answered, "You say I am a king. For this I was born and for this I came into the world, to testify to the truth. Everyone who belongs to the truth listens to my voice." Pilate said to him, "What is truth?"

When he had said this, he again went out to the Jews and said to them, "I find no guilt in him. But you have a custom that I release one prisoner to you at Passover. Do you want me to release to you the King of the Jews?" They cried out again, "Not this one but Barabbas!" Now Barabbas was a revolutionary.

Then Pilate took Jesus and had him scourged. And the soldiers wove a crown out of thorns and placed it on his head, and clothed him in a purple cloak, and they came to him and said, "Hail, King of the Jews!" And they struck him repeatedly. Once more Pilate went out and said to them, "Look, I am bringing him out to you, so that you may know that I find no guilt in him." So Jesus came out, wearing the crown of thorns and the purple cloak. And he said to them, "Behold, the man!" When the chief priests and the guards saw him they cried out, "Crucify him, crucify him!" Pilate said to them, "Take him yourselves and crucify him. I find no guilt in him." The Jews answered, "We have a law, and according to that law he ought to die, because he made himself the Son of God." Now when Pilate heard this statement, he became even more afraid, and went back into the praetorium and said to Jesus, "Where are you from?" Jesus did not answer him. So Pilate said to him, "Do you not speak to me? Do you not know that I have power to release you and I have power to crucify you?" Jesus answered him, "You would have no power over me if it had not been given to you from above. For this reason the one who handed me over to you has the greater sin." Consequently, Pilate tried to release him; but the Jews cried out, "If you release him, you are not a Friend of Caesar. Everyone who makes himself a king opposes Caesar."

When Pilate heard these words he brought Jesus out and seated him on the judge's bench in the place called Stone Pavement, in Hebrew, Gabbatha. It was preparation day for Passover, and it was about noon. And he said to the Jews, "Behold, your king!" They cried out, "Take him away, take him away! Crucify him!" Pilate said to them, "Shall I crucify your king?" The chief priests answered, "We have no king but Caesar." Then he handed him over to them to be crucified.

So they took Jesus, and, carrying the cross himself, he went out to what is called the Place of the Skull, in Hebrew, Golgotha. There they crucified him, and with him two others, one on either side, with Jesus in the middle. Pilate also had an inscription written and put on the cross. It read, "Jesus the Nazorean, the King of the Jews." Now many of the Jews read this inscription, because the place where Jesus was crucified was near the city; and it was written in Hebrew, Latin, and Greek. So the chief priests of the Jews said to Pilate, "Do not write 'The King of the Jews,' but that he said, 'I am the King of the Jews'." Pilate answered, "What I have written, I have written." When the soldiers had crucified Jesus, they took his clothes and divided them into four shares, a share for each soldier. They also took his tunic, but the tunic was seamless, woven in one piece from the top down. So they said to one another, "Let's not tear it, but cast lots for it to see whose it will be," in order that the passage of Scripture might be fulfilled that says: *They divided my garments among them, and for my vesture they cast lots.* This is what the soldiers did. Standing by the cross of Jesus were his mother and his mother's sister, Mary the wife of Clopas, and Mary of Magdala. When Jesus saw his mother and the disciple there whom he loved he said to his mother, "Woman, behold, your son." Then he said to the disciple, "Behold, your mother." And from that hour the disciple took her into his home. After this, aware that everything was now finished, in order that the Scripture might be fulfilled, Jesus said, "I thirst." There was a vessel filled with common wine. So they put a sponge soaked in wine on a sprig of hyssop and put it up to his mouth. When Jesus had taken the wine, he said, "It is finished." And bowing his head, he handed over the spirit.

Here all kneel and pause for a short time.

Now since it was preparation day, in order that the bodies might not remain on the cross on the sabbath, for the sabbath day of that week was a solemn one, the Jews asked Pilate that their legs be broken and that they be taken down. So the soldiers came and broke the legs of the first and then of the other one who was crucified with Jesus. But when they came to Jesus and saw that he was already dead, they did not break his legs, but one soldier thrust his lance into his side, and immediately blood and water flowed out. An eyewitness has testified, and his testimony is true; he knows that he is speaking the truth, so that you also may come to believe. For this happened so that the Scripture passage might be fulfilled: *Not a bone of it will be broken.* And again another passage says: *They will look upon him whom they have pierced.*

After this, Joseph of Arimathea, secretly a disciple of Jesus for fear of the Jews, asked Pilate if he could remove the body of Jesus. And Pilate permitted it. So he came and took his body. Nicodemus, the one who had first come to him at night, also came bringing a mixture of myrrh and aloes weighing about one hundred pounds. They took the body of Jesus and bound it with burial cloths along with the spices, according to the Jewish burial custom. Now in the place where he had been crucified there was a garden, and in the garden a new tomb, in which no one had yet been buried. So they laid Jesus there because of the Jewish preparation day; for the tomb was close by.

One Life for Many

As we continue the liturgy we began on Holy Thursday, we contemplate the passion and death of Jesus. Once again we hear the story of the suffering servant of God, the identity of Jesus as the great High Priest who offers himself as sacrifice, and the long passion narrative from John's Gospel. With these readings, we enter into the heart of Christian mystery. How is it that death can lead to life? What grace and love compels Jesus to lay down his life for the sake of the world?

Isaiah's prophecy paints a picture that Jesus' followers remembered centuries later. This passage is the last of the servant songs in Isaiah. In the first three, the servant is portrayed as the instrument of God's justice (Isaiah 42:1–4), God's prophet (49:1–6), and one who teaches and learns as he speaks to "the weary a word that will waken them" (50:4–9). Each of these hints at some suffering in the servant's life, but the one today describes in detail what will happen and why. "He was pierced for our offenses...by his stripes we were healed" (53:5). With this description Jesus' followers found the words to talk about their experience of the passion and death. They understood that Jesus fulfilled Isaiah's prophecy. It was Jesus who bore their sins and restored their relationship with God.

The Letter to the Hebrews recalls what Christ did and recognizes him as the High Priest who offers sacrifice on behalf of the people. Jesus, of course, gave himself. Hebrews declares that Christ is our High Priest who intercedes for us; we can come to God freely and boldly now. Jesus' obedience to God brought salvation to all of us.

Behold the Cross

In the Good Friday procession we sing out: "Behold the wood of the Cross on which is hung our salvation; O come let us adore..." I don't think it's an accident that the final words of that acclamation echo the refrain of a well-known Christmas hymn: "O come let us adore him, Christ the Lord." We who come to the cradle to adore the Christ child, must also come to the cross, remembering that it is the passion and death of Jesus that frees us from sin and the power of death. Like the beloved disciple and the women at the foot of the cross, we must not be afraid to look death in the face and walk with Jesus in this last part of his earthly life. After all, he was like us in everything but sin. He walked with us, suffered with us, and died for the sake of forgiving our sins and bringing us back to God.

In John's passion, Jesus wastes no time. When his hour comes, there is no agony in the Garden; Jesus lets the guards arrest him and helps his disciples to accept his inevitable death. When Pilate claims power over him, Jesus points out that Pilate wouldn't have power if God hadn't given it to him. When Pilate writes "The King of the Jews" on the cross, he is more accurate than he knows. The duty of the king in Judaism was to be an example of obedience to God's law. Pilate didn't understand; he thought being a king was about power. Jesus knew it was about obedience and service. When he dies, Jesus simply says, "It is finished," and hands over his Spirit.

The Lord's Passion (Good Friday), the Easter Triduum

Good News for All of Us

We hear these stories every Triduum. They're our foundation—the reason we call ourselves Christian. In them, Jesus gives us our example of Christian discipleship. He washes feet and obeys God, even to death on a cross. We're called to do the same. In small and large ways, we must find ways to serve each other. We may well be called to lay down our time, our possessions, or our talents for another. We may even be called to lay down our lives. But we find strength in the knowledge that Jesus did the same for us. It's all the courage we need.

Questions for Reflection and Discussion

➤ *Crosses come in many forms. When you think of a cross, what image comes to your mind?*

➤ *The Stations of the Cross is a Catholic devotion drawn from the four Gospel passion narratives and Christian tradition. Which part of Jesus' passion journey resonates with you today?*

Related Journey of Faith Lesson

E5, "The Way of the Cross"

Themes

Death
    E4, "The Creed"
    E7, "The Meaning of Holy Week"
Pain, Suffering
    E5, "The Way of the Cross"
Sin
    E2, "Living Lent"
    E3, "Scrutinies: Looking Within"
    E8, "Easter Vigil Retreat"

Vigil of the Resurrection (Holy Saturday), the Easter Triduum

READING 1 (ABC), GENESIS 1:1—2:2

In the beginning, when God created the heavens and the earth, the earth was a formless wasteland, and darkness covered the abyss, while a mighty wind swept over the waters.

Then God said, "Let there be light," and there was light. God saw how good the light was. God then separated the light from the darkness. God called the light "day," and the darkness he called "night." Thus evening came, and morning followed—the first day.

Then God said, "Let there be a dome in the middle of the waters, to separate one body of water from the other." And so it happened: God made the dome, and it separated the water above the dome from the water below it. God called the dome "the sky." Evening came, and morning followed—the second day.

Then God said, "Let the water under the sky be gathered into a single basin, so that the dry land may appear." And so it happened: the water under the sky was gathered into its basin, and the dry land appeared. God called the dry land "the earth, " and the basin of the water he called "the sea." God saw how good it was. Then God said, "Let the earth bring forth vegetation: every kind of plant that bears seed and every kind of fruit tree on earth that bears fruit with its seed in it." And so it happened: the earth brought forth every kind of plant that bears seed and every kind of fruit tree on earth that bears fruit with its seed in it. God saw how good it was. Evening came, and morning followed—the third day.

Then God said: "Let there be lights in the dome of the sky, to separate day from night. Let them mark the fixed times, the days and the years, and serve as luminaries in the dome of the sky, to shed light upon the earth." And so it happened: God made the two great lights, the greater one to govern the day, and the lesser one to govern the night; and he made the stars. God set them in the dome of the sky, to shed light upon the earth, to govern the day and the night, and to separate the light from the darkness. God saw how good it was. Evening came, and morning followed—the fourth day.

Then God said, "Let the water teem with an abundance of living creatures, and on the earth let birds fly beneath the dome of the sky." And so it happened: God created the great sea monsters and all kinds of swimming creatures with which the water teems, and all kinds of winged birds. God saw how good it was, and God blessed them, saying, "Be fertile, multiply, and fill the water of the seas; and let the birds multiply on the earth." Evening came, and morning followed—the fifth day.

Then God said, "Let the earth bring forth all kinds of living creatures: cattle, creeping things, and wild animals of all kinds." And so it happened: God made all kinds of wild animals, all kinds of cattle, and all kinds of creeping things of the earth. God saw how good it was. Then God said: "Let us make man in our image, after our likeness. Let them have dominion over the fish of the sea, the birds of the air, and the cattle, and over all the wild animals and all the creatures that crawl on the ground." God created man in his image; in the image of God he created him; male and female he created them. God blessed them, saying: "Be fertile and multiply; fill the earth and subdue it. Have dominion over the fish of the sea, the birds of the air, and all the living things that move on the earth." God also said: "See, I give you every seed-bearing plant all over the earth and every tree that has seed-bearing fruit on it to be your food; and to all the animals of the land, all the birds of the air, and all the living creatures that crawl on the ground, I give all the green plants for food." And so it happened. God looked at everything he had made, and he found it very good. Evening came, and morning followed—the sixth day.

Thus the heavens and the earth and all their array were completed. Since on the seventh day God was finished with the work he had been doing, he rested on the seventh day from all the work he had undertaken.

PSALM 104: 1–2, 5–6, 10, 12, 13–14, 24, 35

READING 3 (ABC), EXODUS 14:15—15:1

The Lord said to Moses, "Why are you crying out to me? Tell the Israelites to go forward. And you, lift up your staff and, with hand outstretched over the sea, split the sea in two, that the Israelites may pass through it on dry land. But I will make the Egyptians so obstinate that they will go in after them. Then I will receive glory through Pharaoh and all his army, his chariots and charioteers. The Egyptians shall know that I am the Lord, when I receive glory through Pharaoh and his chariots and charioteers." The angel of God, who had been leading Israel's camp, now moved and went around behind them. The column of cloud also, leaving the front, took up its place behind them, so that it came between the camp of the Egyptians and that of Israel. But the cloud now became dark, and thus the night passed without the rival camps coming any closer together all night long. Then Moses stretched out his hand over the sea, and the Lord swept the sea with a strong east wind throughout the night and so turned it into dry land. When the water was thus divided, the Israelites marched into the midst of the sea on dry land, with the water like a wall to their right and to their left. The Egyptians followed in pursuit; all Pharaoh's horses and chariots and charioteers went after them right into the midst of the sea. In the night watch just before dawn the Lord cast through the column of the fiery cloud upon the Egyptian force a glance that threw it into a panic; and he so clogged their chariot wheels that they could hardly drive. With that the Egyptians sounded the retreat before Israel, because the Lord was fighting for them against the Egyptians. Then the Lord told Moses, "Stretch out your hand over the sea, that the water may flow back upon the Egyptians, upon their chariots and their charioteers." So Moses stretched out his hand over the sea, and at dawn the sea flowed back to its normal depth. The Egyptians were fleeing head on toward the sea, when the Lord hurled them into its midst. As the water flowed back, it covered the chariots and the charioteers of Pharaoh's whole army which had followed the Israelites into the sea. Not a single one of them escaped. But the Israelites had marched on dry land through the midst of the sea, with the water like a wall to their right and to their left. Thus the Lord saved Israel on that day from the power of the Egyptians. When Israel saw the Egyptians lying dead on the seashore and beheld the great power that the Lord had shown against the Egyptians, they feared the Lord and believed in him and in his servant Moses. Then Moses and the Israelites sang this song to the Lord: I will sing to the Lord, for he is gloriously triumphant; horse and chariot he has cast into the sea.

EPISTLE (ABC), ROMANS 6:3–11

Brothers and sisters: Are you unaware that we who were baptized into Christ Jesus were baptized into his death? We were indeed buried with him through baptism into death, so that, just as Christ was raised from the dead by the glory of the Father, we too might live in newness of life. For if we have grown into union with him through a death like his, we shall also be united with him in the resurrection. We know that our old self was crucified with him, so that our sinful body might be done away with, that we might no longer be in slavery to sin. For a dead person has been absolved from sin. If, then, we have died with Christ, we believe that we shall also live with him. We know that Christ, raised from the dead, dies no more; death no longer has power over him. As to his death, he died to sin once and for all; as to his life, he lives for God. Consequently, you too must think of yourselves as being dead to sin and living for God in Christ Jesus.

PSALM 118:1–2, 16–17, 22–23

GOSPEL (A), MATTHEW 28:1–10

After the sabbath, as the first day of the week was dawning, Mary Magdalene and the other Mary came to see the tomb. And behold, there was a great earthquake; for an angel of the Lord descended from heaven, approached, rolled back the stone, and sat upon it. His appearance was like lightning and his clothing was white as snow. The guards were shaken with fear of him and became like dead men. Then the angel said to the women in reply, "Do not be afraid! I know that you are seeking Jesus the crucified. He is not here, for he has been raised just as he said. Come and see the place where he lay. Then go quickly and tell his disciples, 'He has been raised from the dead, and he is going before you to Galilee; there you will see him.' Behold, I have told you." Then they went away quickly from the tomb, fearful yet overjoyed, and ran to announce this to his disciples. And behold, Jesus met them on their way and greeted them. They approached, embraced his feet, and did him homage. Then Jesus said to them, "Do not be afraid. Go tell my brothers to go to Galilee, and there they will see me."

Vigil of the Resurrection (Holy Saturday), the Easter Triduum

GOSPEL (B), MARK 16:1–8

When the sabbath was over, Mary Magdalene, Mary, the mother of James, and Salome bought spices so that they might go and anoint him. Very early when the sun had risen, on the first day of the week, they came to the tomb. They were saying to one another, "Who will roll back the stone for us from the entrance to the tomb?" When they looked up, they saw that the stone had been rolled back; it was very large. On entering the tomb they saw a young man sitting on the right side, clothed in a white robe, and they were utterly amazed. He said to them, "Do not be amazed! You seek Jesus of Nazareth, the crucified. He has been raised; he is not here. Behold the place where they laid him. But go and tell his disciples and Peter, 'He is going before you to Galilee; there you will see him, as he told you.'"

GOSPEL (C), LUKE 24:1–12

At daybreak on the first day of the week the women who had come from Galilee with Jesus took the spices they had prepared and went to the tomb. They found the stone rolled away from the tomb; but when they entered, they did not find the body of the Lord Jesus. While they were puzzling over this, behold, two men in dazzling garments appeared to them. They were terrified and bowed their faces to the ground. They said to them, "Why do you seek the living one among the dead? He is not here, but he has been raised. Remember what he said to you while he was still in Galilee, that the Son of Man must be handed over to sinners and be crucified, and rise on the third day." And they remembered his words. Then they returned from the tomb and announced all these things to the eleven and to all the others. The women were Mary Magdalene, Joanna, and Mary the mother of James; the others who accompanied them also told this to the apostles, but their story seemed like nonsense and they did not believe them. But Peter got up and ran to the tomb, bent down, and saw the burial cloths alone; then he went home amazed at what had happened.

Scripture readings for the Easter Vigil:
Genesis 1:1—2:2 or 1:1, 26–31a;
Psalm 104:1–2, 5–6, 10, 12, 13–14, 24, 35 or
Psalm 33:4–5, 6–7, 12–13 20–22;
Genesis 22:1–18 or 22:1–2, 9a, 10–13, 15–18;
Psalm 16:5, 8, 9–10, 11;
Exodus 14:15—15:1;
Exodus 15:1–2, 3–4, 5–6, 17–18;
Isaiah 54:5–14/
Psalm 30:2, 4, 5–6, 11–12, 13;
Isaiah 55:1–11;
Isaiah 12:2–3, 4, 5–6;
Baruch 3:9–15, 32—4:4;
Psalm 19:8, 9, 10, 11;
Ezekiel 36:16–17a, 18–28;
Psalm 42:3, 5 and 43:3, 4 or
Isaiah 12:2–3, 4bcd, 5–6 or
Psalm 51:12–13, 14–15, 18–19;
Romans 6:3–11;
Psalm 118:1–2, 16–17, 22–23;
Matthew 28:1–10;
Mark 16:1–7;
Luke 24:1–12

Christ Is Risen—Alleluia

In the college community I serve, I often tell students that once they start celebrating the Triduum, they will never go back to celebrating only on Easter Sunday. The fullness of the ritual, the excitement of the new fire being lit and the Easter candle leading the procession of light into the darkened Church, the celebration of adult initiation into the Church, and all the rich symbolism of candles, water, oil, bread, wine, reading, and song serve to open the mind and heart to the miracle of God's love for us and the desire to return that love in praise, worship, and service.

After the great service of light, we listen to readings from the Law (the first five books of the Bible) and the Prophets. It is fitting to trace God's promise of salvation through the first part of our sacred Scriptures as we prepare to celebrate the fulfillment of that promise in the passion, death, and resurrection of Jesus. With the community and those awaiting initiation, we hear the story of creation; the sacrifice of Isaac and the Exodus;

we take note of the promise of salvation from Isaiah to Ezekiel; and we end this section with God's vow to impart a new spirit in us and give us a heart of flesh to replace our hearts of stone. At that point, the "Gloria" is sung and we know that our celebration has begun in earnest. In our community, all the lights come on, flowers are brought in to decorate the altar and the ambo, and we wait to hear how God has done this. It's not a long wait.

Paul's Epistle to the Romans begins with a question: "Are you unaware?" In baptism we are baptized into the passion, death, and resurrection of Christ. We die with him that we might also rise with him. For the catechumens (those awaiting baptism), this is the last instruction before we hear the Gospel—a reminder of what baptism means to us. For the rest of the community about to renew their baptismal vows—it serves the same purpose.

An Empty Tomb

We sing "Alleluia" for the first time since the beginning of the Lent. But the women who went to the tomb early in the morning saw an empty tomb first and then a young man, no doubt a heavenly visitor. The empty tomb reminds us that God created the world out of emptiness and now recreates it (and us) out of the death of Christ. The young man heralds the Good News. "[Jesus] has been raised; he is not here...He is going before you to Galilee...." In this earliest of the Gospels, Mark narrates that the initial response of the women is fear. Seeing nothing in the tomb is a shock. Was it even possible for someone to survive the death they had witnessed? And certainly the astounding news of the resurrection is strange and hard to grasp. If we read a little further in Mark's Gospel, we see that an additional ending describes post-resurrection appearances of Jesus, so we know the word got out. We might wonder how we would react.

Good News for All of Us

How can we do justice to a celebration of the life, love, and grace we have received through baptism? When we renew our baptismal promises at the vigil or on Easter Sunday, we can rededicate ourselves to our discipleship in Christ. Are there people who need us to offer a comforting word or a warm meal? Is our prayer leading us deeper into our life with God? Are we becoming more forgiving, more loving, more like Christ every day? Being a Christian disciple is a life's work. The Easter Vigil gives us a foretaste of what the destination will be.

Questions for Reflection and Discussion

> In baptism we are anointed to participate in the mission of Christ as priest, prophet, and king. How do you live out these missions in your life? What's the next step you can take? To assist you: the priest always and everywhere offers sacrifice to God; the prophet always and everywhere calls others to faithfulness to God's law; and the king is always and everywhere to be an example of obedience to God.

> Imagine you are the women who come to the tomb and find it empty. What is your reaction? Imagine you are Peter and the other disciples who hear this story for the first time. Do you believe the women?

Related Journey of Faith Lesson

M5, "Our Call to Holiness"

Themes

Life Resurrection
    M1, "Conversion: A Lifelong Process"
    M3, "Your Spiritual Gifts"
    M4, "Discernment"
    M5, "Our Call to Holiness"
Relationships
    M2, "The Role of the Laity"
    M7, "Family Life"
    M5, "Your Prayer Life"
    M8, "Evangelization"

Ascension of the Lord, Seventh Sunday of Easter, or Sixth Thursday of Easter

READING 1, ACTS 1:1–11

In the first book, Theophilus, I dealt with all that Jesus did and taught until the day he was taken up, after giving instructions through the Holy Spirit to the apostles whom he had chosen. He presented himself alive to them by many proofs after he had suffered, appearing to them during forty days and speaking about the kingdom of God. While meeting with the them, he enjoined them not to depart from Jerusalem, but to wait for "the promise of the Father about which you have heard me speak; for John baptized with water, but in a few days you will be baptized with the Holy Spirit." When they had gathered together they asked him, "Lord, are you at this time going to restore the kingdom to Israel?" He answered them, "It is not for you to know the times or seasons that the Father has established by his own authority. But you will receive power when the Holy Spirit comes upon you, and you will be my witnesses in Jerusalem, throughout Judea and Samaria, and to the ends of the earth." When he had said this, as they were looking on, he was lifted up, and a cloud took him from their sight. While they were looking intently at the sky as he was going, suddenly two men dressed in white garments stood beside them. They said, "Men of Galilee, why are you standing there looking at the sky? This Jesus who has been taken up from you into heaven will return in the same way as you have seen him going into heaven."

PSALM 47:2–3, 6–7, 8–9

READING 2, EPHESIANS 1:17–23

Brothers and sisters: May the God of our Lord Jesus Christ, the Father of glory, give you a Spirit of wisdom and revelation resulting in knowledge of him. May the eyes of your hearts be enlightened, that you may know what is the hope that belongs to his call, what are the riches of glory in his inheritance among the holy ones, and what is the surpassing greatness of his power for us who believe, in accord with the exercise of his great might, which he worked in Christ, raising him from the dead and seating him at his right hand in the heavens, far above every principality, authority, power, and dominion, and every name that is named not only in this age but also in the one to come. And he put all things beneath his feet and gave him as head over all things to the church, which is his body, the fullness of the one who fills all things in every way.

GOSPEL (A), MATTHEW 28:16–20

The eleven disciples went to Galilee, to the mountain to which Jesus had ordered them. When they saw him, they worshiped, but they doubted. Then Jesus approached and said to them, "All power in heaven and on earth has been given to me. Go, therefore, and make disciples of all nations, baptizing them in the name of the Father, and of the Son, and of the Holy Spirit, teaching them to observe all that I have commanded you. And behold, I am with you always, until the end of the age."

GOSPEL (B), MARK 16:15–20

Jesus said to his disciples: "Go into the whole world and proclaim the gospel to every creature. Whoever believes and is baptized will be saved; whoever does not believe will be condemned. These signs will accompany those who believe: in my name they will drive out demons, they will speak new languages. They will pick up serpents with their hands, and if they drink any deadly thing, it will not harm them. They will lay hands on the sick, and they will recover." So then the Lord Jesus, after he spoke to them, was taken up into heaven and took his seat at the right hand of God. But they went forth and preached everywhere, while the Lord worked with them and confirmed the word through accompanying signs.

GOSPEL (C), LUKE 24:46–53

Jesus said to his disciples: "Thus it is written that the Christ would suffer and rise from the dead on the third day and that repentance, for the forgiveness of sins, would be preached in his name to all the nations, beginning from Jerusalem. You are witnesses of these things. And behold I am sending the promise of my Father upon you; but stay in the city until you are clothed with power from on high." Then he led them out as far as Bethany, raised his hands, and blessed them. As he blessed them he parted from them and was taken up to heaven. They did him homage and then returned to Jerusalem with great joy, and they were continually in the temple praising God.

The Greatness of God's Power

The Scriptures of Luke, who wrote his Gospel and Acts of the Apostles, are the closest writings we have of a history of Jesus. Luke writes his Gospel as "an orderly account" to Theophilus; he includes names and places; he tries to be chronological in his remembrance. Thus, it's not surprising that Luke gives us the detail that Jesus' ascension is forty days after the resurrection. (The number echoes the forty years in the desert and the forty days Moses was on Mount Sinai, and the forty days Jesus was tempted in the desert.) Interestingly, Jesus gives them no details of their mission other than to tell them that they will be his witnesses in all the world. In an endearing narration, Luke records that Jesus was lifted up out of their sight. The episode has echoes of the Son of Man who appears on a cloud in Daniel 7:13 and of Elijah being taken up in a whirlwind in 2 Kings 2:11.

With a bit of humor, Luke pictures the disciples just staring up into the sky until two men in white robes (usually code for angels) ask them, "Why are you looking up into the sky?" The real event will take place in Jerusalem when, as Jesus says, they will be baptized with the Holy Spirit—the presence of God that guides the Church still today.

The Hope to Which You Have Been Called

Paul's Letter to the Ephesians has one of the most beautiful openings in the Pauline literature. God's gift of faith can open our eyes and enlighten out hearts. Paul names three results: we will know the hope to which we are called, the riches that are given to the communion of saints, and the power of God to do what we think is impossible—even raise someone from the dead. In this letter as well, Paul reveals his theology: Christ has been made head over all things for the Church. We have understood this from the beginning. While we reject nothing of what is true and beautiful in other religions, we believe the fullness of the truth and of salvation subsists in the Catholic Church as the body of Christ. We see the evidence of the Holy Spirit throughout the centuries when the Church has survived even in the face of the sinfulness of its members. Today we need the Holy Spirit more than ever as we try to mend factions and welcome those who are not like us.

The Riches of Our Inheritance Among the Saints

One of the endings of Mark's Gospel records his version of the great commission and the ascension. Mark is the only one who talks about the power of the disciples to cast out demons, heal the sick, handle venomous snakes, and drink poison. There are Christian sects that take this literally and believe in the power of God to keep them from harm in these things. More importantly, Mark notes that the disciples proclaim the Good News everywhere and the Lord worked with them. The disciples may have seen Jesus ascend, but the early Church experienced Christ as alive in their midst. We inherit the faith in the living presence of Christ from this early Church and from the named and unnamed saints who have gone before us and will come after. The Holy Spirit is how we talk about that living presence—a rich inheritance indeed.

Ascension of the Lord, Seventh Sunday of Easter, or Sixth Thursday of Easter

Good News for All of Us

Jesus' great commission is meant for us as well. Being part of the Church means accepting the command of Christ to open our hearts to the Holy Spirit and preach the Good News in word and deed to a waiting world. The Holy Spirit was poured out on the world. In the sacrament of confirmation we receive the grace to do what Jesus asks and to live a life in the Spirit filled with joy and peace even when confronted with trouble. We are blessed, for the Lord works with us. And we have friends and saints to keep us company on the way. How will you share the Good News of Jesus today?

Questions for Reflection and Discussion

> ➤ Vatican II tells us that everyone is called to holiness and that we are to make the world holy. That scares some people and challenges others. Have you thought of yourself as holy? How do/would you reflect that in your life?

> ➤ What is challenging about being Catholic today? Can you point to any places where you see the Holy Spirit active in the Church?

Related Journey of Faith Lesson

Q12 "Who Shepherds the Church?"

Themes

Ascension, Christ, Holy Spirit
    M3, "The Spiritual Gifts"
    M4, "Discernment"
Church
    M2, "The Role of the Laity"
    M5, "Our Call to Holiness"
    M8, "Evangelization"

Birth of St. John the Baptist, June 24

READING 1 (ABC), ISAIAH 49:1–6

Hear me, O coastlands, listen, O distant peoples. The LORD called me from birth, from my mother's womb he gave me my name. He made of me a sharp-edged sword and concealed me in the shadow of his arm. He made me a polished arrow, in his quiver he hid me. You are my servant, he said to me, Israel, through whom I show my glory. Though I thought I had toiled in vain, and for nothing, uselessly, spent my strength, yet my reward is with the LORD, my recompense is with my God. For now the LORD has spoken who formed me as his servant from the womb, that Jacob may be brought back to him and Israel gathered to him; and I am made glorious in the sight of the LORD, and my God is now my strength! It is too little, he says, for you to be my servant, to raise up the tribes of Jacob, and restore the survivors of Israel; I will make you a light to the nations, that my salvation may reach to the ends of the earth.

PSALM 139:1B–3, 13–14AB, 14C–15

READING 2 (ABC), ACTS 13:22–26

In those days, Paul said: "God raised up David as king; of him God testified, *I have found David, son of Jesse, a man after my own heart; he will carry out my every wish.* From this man's descendants God, according to his promise, has brought to Israel a savior, Jesus. John heralded his coming by proclaiming a baptism of repentance to all the people of Israel; and as John was completing his course, he would say, 'What do you suppose that I am? I am not he. Behold, one is coming after me; I am not worthy to unfasten the sandals of his feet.' "My brothers, sons of the family of Abraham, and those others among you who are God-fearing, to us this word of salvation has been sent."

GOSPEL (ABC), LUKE 1:57–66, 80

When the time arrived for Elizabeth to have her child she gave birth to a son. Her neighbors and relatives heard that the Lord had shown his great mercy toward her, and they rejoiced with her. When they came on the eighth day to circumcise the child, they were going to call him Zechariah after his father, but his mother said in reply, "No. He will be called John." But they answered her, "There is no one among your relatives who has this name." So they made signs, asking his father what he wished him to be called. He asked for a tablet and wrote, "John is his name," and all were amazed. Immediately his mouth was opened, his tongue freed, and he spoke blessing God. Then fear came upon all their neighbors, and all these matters were discussed throughout the hill country of Judea. All who heard these things took them to heart, saying, "What, then, will this child be?" For surely the hand of the Lord was with him. The child grew and became strong in spirit, and he was in the desert until the day of his manifestation to Israel.

The Herald of the Lord

It is no accident that we celebrate the birth of John the Baptist six months before Christmas Eve. Luke's Gospel tells us that Elizabeth was in her sixth month when Mary told her of the angel's message. In our sacred calendar, we remember the annunciation on March 24 (the vigil), and three short months later John is born. He would go before the Lord to prepare his way.

As the early Church reflected on the place and figure of John in the New Testament story, they were drawn to the words of Isaiah. Like Jesus, John embodied the image of a servant of the Lord whose mouth is a two-edged sword and who is sent to bring God's light to the world. According to the Gospels, John called people to repent in preparation for the kingdom of God. Matthew and Mark recall the similarity in look between him and the prophet Elijah who was to come before the day of the Lord (Matthew 3:1–6; Mark 1:2–4). When they speak about John, both quote another section of Isaiah about the messenger who prepares the way of the Lord (Isaiah 40:2–3). John simply calls him a man sent by God to testify to the light (John 1:6–8). In all the Gospels, the appearance of John prepares us for the appearance of Jesus and the coming of the kingdom of God.

I Am Not the One

There is no doubt that John had his own disciples and could have made himself far more important. But John's example to all of us is one of humble obedience. He understood that he was a small part of a larger story. His mission was to prepare for the one who was to come, not be the headliner. In every instance, John submitted himself to the one whom he expected. When Jesus came to be baptized by John and begin his public ministry, I imagine that John had a moment of profound awe and knew the humble privilege of serving the Lord in all he did. In the Gospel story, from that moment, John's presence decreases while the presence of Jesus increases. In our memory and imagination, John will always be the one who preceded Jesus and showed us what it is to point to the Lord and get out of the way.

He Shall Be Called John

Every family who welcomes the birth of a child wonders whom this child will take after and what he or she will do with their lives. John was already a surprise because people thought Elizabeth could not have children. When the time came to circumcise and name him, the family learned that he would not bear Zechariah's name, but would be called John, as the Lord commanded. That doesn't seem so unusual today, but in the ancient Near East, not giving the child a family name set him apart and made people wonder. Their questions continued when Zechariah begins to speak again after having been struck mute. Clearly the hand of the Lord was upon this child. "What will this child be?" The neighbors asked this as they watched him grow in grace and spirit. They would know later that he grew into the person God meant him to be from the moment he was created in the womb.

Good News for All of Us

From the beginning, God gave John the gifts to God's presence in our lives and in the world. Every one of us is called by God and baptized into the mission of Christ. We won't all do it like John, nor will we do it exactly like each other. Some of us will share the Good News in families or in schools. Others will work in cities or villages where the presence of God is sometimes hard to find. Still others will find our calling in the service of others or in community with brothers and sisters. The point is everyone has a place in the people of God. We all have gifts that we share. We are all called to build up the community of faith to prepare for the coming of Christ in glory. John is a good model for us.

Questions for Reflection and Discussion

➤ What gifts do you bring to the Church? What have others told you that you are good at?

➤ How do you prepare the way of the Lord in your own heart? How can you do that for others?

Related Journey of Faith Lesson

M1, "Conversion: A Lifelong Process"

Themes

Baptism
    E4, "The Creed"
    M1, "Conversion: A Lifelong Process"
Prophet
    Q13, "The Church as Community"
    M3, "Your Spiritual Gifts"
    M4, "Discernment"
Service
    Q12, "Who Shepherds the Church?"
    Q14, "Mary"
    Q15, "Saints"
    M2, "The Role of the Laity"
    M8, "Evangelization"

Sts. Peter and Paul, June 29

READING 1 (ABC), ACTS 12:1–11

In those days, King Herod laid hands upon some members of the Church to harm them. He had James, the brother of John, killed by the sword, and when he saw that this was pleasing to the Jews he proceeded to arrest Peter also. (It was the feast of Unleavened Bread.) He had him taken into custody and put in prison under the guard of four squads of four soldiers each. He intended to bring him before the people after Passover. Peter thus was being kept in prison, but prayer by the Church was fervently being made to God on his behalf. On the very night before Herod was to bring him to trial, Peter, secured by double chains, was sleeping between two soldiers, while outside the door guards kept watch on the prison. Suddenly the angel of the Lord stood by him and a light shone in the cell. He tapped Peter on the side and awakened him, saying, "Get up quickly." The chains fell from his wrists. The angel said to him, "Put on your belt and your sandals." He did so. Then he said to him, "Put on your cloak and follow me." So he followed him out, not realizing that what was happening through the angel was real; he thought he was seeing a vision. They passed the first guard, then the second, and came to the iron gate leading out to the city, which opened for them by itself. They emerged and made their way down an alley, and suddenly the angel left him. Then Peter recovered his senses and said, "Now I know for certain that the Lord sent his angel and rescued me from the hand of Herod and from all that the Jewish people had been expecting."

PSALM 34:2–3, 4–5, 6–7, 8–9

READING 2 (ABC), 2 TIMOTHY 4:6–8, 17–18

I, Paul, am already being poured out like a libation, and the time of my departure is at hand. I have competed well; I have finished the race; I have kept the faith. From now on the crown of righteousness awaits me, which the Lord, the just judge, will award to me on that day, and not only to me, but to all who have longed for his appearance. The Lord stood by me and gave me strength, so that through me the proclamation might be completed and all the Gentiles might hear it. And I was rescued from the lion's mouth. The Lord will rescue me from every evil threat and will bring me safe to his heavenly Kingdom. To him be glory forever and ever. Amen.

GOSPEL (ABC), MATTHEW 16:13–19

When Jesus went into the region of Caesarea Philippi he asked his disciples, "Who do people say that the Son of Man is?" They replied, "Some say John the Baptist, others Elijah, still others Jeremiah or one of the prophets." He said to them, "But who do you say that I am?" Simon Peter said in reply, "You are Christ, the Son of the living God." Jesus said to him in reply, "Blessed are you, Simon son of Jonah. For flesh and blood has not revealed this to you, but my heavenly Father. And so I say to you, you are Peter, and upon this rock I will build my Church, and the gates of the netherworld shall not prevail against it. I will give you the keys to the Kingdom of heaven. Whatever you bind on earth shall be bound in heaven; and whatever you loose on earth shall be loosed in heaven."

Who Do You Say I Am?

It seems fitting that one day of the year is devoted to the two saints widely acknowledged to have built and led the Church under the guidance of the Holy Spirit from Pentecost until their deaths in the mid-first century. Peter was the rock of the disciples; Paul was the great "Lion of God" who converted to Christianity after a vision of Christ and who was gradually accepted by those early Christians and then proceeded to establish a Christian community in the far-flung corners of the Middle East.

In Matthew's Gospel, Jesus asks all the disciples the question: "Who do you say that I am?" They give him a variety of answers—John the Baptist, Elijah, a prophet. But when Jesus asks them who they say he is, there is silence. It is Peter who offers an answer: "You are the Christ [the anointed one], the son of the Living God." It took tremendous courage to say that. If Jesus had been any of the other figures named, people could have dismissed him. But if Jesus is who we believe he is—the Messiah and Son of God—we will be changed, and we must change our lives for him. That's what happened to Peter. His name was changed; his job was changed. He couldn't have gone back to his old life even if he wanted to.

Poured Out Like a Libation

Paul wasn't one of the Twelve. As Saul, he was passionate about destroying Christians—it gave him purpose and he felt it was right. In the middle of it all, he experienced an encounter with Christ in a vision. When Jesus asked, "Saul, Saul, why are you persecuting me?" Saul changed his life and, like Peter, he took on a new name. As Paul, he traveled throughout the Middle East preaching the Good News, writing letters to the far-flung house churches surrounding the Mediterranean Sea, and ultimately giving up his life to be a follower of Christ. In Paul's Second Letter to Timothy, he is fully conscious that his martyrdom is inevitable. Paul makes it especially clear that losing his life is itself a sacrifice for the sake of Christ. When he talks about being poured out, his words evoke images of worship. Both of Paul's letters to Timothy function as instructions from a mentor to his student or a father to a son. Paul urges him to continue preaching the gospel and to do what he has learned both from his family and from Paul. For Paul, faith in Jesus is more important than any earthly treasure.

Good News for All of Us

The relationship between Peter and Paul was sometimes contentious as both had a strong vision of what the early Church should look like. When we read the Acts of the Apostles and the letters of Paul and Peter, we are reminded that both were committed to spreading the Good News of Jesus. In moments of dispute, they gathered with other elders in the Christian community and worked out their differences with prayer and dialogue. Read the story of the first Council of Jerusalem, which answered the question surrounding circumcision (Acts 15).

We should look at the lives of these men as an example for us. Peter followed Jesus from the beginning of his ministry. He still went through a conversion. He had to be with Jesus for a year or more before coming to say, "You are the Messiah..." and even after that, he denied Jesus three times when he was afraid. He kept going even until his own death. Paul didn't know Jesus at all and had to undergo a different kind of conversion experience. He was struck blind, knew the enormity of what he had done, and immediately changed his life. Whether we grow to know Jesus over time like Peter or come to a sudden understanding like Paul, we come to the same conclusion: they knew Jesus and we should, too.

Questions for Discussion and Reflection

➤ Are there any disputes in the Church today that would benefit from a council devoted to prayer and dialogue?

➤ What other figures in the Scriptures of the early Church provide examples of Christian leadership and service?

Related Journey of Faith Lesson

M8, "Evangelization"

Themes

Authority
    Q12, "Who Shepherds the Church?"
Gifts
    M3, "Your Spiritual Gifts"
Ministry
    Q13, "The Church as Community"
    M2, "The Role of the Laity"
    M8, "Evangelization"

Transfiguration of the Lord, August 6

READING 1 (ABC), DANIEL 7:9–10, 13–14

As I watched: Thrones were set up and the Ancient One took his throne. His clothing was bright as snow, and the hair on his head as white as wool; his throne was flames of fire, with wheels of burning fire. A surging stream of fire flowed out from where he sat; Thousands upon thousands were ministering to him, and myriads upon myriads attended him. The court was convened and the books were opened. As the visions during the night continued, I saw: One like a Son of man coming, on the clouds of heaven; When he reached the Ancient One and was presented before him, The one like a Son of man received dominion, glory, and kingship; all peoples, nations, and languages serve him. His dominion is an everlasting dominion that shall not be taken away, his kingship shall not be destroyed.

PSALM 97:1–2, 5–6, 9

READING 2 (ABC), 2 PETER 1:16–19

Beloved: We did not follow cleverly devised myths when we made known to you the power and coming of our Lord Jesus Christ, but we had been eyewitnesses of his majesty. For he received honor and glory from God the Father when that unique declaration came to him from the majestic glory, "This is my Son, my beloved, with whom I am well pleased." We ourselves heard this voice come from heaven while we were with him on the holy mountain. Moreover, we possess the prophetic message that is altogether reliable. You will do well to be attentive to it, as to a lamp shining in a dark place, until day dawns and the morning star rises in your hearts.

GOSPEL (A), MATTHEW 17:1–9

Jesus took Peter, James, and his brother, John, and led them up a high mountain by themselves. And he was transfigured before them; his face shone like the sun and his clothes became white as light. And behold, Moses and Elijah appeared to them, conversing with him. Then Peter said to Jesus in reply, "Lord, it is good that we are here. If you wish, I will make three tents here, one for you, one for Moses, and one for Elijah." While he was still speaking, behold, a bright cloud cast a shadow over them, then from the cloud came a voice that said, "This is my beloved Son, with whom I am well pleased; listen to him." When the disciples heard this, they fell prostrate and were very much afraid. But Jesus came and touched them, saying, "Rise, and do not be afraid." And when the disciples raised their eyes, they saw no one else but Jesus alone. As they were coming down from the mountain, Jesus charged them, "Do not tell the vision to anyone until the Son of Man has been raised from the dead."

GOSPEL (B), MARK 9:2–10

Jesus took Peter, James, and his brother John, and led them up a high mountain apart by themselves. And he was transfigured before them, and his clothes became dazzling white, such as no fuller on earth could bleach them. Then Elijah appeared to them along with Moses, and they were conversing with Jesus. Then Peter said to Jesus in reply, "Rabbi, it is good that we are here! Let us make three tents: one for you, one for Moses, and one for Elijah." He hardly knew what to say, they were so terrified. Then a cloud came, casting a shadow over them; from the cloud came a voice, "This is my beloved Son. Listen to him." Suddenly, looking around, they no longer saw anyone but Jesus alone with them. As they were coming down from the mountain, he charged them not to relate what they had seen to anyone, except when the Son of Man had risen from the dead. So they kept the matter to themselves, questioning what rising from the dead meant.

GOSPEL (C), LUKE 9:28B–36

Jesus took Peter, John, and James and went up a mountain to pray. While he was praying his face changed in appearance and his clothing became dazzling white. And behold, two men were conversing with him, Moses and Elijah, who appeared in glory and spoke of his exodus that he was going to accomplish in Jerusalem. Peter and his companions had been overcome by sleep, but becoming fully awake, they saw his glory and the two men standing with him. As they were about to part from him, Peter said to Jesus, "Master, it is good that we are here; let us make three tents, one for you, one for Moses, and one for Elijah."

But he did not know what he was saying. While he was still speaking, a cloud came and cast a shadow over them, and they became frightened when they entered the cloud. Then from the cloud came a voice that said, "This is my chosen Son; listen to him." After the voice had spoken, Jesus was found alone. They fell silent and did not at that time tell anyone what they had seen.

An Everlasting Dominion

The transfiguration of Jesus is told twice during the Church year. It's the Gospel for the second Sunday of Lent—a foretaste of the resurrection and revelation of Jesus' divine nature. Here in Ordinary Time, the story reminds us that Jesus is God and we're called to be disciples. Both the first reading and the Gospel fall about halfway through their respective books and mark a turning point of sorts.

In Daniel's prophetic vision, he sees a glimpse of the "Ancient of Days," and one like a "Son of Man." Daniel does not give more specific names, but his description of thrones and dominion, servants and kingship, immediately makes us think of descriptions of God and Jesus. John's Book of Revelation quotes this section of Daniel to refer to Jesus. Daniel's vision closes the first half of the book and prepares us for the apocalyptic battles he will talk about in the second half.

Daniel lived in a time of persecution when, attacked on all sides, the Israelites could only cling to the hope that God would triumph over the evil surrounding them. Apocalyptic literature imagines a great battle between good and evil. The outcome is never in doubt. God will reign, even if that reign seems far away. The throne, the multitudes that worship and serve, and the judgment on all people signal the victory. Moreover, God's reign is an everlasting one. In the case of both Daniel and Revelation, it is the "one like a Son of Man" who is given dominion over all creation by the Ancient of Days.

Glory and Discipleship

In Mark's Gospel, the transfiguration follows the confession of Peter who has come to accept that Jesus is the Messiah and the first prediction of the passion to which Peter has objected vehemently. Jesus tells Peter and us that the challenge of discipleship is taking up the cross and following Jesus. Many had qualms about such a demand. The transfiguration is Jesus' response.

Peter, James, and John follow him up the mountain and witness his glorified self. We note the similarity between the whiteness of Jesus' clothes and the white clothing on the "Ancient of Days." Along with the disciples, we see Moses, who represents the Law, and Elijah, who represents the prophets, conversing with the Jesus who is the fulfillment of both. The voice of God tells us "This is my beloved Son," an echo of the Son of Man in Daniel and the way Jesus often refers to himself in Mark's Gospel.

Peter wanted to stay on that mountain. His offer to build tents was genuine, even if misguided. Jesus knew that his time of suffering was coming. Would the brief glimpse of glory they had be enough to get them through what was to come? Would they understand that it was God who was emptying himself for their sakes and the sake of the world, even if it meant his death on the cross? He needs them to ponder the experience in their hearts and so they continue their journey down the mountain, not telling anyone until they themselves understand it after the resurrection.

Eyewitness

In his epistle, Peter tells his own account of that day from the vantage point of hindsight. Peter is eager to share his understanding and his experience. Jesus was the Son of Man glorified by the Father. He is coming again in power and majesty. His words are a lamp shining in our darkness. Moreover, Peter comprehends that it is only through God's grace that he can preach this message at all.

Transfiguration of the Lord, August 6

Good News for All of Us

Mountaintop experiences are moments when we come to sudden clarity about who we are, who God is, and where we are going. We are tempted to stay on the mountain rather than immerse ourselves in the daily business of living, waiting for something that hasn't come. We want to stay to avoid suffering and pain, which are part of the journey. Jesus reminds us we can't get to the mountaintop without walking through the valley and the dark places, but sometimes the smallest vision can give us hope, and we know that Jesus walks with us to guide our steps.

Questions for Reflection and Discussion

- ➤ *What are the mountaintop experiences that you have had that have revealed something about God or yourself?*

- ➤ *What helps you get over the small and large challenges in your life?*

Related *Journey of Faith* Lesson

M5, "Our Call to Holiness"

Themes

Revelation
    Q13, "The Church as Community"
    M1, "Conversion: A Lifelong Process"
Second Coming
    E4, "The Creed"
    M8, "Evangelization"
Transfiguration
    Q6, "Divine Revelation"
    M7, "Family Life"

**READING 1 (ABC),
REVELATION 11:19A; 12:1–6A, 10AB**

God's temple in heaven was opened, and the ark of his covenant could be seen in the temple. A great sign appeared in the sky, a woman clothed with the sun, with the moon under her feet and on her head a crown of twelve stars. She was with child and wailed aloud in pain as she labored to give birth. Then another sign appeared in the sky; it was a huge red dragon, with seven heads and ten horns, and on its heads were seven diadems. Its tail swept away a third of the stars in the sky and hurled them down to the earth. Then the dragon stood before the woman about to give birth, to devour her child when she gave birth. She gave birth to a son, a male child, destined to rule all the nations with an iron rod. Her child was caught up to God and his throne. The woman herself fled into the desert where she had a place prepared by God. Then I heard a loud voice in heaven say: "Now have salvation and power come, and the Kingdom of our God and the authority of his Anointed One."

PSALM 45:10, 11, 12, 16

READING 2 (ABC), 1 CORINTHIANS 15:20–27

Brothers and sisters: Christ has been raised from the dead, the firstfruits of those who have fallen asleep. For since death came through man, the resurrection of the dead came also through man. For just as in Adam all die, so too in Christ shall all be brought to life, but each one in proper order: Christ the firstfruits; then, at his coming, those who belong to Christ; then comes the end, when he hands over the Kingdom to his God and Father, when he has destroyed every sovereignty and every authority and power. For he must reign until he has put all his enemies under his feet. The last enemy to be destroyed is death, for "he subjected everything under his feet."

GOSPEL (ABC), LUKE 1:39–56

Mary set out and traveled to the hill country in haste to a town of Judah, where she entered the house of Zechariah and greeted Elizabeth. When Elizabeth heard Mary's greeting, the infant leaped in her womb, and Elizabeth, filled with the Holy Spirit, cried out in a loud voice and said, "Blessed are you among women, and blessed is the fruit of your womb. And how does this happen to me, that the mother of my Lord should come to me? For at the moment the sound of your greeting reached my ears, the infant in my womb leaped for joy. Blessed are you who believed that what was spoken to you by the Lord would be fulfilled." And Mary said: "My soul proclaims the greatness of the Lord; my spirit rejoices in God my Savior for he has looked with favor on his lowly servant. From this day all generations will call me blessed: the Almighty has done great things for me and holy is his Name. He has mercy on those who fear him in every generation. He has shown the strength of his arm, and has scattered the proud in their conceit. He has cast down the mighty from their thrones, and has lifted up the lowly. He has filled the hungry with good things, and the rich he has sent away empty. He has come to the help of his servant Israel for he has remembered his promise of mercy, the promise he made to our fathers, to Abraham and his children forever." Mary remained with her about three months and then returned to her home.

A Reasonable Assumption
On November 1, 1950, Pope Pius XII declared the assumption of Mary to be a dogma, requiring the full faith and assent of the Catholic Church. It's the most recent dogma (and the only infallible statement since the proclamation of papal infallibility), but it proclaimed and articulated a belief that had been present at least since the fifth century or possibly since Mary's passing, since there is no body.

Mary has always enjoyed a special place as the Mother of God. Though the stories of her in Scripture are limited, the memory and imagination of her in Catholic tradition (and in the traditions of other Christians and of Muslims) have made her the subject of prayer and devotion. When I was a child, we were told that if St. Peter barred the gate of heaven and we were wearing a scapular, Mary would pull us up through the window. (The scapular is attributed to Our Lady of Mount Carmel, in which she is believed to have promised St. Simon Stock, "Those who die wearing this scapular shall not suffer eternal fire.")

It makes sense that the Church in the first centuries would hold Mary in a special regard. Early on, stories were told that at her death, the apostles were miraculously transported to her deathbed from wherever they were preaching. Reportedly, St. Thomas was late to that event and insisted that the tomb be opened. When they opened the tomb, there was no body there. While there is no proof for this story, the Church reflected on what would be the best honor that God would bestow on the Mother of Jesus. As they searched the Scriptures, they kept coming back to the passage in Genesis that prophesied that the offspring of the woman would crush the serpent with his heel (Genesis 3:15). Echoes of that prophecy can be found in the vision of the "woman clothed with the sun" whose offspring defeats the dragon in Revelation. Pope Pius also cited our epistle for today, seeing in Paul's First Letter to the Corinthians the promise of victory over death. It seemed logical that the Mother of Jesus would be the first among us to experience the eternal life that Jesus' passion and death won for us.

Mary, Elizabeth, and the Promise of Ages

The assumption of Mary is not specifically relayed in any part of the New Testament. Instead, Luke's Gospel lifts up the account of Mary's visit to Elizabeth, who recognizes her as the Mother of the Lord. The Scripture says that Elizabeth was filled with the Holy Spirit, a description used frequently of prophets and holy men and women. Her utterance tells us all we need to know: "Blessed are you and blessed is the fruit of your womb." From the first moment of Mary's assent to God's will, others knew her as set apart and they marveled at her faith in God's promises. Mary herself sings the song of God's favor and the divine mercy that lifts the oppressed and brings justice to the earth.

Good News for All of Us

It seems that August 15 is often a forgotten holy day. People may be on vacation or getting ready to go back to school. The middle of August always sneaks up on us and surprises us when we least expect it. That's as it should be. No doubt the archangel Gabriel surprised Mary when he came. The events of Jesus' life took a turn she may not have expected. She held her dead Son in her arms, something no mother should have to do. She was, and is, a model for us all and Mother to the Church. When we celebrate the assumption, we honor her and look forward to the day when we can share in the gift of eternal life that she was given at the end of hers. We can rejoice in that hope.

Questions for Reflection and Discussion

> *What images or stories about Mary are meaningful to you as a Catholic?*

> *John's Gospel records that Jesus gave his mother into the keeping of John (and so to the whole Church) just before he died. What inspiration do you find in Mary, Mother of the Church? How can she guide your life?*

Related Journey of Faith Lesson

Q14, "Mary"

Themes

Assumption, Mary
  Q14, "Mary"
  M5, "Our Call to Holiness"
Redemption
  E4, "The Creed"
  M1, "Conversion: A Lifelong Process"

Exaltation of the Holy Cross (Triumph of the Cross), September 14

READING 1 (ABC), NUMBERS 21:4B–9

With their patience worn out by the journey, the people complained against God and Moses, "Why have you brought us up from Egypt to die in this desert, where there is no food or water? We are disgusted with this wretched food!" In punishment the LORD sent among the people saraph serpents, which bit the people so that many of them died. Then the people came to Moses and said, "We have sinned in complaining against the LORD and you. Pray the LORD to take the serpents from us."

So Moses prayed for the people, and the LORD said to Moses, "Make a saraph and mount it on a pole, and if any who have been bitten look at it, they will live." Moses accordingly made a bronze serpent and mounted it on a pole, and whenever anyone who had been bitten by a serpent looked at the bronze serpent, he lived.

PSALM 78:1BC–2, 34–35, 36–37, 38

READING 2 (ABC), PHILIPPIANS 2:6–11

Brothers and sisters: Christ Jesus, though he was in the form of God, did not regard equality with God something to be grasped. Rather, he emptied himself, taking the form of a slave, coming in human likeness; and found human in appearance, he humbled himself, becoming obedient to death, even death on a cross. Because of this, God greatly exalted him and bestowed on him the name that is above every name, that at the name of Jesus every knee should bend, of those in heaven and on earth and under the earth, and every tongue confess that Jesus Christ is Lord, to the glory of God the Father.

GOSPEL (ABC), JOHN 3:13–17

Jesus said to Nicodemus: "No one has gone up to heaven except the one who has come down from heaven, the Son of Man. And just as Moses lifted up the serpent in the desert, so must the Son of Man be lifted up, so that everyone who believes in him may have eternal life." For God so loved the world that he gave his only Son, so that everyone who believes in him might not perish but might have eternal life. For God did not send his Son into the world to condemn the world, but that the world might be saved through him.

For God So Loved the World

Today's Gospel includes the famous citation often seen at sporting or other events with large crowds: John 3:16. The quotation reminds us that the Father sent Jesus because he loved us and so we might have eternal life through him. The cross is at the center of our faith. Why, then, do we need to have a special feast dedicated to the cross? The feast of the Exaltation of the Holy Cross celebrates the discovery of the True Cross in 326 by St. Helena, the mother of Constantine. The Church of the Holy Sepulcher was built on the site of the discovery, and today's pilgrims enter the Church to view the site of the crucifixion, the rock on which Jesus' body was anointed, and the burial site itself. When it was complete, the church was dedicated with a portion of the cross on September 14 in 335.

The long period between Pentecost and the feast of Christ the King, which marks the end of the Church year, encourages us to move more deeply into our lives as followers of Christ. With its feasts and holy days, the Church punctuates its year with reminders that God entered into human history. The feast of the Cross helps us reflect on the paradox of the Cross itself. Paul says it well in Philippians: Jesus humbled himself in obedience and God exalted him. In his moment of greatest weakness, Christ was stronger than death itself. The cross was an instrument of torture for Rome, designed to impress people with Rome's power; in God's hands it becomes the sign of victory over death and divine justice for the oppressed.

Looking at the One Who Can Save Us

Both the Old Testament lesson and the Gospel share a common motif. For the Israelites, plagued by serpents that bite them as a result of their complaining, Moses lifts up a "seraph," on a pole. The root of the word means "fiery one." It could be a venomous snake, but it's the same root that's used for "Seraphim," the fiery angels around the throne of God in Isaiah 6. In either case, fire is a sign of purification, and the Israelites who gaze at the serpent are cured of their bites.

In the Gospel, John alludes to the episode from Numbers as Jesus talks about the Son of Man being lifted on a tree to bring salvation to the world. When we look at Jesus, we remember that we have been freed from sin and are encouraged to continue our way as disciples.

A Hymn to Jesus

Bridging the first reading and the Gospel, Paul's Letter to the Philippians contains the remnants of an early Christian hymn. Paul makes it clear that Jesus did not think that equality with God was something to be grasped; but hidden in that is the opposite statement. Jesus did not think human beings were something to be despised. The Incarnation (God taking flesh) sets Christianity apart from all other religions. In an act of wondrous love, God emptied himself to become one of us. The only proper response is to bow before him. Paul repeats a portion of Isaiah in his final verses. The speaker is God: "…I am God; / there is no other!…. / To me every knee shall bend; / by me every tongue shall swear" (Isaiah 45:22, 23). Paul's letter adds the acclamation that "Jesus Christ is Lord," showing that the early Church was already articulating the identification of Jesus with God.

Good News for All of Us

"Behold the wood of the cross on which is hung our salvation." Thus the veneration of the cross on Good Friday begins as the cross is processed throughout the Church. The words beg us to look at the cross, to ponder what it means in our lives as Christians, and to repent and be healed. The very fact that we can do that is the Good News that we can share with everyone. The death and resurrection of Jesus is the beginning of eternal life in God. The challenge is to reflect that life in all we do.

Questions for Reflection and Discussion

> *Some crosses can be plain or elaborate, with a body or without, depicting Jesus as suffering or triumphant. Is there a particular representation of the cross that is meaningful to you for prayer or reflection?*

> *How do you embody the love of God to others every day?*

Related Journey of Faith Lesson

E4, "The Creed"

Themes

Cross, Lord, Salvation
   E4, "The Creed"

READING 1 (ABC), REVELATION 7:2–4, 9–14

I, John, saw another angel come up from the East, holding the seal of the living God. He cried out in a loud voice to the four angels who were given power to damage the land and the sea, "Do not damage the land or the sea or the trees until we put the seal on the foreheads of the servants of our God." I heard the number of those who had been marked with the seal, one hundred and forty-four thousand marked from every tribe of the children of Israel. After this I had a vision of a great multitude, which no one could count, from every nation, race, people, and tongue. They stood before the throne and before the Lamb, wearing white robes and holding palm branches in their hands. They cried out in a loud voice: "Salvation comes from our God, who is seated on the throne, and from the Lamb." All the angels stood around the throne and around the elders and the four living creatures. They prostrated themselves before the throne, worshiped God, and exclaimed: "Amen. Blessing and glory, wisdom and thanksgiving, honor, power, and might be to our God forever and ever. Amen." Then one of the elders spoke up and said to me, "Who are these wearing white robes, and where did they come from?" I said to him, "My lord, you are the one who knows." He said to me, "These are the ones who have survived the time of great distress; they have washed their robes and made them white in the Blood of the Lamb."

PSALM 24:1BC–2, 3–4AB, 5–6

READING 2 (ABC), 1 JOHN 3:1–3

Beloved: See what love the Father has bestowed on us that we may be called the children of God. Yet so we are. The reason the world does not know us is that it did not know him. Beloved, we are God's children now; what we shall be has not yet been revealed. We do know that when it is revealed we shall be like him, for we shall see him as he is. Everyone who has this hope based on him makes himself pure, as he is pure.

GOSPEL (ABC), MATTHEW 5:1–12A

When Jesus saw the crowds, he went up the mountain, and after he had sat down, his disciples came to him. He began to teach them, saying: "Blessed are the poor in spirit, for theirs is the Kingdom of heaven. Blessed are they who mourn, for they will be comforted. Blessed are the meek, for they will inherit the land. Blessed are they who hunger and thirst for righteousness, for they will be satisfied. Blessed are the merciful, for they will be shown mercy. Blessed are the clean of heart, for they will see God. Blessed are the peacemakers, for they will be called children of God. Blessed are they who are persecuted for the sake of righteousness, for theirs is the Kingdom of heaven. Blessed are you when they insult you and persecute you and utter every kind of evil against you falsely because of me. Rejoice and be glad, for your reward will be great in heaven."

Singing About the Saints of God

The last stanza of an old hymn by Lesbia Scott, now in the public domain, goes: "[Saints] lived not only in ages past; there are hundreds of thousands still; the world is bright with the joyous saints who love to do Jesus' will. You can meet them in school, or in lanes, or at sea, in church, or in trains, or in shops, or at tea; for the saints of God are just folk like me, and I mean to be one too." The verse has always made me smile because it combines the understanding that to be a saint, we must love to do Jesus' will above all else and because, in 1929, Ms. Scott understood that we are all called to holiness no matter who or where we are.

On All Saints' Day, we celebrate the great communion of saints—those who have been sure examples of God's love and presence in the world to generations of believers. The saints heard and responded to God's voice in their lives. They trusted in God even when the world seemed dark and they were challenged to continue. As Catholics, we believe they stand before God now as John's vision in the Book of Revelation describes.

It may be more important, however, to remember that the Saints were not perfect. Many, like St. Augustine or St. Paul, led sinful lives before their conversion experience. Some had bad tempers like Sts. Peter and Jerome. Those who knew her also remember Dorothy Day, whose cause for canonization is in progress, as being very fiery. Still other saints, like Mother Teresa, suffered long periods of doubt when they wondered if God heard them at all.

We Are God's Children Now

The First Letter of John is an extended reflection on the understanding that God is Love. The medieval mystic Julian of Norwich once wrote that before God ever made us, he loved us. That foundation of love has given courage and trust to everyone who follows the path of discipleship. But I like what John says: "Beloved, we are God's children now; what we shall be had not yet been revealed." Only God knows how he will work in us and what path we will take. Our trust is in our identity as God's children. As the children of God who is Love, we are bound to love one another. The rest will follow.

How to Be a Saint

In spite of these things, saints continued to do what they thought God wanted, whether it was founding a religious order to help the poor or simply living lives of such holiness in their towns and villages that others looked at them and knew that God was present in them. They allowed God to work through them.

Good News for All of Us

The universal call to holiness is challenging for all. Our tendency is to think of holiness as belonging solely to our public figures: the pope, priests, sisters, and the saints. And yet, all of us know someone who embodies the Christian life. They are compassionate, loving, and just. They care about everyone they meet. They find comfort and strength in their relationship with God. They aren't perfect, but a light shines in them, which makes us want to know more about them. They are God's witness in the world and, God willing, we'll be one, too.

Questions for Reflection and Discussion

> *Do you, your friends, or family have a special saint that you turn to for strength or see as a role model for how to live the Christian life?*

> *Saint Paul called the people of God "saints," which means "holy" or "set apart." Why would Paul refer to Christians as "set apart"?*

Related Journey of Faith Lesson

Q15, "The Saints"

Themes

Freedom
    M3, "Your Spiritual Gifts"
    M5, "Our Call to Holiness"
Revelation
    Q6, "Divine Revelation"
    Q7, "Your Prayer Life"
    Q13, "The Church as Community"
    M4, "Discernment"
Saints
    Q15, "The Saints"
    M2, "The Role of the Laity"

READING 1 (ABC), WISDOM 3:1–9

The souls of the just are in the hand of God, and no torment shall touch them. They seemed, in the view of the foolish, to be dead; and their passing away was thought an affliction and their going forth from us, utter destruction. But they are in peace. For if before men, indeed, they be punished, yet is their hope full of immortality; chastised a little, they shall be greatly blessed, because God tried them and found them worthy of himself. As gold in the furnace, he proved them, and as sacrificial offerings he took them to himself. In the time of their visitation they shall shine, and shall dart about as sparks through stubble; they shall judge nations and rule over peoples, and the LORD shall be their King forever. Those who trust in him shall understand truth, and the faithful shall abide with him in love: because grace and mercy are with his holy ones, and his care is with his elect.

PSALM 23:1–3, 3–4, 5, 6

READING 2 (ABC), ROMANS 5:5–11

Brothers and sisters: Hope does not disappoint, because the love of God has been poured out into our hearts through the Holy Spirit that has been given to us. For Christ, while we were still helpless, died at the appointed time for the ungodly. Indeed, only with difficulty does one die for a just person, though perhaps for a good person one might even find courage to die. But God proves his love for us in that while we were still sinners Christ died for us. How much more then, since we are now justified by his Blood, will we be saved through him from the wrath. Indeed, if, while we were enemies, we were reconciled to God through the death of his Son, how much more, once reconciled, will we be saved by his life. Not only that, but we also boast of God through our Lord Jesus Christ, through whom we have now received reconciliation.

GOSPEL (ABC), JOHN 6:37–40

Jesus said to the crowds: "Everything that the Father gives me will come to me, and I will not reject anyone who comes to me, because I came down from heaven not to do my own will but the will of the one who sent me. And this is the will of the one who sent me, that I should not lose anything of what he gave me, but that I should raise it on the last day. For this is the will of my Father, that everyone who sees the Son and believes in him may have eternal life, and I shall raise him on the last day."

A Hope Full of Immortality

While November 1 celebrates all the named saints of the Catholic Church, the feast of All Souls remembers all those who died in faith and in the expectation that they would at last see God face to face. An anonymous prayer urges us to be one in Christ so as not to be far from each other, though some are in heaven and some on earth. That call to oneness in Christ begins at our baptism and is part of the journey of our lives. We have hope in the resurrection and everlasting life because of our faith.

The Book of Wisdom expresses confidence that those who live according to God's law are "in the hand of God" and "no torment shall touch them." The book imagines the persecution the Israelites suffered as a time of purification after which they will shine out to the world and, ultimately, will come to judge the nations under the watchful eye of the Lord. The reading ends with an exhortation to "abide with [God] in love," because God takes care of those who are his own.

Christians understand the first reading to describe the hope of our faith. Our Creed says we look forward to the resurrection of the dead and life everlasting. Our funeral rites call on the saints and angels to accompany us to paradise and our final purification (purgatory) before we live with God forever.

Saved by His Life

Psalm 23 is the psalm most frequently used in funeral Masses. It expresses absolute trust in God even though we "walk through the valley of the shadow of death." God will lead us to a place of rest, anoint our heads with oil (a sign of favor), and we shall dwell with God forever. Both Jews and Christians find great comfort in this hope. Christians believe this hope was fulfilled by the passion, death, and resurrection of Jesus Christ for the world. The reading from Romans describes the wonder of Jesus' action: "While we were still sinners Christ died for us." Paul connects the death of Christ with our reconciliation with God and our salvation, which comes through Christ. What's the result? Even now, God has poured out his love into our hearts through the Holy Spirit. The beginning of our eternal life was our baptism into Christianity. We can't see the end yet, but our hope is that we live out our faith in fullness until that day when we live it fully in the presence of God.

Raised Up on the Last Day

In the middle of the great teaching on the Bread of Life, Jesus explicitly promises that "everyone who sees the Son and believes in him may have eternal life, and I shall raise him on the last day" (John 6:40). John understood that those who believed in Jesus already had eternal life in them. The promise of Jesus to raise them up meant that death of the body was not the end of all things. Rather, they would continue their lives in God after death. Resurrection was not a widely accepted belief and Jesus' claims must have seemed strange to many. But for those who followed him remembered passages like that in the Book of Wisdom, which promised the same thing. They saw Jesus' words as continuing the promise of God from ancient days. And in the end, Jesus' resurrection confirmed their trust.

The readings here are suggestions only. Any readings from the liturgical Masses for the Dead, numbers 1011–1016, may be used today.

Good News for All of Us

It's a custom in some families to visit the graves of family members who have died and remember them, laughing at the good memories or crying at their loss. Through it all, we believe in God's promise that he will raise us up and we will stand before him. We know we're all sinful and we know that God will judge us with justice, mercy, and compassion. We look forward to that. In the meantime, we have the lives of our family and friends who are examples of Christian discipleship, and we strive to do what they do. One of God's blessings is that they were part of our lives.

Questions for Reflection and Discussion

➤ *Who in your family is an example of Christian life and values?*

➤ *How do you remember those family and friends who have died? Do you remember them in prayer?*

Related Journey of Faith Lesson

Q16, "Eschatology: The 'Last Things'"

Themes

Death
   E4, "The Creed"
Life
   Q15, "The Saints"
   M1, "Conversion: A Lifelong Process"
Remembrance
   Q9, "The Mass"
   Q10, "The Church Year"

Dedication of St. John Lateran, November 9

READING 1 (ABC), EZEKIEL 47:1–2, 8–9, 12

The angel brought me back to the entrance of the temple, and I saw water flowing out from beneath the threshold of the temple toward the east, for the façade of the temple was toward the east; the water flowed down from the southern side of the temple, south of the altar. He led me outside by the north gate, and around to the outer gate facing the east, where I saw water trickling from the southern side. He said to me, "This water flows into the eastern district down upon the Arabah, and empties into the sea, the salt waters, which it makes fresh. Wherever the river flows, every sort of living creature that can multiply shall live, and there shall be abundant fish, for wherever this water comes the sea shall be made fresh. Along both banks of the river, fruit trees of every kind shall grow; their leaves shall not fade, nor their fruit fail. Every month they shall bear fresh fruit, for they shall be watered by the flow from the sanctuary. Their fruit shall serve for food, and their leaves for medicine."

PSALM 46:2–3, 5–6, 8–9

READING (ABC), 1 CORINTHIANS 3:9C–11, 16–17

Brothers and sisters: You are God's building. According to the grace of God given to me, like a wise master builder I laid a foundation, and another is building upon it. But each one must be careful how he builds upon it, for no one can lay a foundation other than the one that is there, namely, Jesus Christ. Do you not know that you are the temple of God, and that the Spirit of God dwells in you? If anyone destroys God's temple, God will destroy that person; for the temple of God, which you are, is holy.

GOSPEL (ABC), JOHN 2:13–22

Since the Passover of the Jews was near, Jesus went up to Jerusalem. He found in the temple area those who sold oxen, sheep, and doves, as well as the money-changers seated there. He made a whip out of cords and drove them all out of the temple area, with the sheep and oxen, and spilled the coins of the money-changers and overturned their tables, and to those who sold doves he said, "Take these out of here, and stop making my Father's house a marketplace." His disciples recalled the words of Scripture, *Zeal for your house will consume me*. At this the Jews answered and said to him, "What sign can you show us for doing this?" Jesus answered and said to them, "Destroy this temple and in three days I will raise it up." The Jews said, "This temple has been under construction for forty-six years, and you will raise it up in three days?" But he was speaking about the temple of his Body. Therefore, when he was raised from the dead, his disciples remembered that he had said this, and they came to believe the Scripture and the word Jesus had spoken.

Mother Church

The Lateran Basilica is the cathedral Church of Rome and the oldest of the four basilicas in the city, dating from the fourth century. The site was originally a palace for the family of the *Laterani*. Ultimately, the emperor Constantine took control of it and gave it to the Church, which began to use the great hall and adjoining areas as a basilica. The dedication to St. John the Baptist and St. John the Evangelist quickly gained favor, and it became the center of Roman Christian life. The popes even lived there for decades. While the Church itself has been rebuilt or renovated several times in its long history, its pride of place as the Mother Church of Rome and of the world has remained intact, and so we celebrate the feast of its dedication each year.

It is fitting that the reading from Ezekiel contains a vision of the heavenly temple of God from which a river flows with life-giving water. Ezekiel's vision is of a renewed Garden of Eden where life is abundant and plentiful for believers. The Old Testament prophets frequently imagine the day of the Lord as a great feast that welcomes all who serve the Lord and in which the peace and justice of God reign forever. The early Christians experienced their communities in the same way—as life-giving and just. They knew that Jesus Christ was alive in their midst and his Spirit was poured out over the world. When they preached the Good News, it was about salvation and the abundant life found in Christ, and lived out in the Christian community. It made sense that they saw the Church as a mother who preached about salvation to all her children. Today's psalm underscores the prophetic vision with its refrain about the waters of the river, which gladden the city of God. The important message that God is our refuge draws people to the Church, whose members proclaim their trust and faith in him.

You Are God's Temple

No one knows better than Christians that the Church is more than just a building. The Lateran Basilica was destroyed and rebuilt several times in its long centuries of existence. If the Vatican were destroyed tomorrow, Catholicism would continue because it's the community of the faithful that spreads the Good News, takes care of one another, and reaches out to the world. Paul tells his listeners, "You are the temple of God." Paul knows that the Christian community can stand strong because of its foundation in Christ. We all might build upon that, but the more we forget that Jesus is our founder and source, the shakier the building becomes.

When Jesus comes upon the Temple marketplace in John's Gospel, he gets angry because they have forgotten the purpose of the temple—to offer prayer and sacrifice to God, not make money. He challenges them to renew their place of worship and when the people ask why, he moves the conversation to a coming miracle—a temple that is destroyed and raised up after three days. They didn't understand that he meant himself until after the resurrection. But when the disciples reflected on the events, they believed in him and in a faithful community that is constantly renewed by grace.

At the end of Paul's letter, he also draws an analogy to individuals. We are all temples of the Holy Spirit. The good work that God has begun in each one of us has to be nurtured by our openness to God's grace and willingness to follow God's path rather than our own. That can be challenging in today's world, but we are promised the grace and strength to do it.

Good News for All of Us

We're not alone. As Catholics, we are part of a world Church whose members support, care for, and love one another. We're not a perfect society. Vatican II called the Church the People of God and the Refuge of Sinners. We are certainly people and sinners who strive for holiness and renewal. But it's comforting to know that we're in it together, brothers and sisters, walking this path to God and looking forward with the same vision.

Questions for Reflection and Discussion

> *What is comforting and what is challenging about being a part of the Church today?*

> *What are some of the things you can do in your local church to make it a place of welcome for all?*

Related Journey of Faith Lesson

Q11, "Places in a Catholic Church"

Themes

Church
    Q10, "The Church Year"
    Q11, "Places in a Catholic Church"
    M2, "The Role of the Laity"
Holiness
    Q15, "The Saints"
    M3, "Your Spiritual Gifts"
    M5, "Our Call to Holiness"
Salvation
    Q2, "What Is Faith?"
    M1, "Conversion: A Lifelong Process"

Gathering Prayers

Gathering Prayers During Inquiry

Prayer

Good and gracious God, something has drawn us here to share with one another our search for you. We long to know you. We long to see where you have been present in our lives and in our hearts. Give us the grace to help each other grow in faith as we travel this way together. Be present to us now, O Lord, our God. Amen.

Prayer

Loving God, we gather to share the life we find with you. We gather to find your presence in this community of faith, your Church. Give us courage to ask questions and voice doubts. Also give us an open heart and mind to see the life you offer us as a part of this communion of souls. Never let us give up searching for you. Amen.

Prayer

Lord of all, as we come to know more about you, we see your presence in all creation and we share the awe and wonder that comes from knowing you created us in love and that you desire nothing more than that we become one with you. Fill our hearts with prayer, our lives with service, and our souls with longing. Amen.

Prayer

Gracious God, Father of our Lord, Jesus Christ, as we continue to walk with you and each other in this journey, help us follow Jesus more closely and know you by knowing him. May Jesus be with us as we commit to the next step of living our faith in the Catholic Church. May that step fill us with joy and peace and may we never cease coming to you with praise and gratitude. We pray this through Christ, our Lord. Amen.

Gathering Prayers During Catechumenate

Prayer

God of all nations, your Word is life. Bless us now as we gather to reflect on sacred Scripture. In these words let us find your Truth. Help us to know you not only with our minds, but also with our hearts. When our learning is finished, bring us into your presence rejoicing. We pray this through Christ, our Lord. Amen.

Prayer

Draw near to us, O Lord, in these passages from Scripture. May our hearts grow in the desire to know you in these stories and to see ourselves as part of them. Jesus, speak to us as you spoke to those who followed you. Open the Scriptures to us as you did to the disciples on the road to Emmaus that we might recognize our presence in our lives. Amen.

Prayer

Eternal God, our hearts are hungry for your word. Teach us the story of Jesus and let us know it as our story. Give us ears to hear what you have to say to us. Always and forever be our guide and comfort us as we make our way in this journey to life in your Church. And, Lord, teach us to bring your Good News to others along the way. Amen.

Prayer

Good and gracious God, this time of learning has challenged us as we have listened to your Scriptures more deeply than ever before. As we begin following your footsteps to the cross, let your words so fill us that our every longing might be for you. Increase our faith in you and help us know we do not walk alone for you are always with us. May our discipleship be fruitful now and forever. Amen.

Gathering Prayers During Lent

Prayer

Compassionate and loving God, in Jesus you entered human experience. You were tempted and didn't despair, betrayed and didn't turn to hate, killed and spoke words of forgiveness. Be with us now in our desert experience so we can learn to walk in our trials as you did, clinging to the faith that you will us through it all. Amen.

Prayer

Lord Jesus, be the living water in the dryness of our lives. Be our sight when we are blind. Hear our prayer as we place our faith in you and in your Church. Let the communion of saints walk with us in this journey. Above all, Lord, let us know you in the depths of our hearts even as you know us. Amen.

Prayer

Jesus, our Savior, to whom else can we go? You are the source of eternal life for us. With you, death loses its sting and we await the resurrection that faith in you promises. Give us hope to walk in dark places and strength to follow faithfully in your path to the radiant light of your presence. Amen.

Prayer

Jesus, Lord of all, we sing out your praise with the rest of the crowd and then follow you to your death, uncertain, afraid that our hopes have died with you. We see where they have laid you and wonder if our lives will ever be the same. But in you we trust. You make all things new. Give us the confidence to believe with our whole being as we wait in hope for you. Amen.

Gathering Prayers During Mystagogy

Prayer

Glorious God, Lord Jesus—like the women at the tomb, we saw only emptiness at first but then you appeared to your disciples and to Mary Magdalene. You opened our hearts and filled them with joy. We now recognize you not only by the wounds in your body, but by the miracle of your rising. Be with us now as we walk into your light. Amen.

Prayer

Gracious Lord, as we come together to reflect on the mystery of your passion, death, and resurrection, we pray to be filled with your Good News. Help us share it with everyone we meet. Help us live it out in every facet of our lives. And when our lives are over, grant us to live in your presence forever. Amen.

Prayer

Jesus, you call to us to follow in your path and be your disciples. Teach us the way of truth and light. Let us be your hands, your feet, your compassion in the world. Let us see your face in all we meet and be your face to all we meet. Give us grace not to waver in our commitment to you. Amen.

Prayer

Blessed are you, Lord, our God, ruler of the universe. In this OCIA journey, we have traveled far together. We have given support and comfort to one another. As we come together these last times, strengthen our resolve to be a light on the path for each other and to carry that light out into the world. We pray this through Christ, our Lord. Amen.

Dismissal Prayers

Dismissal Prayers During Inquiry

Prayer

Merciful God, we have begun this journey of faith together. We are grateful for the companions on our way, for the openness with which we receive one another, and most of all, for your love, which brought us here. As we leave today, fill our hearts with a desire to know you even more and when we return, let it be with joy and eagerness. Amen.

Prayer

God of all people, sometimes questions and doubts fill our minds and we can only ask, listen, and reflect on the response. Be patient with us as we hesitate and seek. Continue to call our names so we might find our way in the dark. We know we are never alone when we are with you and one another. Be present to us in our searching for you. Amen.

Prayer

Faithful God, the stories of our journey to faith bring us together in the great story of your salvation. Help us bear witness to your presence as we leave here today. Give us courage to continue the path if the way gets harder, to support one another, and to reach out in prayer to you whenever we are able. Amen.

Prayer

We give you praise, O God, for your faithful presence in our lives. Your Holy Spirit moved us to seek you in new and different ways. Walk with us as we commit ourselves to go deeper into your mystery. Draw us closer to you with the stories of your presence, the grace of your peace, and the love you expressed through your Son, Jesus Christ. We long to see you face to face. Amen.

Dismissal Prayers During Catechumenate

Prayer

God, Father of us all, the stories of faith in your sacred Scripture tell us the story of your presence to your people from the moment of creation to the resurrection of Jesus and even now. Give us insight to learn from them and faith to see them not just as stories of people who lived a long time ago but also as stories that speak to us of your presence so many centuries later. Help us to share what we are learning with others. Amen.

Prayer

Open our minds and heart, O Lord, to learn the truth of your love for us. Let us see in these Scriptures the evidence that you have cared for us and called us from the very beginning of our lives. When questions and doubt seek to overcome us, let us remember that you have the words of life. Amen.

Prayer

Good and gracious Lord, we are hungry for your grace and truth. We long to hear your voice calling us in every place in our lives. Now that we have shared your words in sacred Scripture, let them so fill us that we try to live them in our lives and thus give honor to you. Amen.

Prayer

Loving God. We leave this gathering ready to take the next step of following your Son, Lord Jesus Christ, into the story of his life, death, and resurrection. We thank you for being with us since the beginning. Be present to us now as we begin to learn what discipleship really means. Watch over us as we place our trust in you. Amen.

Dismissal Prayers During Lent

Prayer

Loving Jesus, when you were tempted in the desert, you spoke only of trust in God the Father. We may be tempted many times in this journey. As we go on our way today, give us the confidence to trust God as you did and feel his presence when we find ourselves in a desert place. Amen.

Prayer

God of all, we are thirsty for your peace and presence in our lives. Through the Incarnation, you walked among your people as Jesus Christ. You reminded us that you are living water and light to the blind. Help us remember that you are with us still in your body, the Church. Help us see the signs of your presence in every place we go and in every person we meet. Amen.

Prayer

Lord, we will continue to walk with you this Lent and throughout the rest of our lives. Give us your grace to follow your path and not our own. Give us strength and courage to face what lies ahead. Fill us with your life that we might enter into eternal life when we see you at the end. We pray all these things in your holy name. Amen.

Prayer

Jesus, our Brother and Savior, we are about to make a final commitment to live our lives as disciples. We are eager to follow your path, proclaim your Good News, and witness to your love by our actions. We are filled with gratitude that you have brought us this far. Let us rejoice in this new step in faith. Amen.

Dismissal Prayers During Mystagogy

Prayer

Jesus, Lord of Life, you have risen into our broken world and brought grace and healing with your presence. In your life, we have become a new creation, a people set apart to do your will and witness to your presence to all we meet. Pour out your grace on us that we may live into that new life with faith in you always. Amen.

Prayer

Gracious God, source of all good things, as we reflect on what it means to be your daughters and sons; we know we will face dark times and difficult paths and that the way will not always be easy. When that happens fill us with the desire to bring our troubled hearts to the cross of Jesus, that he might take them up, calm our fears, and send us out rejoicing once more. Amen.

Prayer

Brother, Jesus, we are new at being your disciples. Like Peter, Andrew, James, John, Mary Magdalene, the woman at the well, and countless others, we strive to do your will. Please give us courage us to do what is right. Forgive us when we fail. Have mercy on our efforts to please you. But above all, let us never forget that you love us and that our only good rests in becoming one with you. Amen.

Prayer

Loving God, our hope and light, we have shared a journey of faith with one another. Our stories have joined the stories of the prophets and people of the Old Testament and those of the early followers of Jesus. We have come to know that they are all one story of your divine grace breaking into our imperfect world and making something holy of us. We praise you for this miracle now and forevermore. Amen.

Thematic Index

Numbers in bold type refer to pages in this book.
Numbers preceded by a letter refer to Lessons:
   Q = Inquiry; C = Catechumenate;
   E = Enlightenment and Purification; M = Mystagogy.

Example: Anointing...**34-35**, C3, C4, C7. Information on anointing may be found in The Word Into Life, Year B on pages 34-35.
   Further information may be found in the Catechumenate Lessons, numbers 3, 4, and 7.